CHECKMATE IN CLEVELAND

CHECKMATE IN CLEVELAND

The Rhetoric of Confrontation During the Stokes Years

ESTELLE ZANNES
Assisted by Mary Jean Thomas

THE PRESS OF CASE WESTERN RESERVE UNIVERSITY
CLEVELAND/LONDON
1972

Printed in the United States of America.
International Standard Book Number: 0–8295–0231–9.
Library of Congress Catalogue Card Number: 72–187013.

To my children
Tom, Timothy, and Maria

CONTENTS

OVERVIEW

I REMEMBER one morning at daylight in the early fifties. My husband came home, very tired and very happy. He had just "flown" the first successful ICBM, and he spoke of the great team of men who worked with him and of the beauty of the flight. We knew there would be many more flights and many more important events in man's travel into space. But this was a "first," and he thought there was a special feeling about being the first man to accomplish a feat. "They never can take that away from you," he said.

No matter how events of the past years are reported or analyzed, Cleveland will always be the first major American city to have elected a black mayor, and Carl Stokes will have been that first black mayor.

I have recorded, as objectively as possible, the events of the past ten years. Furthermore, I have tried to look at the problems in Cleveland as a moving part of a much bigger scene, to cover trends as well as events, to explain rather than expose. Although the problems of transportation, crime, racial relations, poverty, housing, and politics have not been solved, I have been able to draw some conclusions about the city's inability to resolve its internal difficulties. Much of the difficulty resides in the rhetoric employed in all quarters and all levels, the language, the modes, and the types of arguments used to advance causes and to check their advances.

This book deals only with events as they occurred, for I recorded oral history. Events were recorded when they happened, and interviews were taken while the event was occurring, or very shortly thereafter. All quoted material not cited comes from interviews I personally conducted over the past five years. In every instance I used the tape recorder, and the interviewee was aware that the material would be published. I have recorded many changes of attitude that occurred during the years. I have also recorded the changes in language. Early in the sixties the word Negro was more often used than colored; by the late sixties black became more accepted and preferred. Generally, I have used black to identify a race and Negro to identify an individual, especially if I knew that that individual preferred it.

I recorded an era in the history of Cleveland. I listened to the city, the people, the opinion leaders.

One of the most flamboyant of the leaders was Carl Stokes. Stokes always saw himself as a part of a historical movement. "A Carl Stokes can do it because a La Guardia did it," he would say. All the history he had read made him believe that he had a part to play in the story of Cleveland politics. He could see the beginning and the ending of a historical movement. The problem, of course, is that a politician who sees the world events in this light often writes his own tragic ending.

Carl Stokes is the eternal campaigner. He enjoys the rhetoric of conflict. He is at his best on a platform, in an arena, before a television camera. By his own admission he is revitalized before an audience. And also by his own admission, he is no administrator. I remember a luncheon at Cleveland State University that he attended. Julian Bond was the guest of honor and until the moment Carl Stokes arrived, all attention had focused on Bond. Carl Stokes arrived late, opened the door, smiled, apologized for being tardy, and began immediately to charm the audience. Bond remained reserved, and for a while there seemed to be some tension in the room. The talk turned to the presidency, and the two men were asked whether they aspired to it. Bond shook his head. Stokes said he did not seek it. Besides, Stokes said he felt a black *woman* would have a better chance. "Not me," he laughed, "I'm no administrator. When I was elected in '67 I didn't know what to do first." It was said in a joking manner, but the truth of the statement gave the audience pause.

Thomas Guthrie of the *Plain Dealer* remarked that things would have worked if only Stokes had had a political adviser, a strong administrator as his right-hand man to take over when he was out of town. The men around Stokes were well-meaning amateurs, Guthrie indicated. Certainly part of the dissatisfaction with the Stokes administration was that the men in key positions constantly embarrassed their boss or, frustrated in their inability to work with him, simply left him. "A king is known by his ministers," said a knowledgeable member of the old Cleveland dynasty. "If they're good, they elevate him."

Stokes was not elevated by many of the men around him, nor was it felt that he tried to elevate any, particularly a black man. Yet the record shows that there were more blacks at City Hall during the Stokes years than at any time in history. Also the opportunity for blacks to elevate themselves through civil service examinations was greatest at that time. Two hundred sixty men and women with salaries over ten thousand dollars made over three million dollars—dollars that were poured into their neighborhoods, dollars that improved the tax duplicate and raised the economic position of the black community.

There was also more housing for the poor and the elderly completed during the Stokes administration (although the planning for these housing projects was initiated in other administrations) than during the past thirty years. But people still remember the fight over Lee-Seville and the housing for the elderly that was sometimes ill conceived. As an example, the high-rise for the elderly at Fifty-fifth and Chester has only 15 percent occupancy, because old people are afraid to live in a high crime area away from convenient shopping.

As Ralph Locher had predicted, the Erieview projects started as far back as the Burke administration were either completed or nearing completion during the Stokes administration. Community Development Director Richard Green concentrated more upon downtown urban renewal than upon neighborhood assistance. An example was the downtown ward. People who lived downtown felt they needed attention. They had demonstrated their goodwill by putting new siding on their homes, painting, and repairing. Green visited them, told them to keep up the good work, and said they would be considered next after the other top priority projects were completed. But the people considered themselves top priority. They needed help. They needed, particularly, the recreation center which had been promised to them, the money for which had been channeled into another fund. With the cooperation of Cleveland State University they learned to put out a newspaper, and they sent the first edition to the mayor. On the front page was the picture of the proposed model of the recreation center and the caption "When, Mr. Mayor?" After three years of attending community meetings, becoming involved in the political process, visiting City Council meetings, the people finally did obtain their recreation center, and the day came to turn over that first shovel of dirt. The people changed the time of the ceremonies twice in order to accommodate their mayor. A banner was painted with the words "Thank you Mr. Mayor" printed upon it. The children were dressed and ready to recite; the babies were in their carriages. The rain came, and the wind blew the sign down, but the people waited and waited. Only after an hour and a half did they accept the fact that the mayor would not make it to the ceremonies.

That was the problem—the bitterness at the end. The Erieview projects were completed and the recreation center was being started, but the man who was supposed to be so good at public relations seemed not to care.

During the last year his own bitterness became apparent. An event over which he had no control greatly affected his administration. Glenville put an end to many things, but especially to Cleveland: NOW! This project originally proposed an investment of $90 million in neighborhood housing rehabilitation, $60 million in accelerated urban renewal construction, the creation of 16,000 jobs, aid to small businesses, twenty welfare and child day-care centers, recreation programs for youth, and the construction of Camp Cleveland for disadvantaged youth. A grant of $10,000 to Ahmed Evans destroyed the entire project. The money stopped coming in. Worse, the stigma of mismanagement was attached to the project. Though the public constantly inquired where the money already collected had gone, no real accounting was forthcoming. When the newspapers published an alleged report of expenditures, the public didn't believe it. They were sure the funds had been mishandled. The business leaders who had originally accepted the responsibility of disbursing the funds were not available for comment. To this day, people will call talk shows and ask, "Whatever happened to Cleveland: NOW?" and the disc jockeys will shrug and wonder too, adding to the mystery. No one has the answer. But people haven't forgotten the money that went to the militants.

The mayor and the militants were constantly discussed. Stokes tried to explain that there was a difference between one black nationalist and another. He argued that black nationalism wasn't any different from white nationalism. The militants of the early sixties were hired by the system and tried to work within it. Baxter Hill got a job in the Department of Community Relations and tried to keep the peace in the community, but someone was always shooting at him. Harllel Jones helped in campaigns but eventually was arrested for murder. DeForest Brown became director of a $1.6 million federal grant and Lewis Robinson, the first militant of the sixties, became its economic director. Brown unfortunately allotted Cleveland: NOW! money to Ahmed Evans. Another group of militants then entered the picture. They were the men who did not wish to work within the system. They were the men who distributed the literature of Ho Chi Minh, organized rifle clubs, and labeled the police the enemy. Many of Stokes's friends wanted him to move against these militants, but he would not interfere. In the end, these militants did more to destroy Stokes's administration than the citizens, white and black, who finally refuted him.

His decision not to openly censure the various militant groups further irritated an already alienated police force. There were members of the black community who were victims of extortion gangs and rising crime and who became irritated at the lack of police protection. The police, caught between City Hall and the community, felt abandoned. They began taking care of each other.

I rode with the Fifth District police who really believe certain militant groups are preparing more sniper attacks upon them. They point out buildings where cement bags were hauled in. There are fortresses in the black community which they claim the police will never be able to penetrate. I have seen the constant confrontation of police and militants where the slightest encounter is a potential riot situation. One night on a routine run, we stopped to investigate a car parked near a fireplug. The police proceeded to check it out to see if it was stolen and asked whether the owner was about. A young boy came out of store nearby and said he had driven it to the store, but that it was his uncle's car. The boy had no license. While the police were asking the boy to find his uncle and get the car moved, several militants with rifles over their shoulders moved in, separated the two officers, and demanded to know what the problem was. A crowd gathered. Were the police harassing the boy? Within ten seconds four police cars were on the scene. "Anything wrong?" asked the captain. It was a standoff, and police and militants retired.

"How long have you been backing each other up?" I asked one policeman. "Since Glenville," was the reply.

Other things have happened since Glenville. For the first time, the citizens have asked the police to come into their neighborhoods and open up shop. Four outreach centers located in store fronts, supported by the local citizenry, staffed with special policemen are located on the east side of Cleveland. "We're here for as long as they want us," said Sergeant Jack Latko of the Community Relations Unit. The men recommended for these centers have narcotics experience, experience working with juveniles, tactical-unit experience, ability to relate to groups of people, awareness of the social and economic character of the area, ability to set up meetings and conduct safety programs and, preferably, are black.

The men selected for this unit have been responsible for easing tensions in many instances. When a school bus was stoned on Murray Hill, it was the officers from the outreach center who helped negotiate a peace.

The negotiators, the people who requested discussion instead of dissent, are too few. Who knows about them? For the main part, they are quiet men. They move silently in the community. Men like Patrolmen Joseph Jasper, Gus Zukie, Curtis Scott, Rudolph Turner, Edward Coleman, Creed Williams. These men are helping us to survive.

This book records a city's survival in a turbulent decade. America emerged from the sixties a nation bruised, scarred, and still trying to bind her open wounds. A passion play began in 1960 which lasted the full ten years. We began with an awakening, moved to the mountain where we crucified our heroes, burned our cities, and cried out in protest at what we had done. But we survived.

But the question remains: Is survival enough? Mayor John Lindsay, when asked about the priorities for municipal action, said, "Survival." Other mayors, however, have abandoned the fight, stating that the problems are insurmountable. Terry D. Schrunk, mayor of Portland, Oregon, and president of the U.S. Conference of Mayors, said, "When we went home from Chicago in 1968 we had designated thirty-nine mayors to sit in places of leadership. . . . Today nearly half of them are either out of office or going out . . . most of them by their own decision not to run again." These men echo Henry Ford's statement, "We shall solve the city problem by leaving the city."*

But what of those who do not wish to abandon the city? In the center of Cleveland, a short walk from City Hall and the Central Police Station, are clusters of citizens—mostly white—who stubbornly cling to their ancestral homes, who have simply refused to be written off when all surveys in the fifties assured them their neighborhood would be extinct in the sixties. Dwelle Butts—a black man—introduces visitors to the city through his touring service and points to the greatness, past and present, of a city he loves. He preaches the gospel of neighborhood pride and determination to the black community, the gospel of stay and build rather than abandon and destroy. Unfortunately these small voices which say, "Let's take stock of our resources and see what we can make of them," have been drowned out by the shouts of those who seek to castigate, lay blame, and find scapegoats for all our ills. For every voice which suggests, "Here is the problem; what shall *we* do about it?" there are ten voices who answer, "The problem is *their* fault; we're not going to do anything until *they* do something."

The rhetorical game has now evolved into a new and dangerous stage. The object is no longer a straightforward progress towards a political victory. The game has degenerated into bickering, name-calling, and manipulating all means of persuasion. Each group waits for the crucial opportunity to stymie opposition once and for all—the final brilliant ploy—checkmate!

*Gus Tyler, "Can Anyone Run a City?," *Saturday Review*, November 8, 1969, p. 22.

ACKNOWLEDGMENTS

I MUST ACKNOWLEDGE first my gratitude to the many persons whose names appear in the pages that follow—the many persons who "granted audience" to me and my tape recorder. For upon their contribution depends my own effort.

Specifically I want to thank my brother, Arthur P. Lambros, whose knowledge of politics and politicians proved invaluable; my first adviser, Dr. Claire Henderlider, who encouraged my enthusiasm to pursue the 1967 campaign for a doctoral dissertation; and Dr. Carroll C. Arnold, whose theory greatly influenced the direction of this book. While all the politicians I interviewed were extremely cooperative, I would like particularly to thank Carl B. Stokes, Ralph Locher, Robert Kelly, William Franklin, Dennis Kucinich, Bronis Klementowicz, Arnold Pinkney, Seth Taft, Patrick Sweeney, William Hendrickson, Patrick Gerity, and General Benjamin O. Davis.

CHECKMATE IN CLEVELAND

CHAPTER 1

THE COMING TO BE

JEAN MURRELL CAPERS, a Negro attorney with an advanced degree in law, knew the power of the ballot, having been a member of the City Council for many years. She felt that more Negro councilmen were not the answer. "I decided the only thing that could be done was to run a Negro for mayor." She was politically astute and always abreast of the times, which perhaps could account for the fact that others besides Jean Capers were having the same "original" idea at the same time. Lewis G. Robinson, a civil rights figure, today claims that a group called the Freedom Fighters under his leadership tried to recruit a black mayor in 1964—attorney Stanley Tolliver. Reportedly, Carl B. Stokes, the first Negro Democrat ever elected to the Ohio legislature, told the group at that time that they were dreaming.

The significant difference between other claimants and Jean Capers is that she had both the political acumen and the enthusiasm to spearhead the drive. In the black community today there is agreement that it was she who helped many of the black politicians become more sophisticated in their approaches to politics.

Jean Capers described how she first set the stage for the "Draft Carl Stokes" movement. Right after the national election in 1964 a group of her friends were "chewing the fat" at the Thirty Second Cedar Club on Cleveland's east side. She told one of her friends, Geraldine Williams, that the only way to give the Negro status and dignity was to have a Negro mayor. Geraldine Williams replied: "You've come forward with a whole lot of crackpot ideas, but this is undoubtedly the worst." However, the two women agreed to plant the idea while sitting around the club, and in about thirty minutes everyone was discussing the pros and cons of running a Negro for mayor. Generally the response was good, but Jean Capers felt that the people did not understand the full power of the ballot. Even the enthusiasts countered with "*They* won't let a Negro be mayor." But Jean Capers argued that the voting booth was the one place where the Negro was truly equal, where he could walk in, pull a curtain, and make a decision without being intimidated.

"This is the place the Negro is least concerned about democracy and the only place where he will always be equal," she emphasized. By the time the discussion ended, Geraldine Williams agreed with Jean Capers: "I think you have something." It is interesting to note that since that time Geraldine Williams has become an astute and much sought-after political campaign manager.

After agreeing that the push could not come from the rank and file but from those in the black community who possessed higher formal education, the two women called a meeting of selected professional people and knowledgeable political workers. The idea was to keep the drive nonpartisan because many of the Negro voters were registered Republicans. The initial group met every Sunday from November to February.

There had never been a *genuine* draft of a candidate in Cleveland, and no one had contacted Carl Stokes. Carl Stokes seemed the only likely choice because of his ability to campaign and rally white voters as well as black. Carl Stokes was in Columbus at the time serving his third term as state representative and making a name for himself as an eloquent speaker. Jean Capers confronted Carl Stokes with the idea of running for mayor only *once* before offering him the petitions. Stokes responded angrily, "I am on my way up the ladder, and you are trying to pull me down!" The two exchanged strong words on the subject, but Jean Capers was not to be deterred from her purpose.

The date set for issuing the petition was January 15, 1965. Jean Capers drafted the petition, and copies were run off in the back room of the Thirty Second Cedar Club on a machine owned by Geraldine Williams.

Many people were involved in gathering the names for the petitions. "The man who got the most names was a beer salesman going into bars," Jean Capers recalled. Knowing that all signatures would not be legally valid, the group tried to find professional people to sign the petitions but had little success. The group had difficulty at first obtaining recognition from the media, but as word of the draft petitions circulated, newspapermen started calling Carl Stokes in Columbus for comment. Stokes became more receptive to the idea and called upon the League of Non-Partisan Voters to give him the petitions. At that time the group, which had been aiming for 100,000 signatures, had obtained only 21,000. The eight people who had circulated the petitions had contacted 200,000 people. The league refused to give Stokes the petitions, insisting on observing their May fifteenth deadline for the delivery of petitions to candidates.

The league recognized the need to have the public take the Stokes petitions effort seriously, and Jean Capers took over the task of publicizing the drive. "In March of 1965 we got out a paper. We carried an article. I wrote the whole thing. Five thousand copies were delivered door to door." The group had decided to take care of its own public relations and not to rely upon the established media.

Enthusiasm grew. Election law required 34,000 signatures on the petitions to qualify the candidate. The group actually obtained over 51,000—signed in every conceivable, some in quite peculiar, fashion. Newspaper articles unfavorable to Stokes began to appear and, according to Jean Capers, this made Stokes angry. He pushed up the date for filing his candidacy, and this time the Capers group cooperated.

The campaign *almost* succeeded in 1965. Carl Stokes came within 2,100 votes of defeating Mayor Ralph S. Locher. Stokes, a Democrat, had taken advantage of a City Charter provision that allows a candidate to file as an Independent, bypassing the partisan primaries. The Reverend Charles Rawlings admitted, "It was the Negro political pros who made the technical arrangements, and it was all of us who were the alumni of the civil rights movement who almost pulled it off in 1965." He added sadly, "I'm very sorry it didn't happen in 1965 because, if it had, the liberal community could have owned Stokes. It happened in 1967, and the business community owns him."

In 1965, after the petitions were filed, the enthusiasm of the black community reached fever pitch. The early civil rights leaders who joined the campaign worked day and night. It was the American dream. There was little money and no business or newspaper support, but as Rawlings expressed it: "There are very few times in history when you can identify strands deeper than money. . . . That was one of those periods in history when the people said the hell with cost, we're going to go." Though Carl Stokes did not win in 1965, the campaign was a major victory for the black community of Cleveland. It demonstrated that unity was power, and that unity could be attained with an attractive, eloquent leader.

THE CLEVELAND LEGACY

Once before Cleveland had had such a unity—as the result of a strong, appealing leader. Cleveland's rebirth as a progressive city is usually identified with the election of Tom L. Johnson who became mayor in 1901. Cleveland has since wrapped itself in the legend of Johnson's liberalism and, though some claim there is nothing left of that liberalism except the legend, the aura of his "Golden Age" exerts itself whenever Clevelanders decide it's time for a change.

Johnson served two terms in Congress and in 1901 was elected mayor of Cleveland. During his eight years as mayor there were few dull months. Among other things, Johnson built a thousand miles of streets, cleaned up dishonest weights and measures, established meat and dairy inspection, reformed the jails and prisons, founded the nation's first farm for deprived boys, removed all Keep Off the Grass signs, and built parks and playgrounds. When Johnson later failed to be reelected, he explained that he had been mayor for so many years people had lost sight of conditions as they existed before his time. "The man who is worthy of being a leader of men," he remarked in retrospect, "will never complain of the stupidity of his helpers or the ingratitude of mankind, nor of the inappreciation of the public. These things are all part of the great game of life and to meet them and not go down under them is the final proof of power."[1]

The spirit of progressiveness engendered by Cleveland's Johnson administration thrived for a few years. In the early twenties Tom Johnson's old police chief, Fred Kohler, won an upset mayoral election on the strength of his promises to "make life and property safe, clean up the town, and live within his income."[2] From 1924 through 1931 Cleveland carried out an experiment in municipal government which captured the attention of the nation—the city manager form. But a city administration without politics did not capture the fancy of Cleveland voters who demanded and brought about the return of a modified federal plan of government.

Ray T. Miller, Harry L. Davis, and Harold H. Burton served as mayors during the 1930s, and their apparent inability to cope with the problems of the labor movement, unemployment, slums, and housing led Walter Abbott to write an article for *Forum Magazine* in 1938 entitled "Cleveland: A City Collapses." Abbott spoke of the sack of the city by a long line of "hack and quack administrations" and described the city, for all its cosmopolitan ingredients, as a kind of witches' cauldron: "[E]ssentially a group of juxtaposed tribes more or less at war with one another. . . . She is a melting pot that has never melted but continues to boil, casting up hard racial lumps in indigestible form."[3] Immigration from Europe had declined after the discriminatory immigration laws of 1924, but apparently the settling-in process did not result in an amalgamation of the various ethnic groups.

In a recent interview George Condon, Cleveland's humorist-journalist-historian, said that during the forties, fifties, and first half of the sixties Cleveland had a succession of "real good guys that were deadly." Condon felt that while Mayors Harold H. Burton (1935–40), Edward Blythin (1940–41), Frank J. Lausche (1942–45), Thomas A. Burke

(1945–53), Anthony J. Celebrezze (1953–62), and Ralph Locher (1962–67) were all men of great integrity, they were "deadly because they were not innovators." These men were so anxious to please the establishment that they would not stick their necks out and try to achieve something big. He admired the type of man Tom Johnson was—the type of man who thought in large pictures, in large concepts. "All these men were proper and trivial," was Condon's summation of the administrations of the forty years that preceded the election of Carl Stokes.

His judgment is perhaps harsh and certainly does not recognize the phenomenal change in Cleveland itself during those years. World War II brought a large group of transient workers into the industrial valley, and southern Negroes came North looking for work. Inadequate housing became an enormous problem at a time when materials were not available for housing construction. While trying to cope with the increased problems at hand, the administrations of Blythin and Lausche did indeed do some "big thinking" about postwar programs. One such plan was a $240 million long-range express highway plan. Lausche set up six panels in 1944 to study the problems of returning servicemen, transportation, traffic, transit, public works, and labor-management relations. By 1946 the recommendations of these six panels had been translated into twenty-four proposals for public improvements at a cost of $57 million. That Cleveland citizens were eager for these programs is evidenced by the fact that the vote carrying each proposal ranged from 72.5 percent to 84.9 percent of all votes cast. The list of improvements included hospitals, schools, a new viaduct, a county administration building, a new central market, recreation centers, park improvements, airport expansion, and many other projects affecting the health, welfare, safety, public service, as well as the industrial expansion of Greater Cleveland.

It is hard to imagine a more ambitious scheme on a larger scale than Celebrezze's urban renewal program which began in 1955 with council's approval of the Garden Valley project. By 1960 six more areas of the city had been brought under urban renewal. With the addition of two downtown renewal projects, Cleveland could claim by 1965 the somewhat dubious honor of having more acreage officially designated as slum and blighted than any other city in the nation.

Perhaps the real problem was not that Mayors Blythin, Lausche, Burke, Celebrezze, and Locher did not think in large pictures and large concepts, but that they did not attend carefully enough to the trivial work-a-day details which cumulatively transform dreams into realities.

The most remarkable changes which took place in the city and which might have stunned even the great Tom Johnson were the demographic ones. In 1930 there were 37,000 Negroes living in the central area south of Euclid Avenue. In 1940 about 10 percent of Cleveland's population was Negro, and in 1950, 16.3 percent of Cleveland's population was Negro. But from 1950 to 1965, while Cleveland's total population decreased by 100,000 to 810,858, the Negro population more than doubled, from 147,847 to 297,352—an increase from 16.5 percent to 36.6 percent of the city's population. Cleveland, despite a certain amount of discrimination, had acquired a reputation as a "good" city for Negroes.[4] Many Cleveland Negroes who migrated from the South reported that it was generally believed that "if you can't make it in Cleveland, you can't make it anywhere up North."

Cleveland's east side neighborhoods were changing rapidly between 1950 and 1960. A report issued by the Urban League in 1964 made the observation that heavy home purchases were made by Negroes in previously all-white foreign nationality neighborhoods—mostly of Eastern European extraction—along St. Clair Avenue towards East Cleveland and southeast along Lee, Miles, and Harvard avenues near the city limits and towards the eastern suburbs near the borders of Shaker Heights, Warrensville Heights, and Maple Heights. By October, 1963, the area lying between Shaker Heights, Kinsman, and Buckeye roads that had been mostly white in the late fifties had become 80 percent Negro. The neighborhoods south of Kinsman and north of Harvard between 104th and 154th streets had become 95 percent Negro. The community east of Lee Road and extending from Shaker Heights to Harvard Avenue had changed from a practically all-white neighborhood in 1960 to nearly 70 percent Negro by October, 1963.[5]

The new Negro immigrants followed the same pattern which the European immigrants had established a century before, the creation of autonomous neighborhoods in which their own customs and traditions could be retained. By the early 1960s economic discrimination against the Negro had declined in Cleveland. A substantial number of Negroes had achieved an adequate standard of living and realized the benefits of the modern industrial society. Few, however, really scaled the ghetto wall, because the wall kept moving further and further out. While poverty was declining among most Negro households with male heads, the gap between the haves and have-nots was widening. Poverty was more visual—the garbage was gathering in the streets and rats flaunted their own tenancy over that of human slum dwellers.

Unrest over the obvious inequalities between Cleveland's white and black citizens did not *begin* in the 1960s, although the unrest reached its most explosive heights in that decade. In 1933 members of the NAACP complained of the inequalities in education imposed on Negro children by their confinement to Central High School where course offerings and facilities were inferior to those of other high schools in the city. Longwood and Outhwaite Elementary schools were designated for black children from the South who needed "urbanizing." The NAACP complained that most of the Negro children attending these two schools were Cleveland natives, not southern immigrants. These schools, called "dumbbell schools" by the NAACP, not only stigmatized the pupils but also created discipline problems.

In theory, Cleveland had integrated public schools; however, because of the "neighborhood" concept of pupil assignment and the ease with which white students could transfer out of a primarily black neighborhood school, de facto segregation had existed for half a century. School controversies with racial overtones were frequent occurrences between the 1930s and the early 1950s. The Board of Education usually responded to such protests by taking the matter under consideration or referring it to the inevitable study committee.

THE BULLDOZER INCIDENT

In retrospect it seems quite natural that the first stirrings of racial unrest in Cleveland in the early sixties would center on the schools. Leadership among an economically emancipated Negro core had been exercised in past disputes about segregation and equality of educational opportunities. Eventually this Negro core group was joined and aided in its efforts by white citizen groups generally headed by religious leaders.

At the same time, Cleveland was beginning to pick up vibrations from without its boundaries. In 1963, when "Bull" Connor turned the fire hoses and dogs on the group led by Martin Luther King, Jr., a Cleveland group hitherto engaged in rather passive protests was catalyzed into action. Small militant organizations began to spring to life. The Congress of Racial Equality developed a local chapter which attracted people who, in those days, could have been considered radicals. Today they would be called moderates. Leadership of that organization was headed by Ruth Turner and Antoine Perot (both black), and two white men—David Cohen, professor, and Bruce Klunder, a campus minister of Western Reserve University. Black Muslims established a mosque on Superior Avenue. Many other groups were formed, but their efforts were fragmented and none had enough strength to be really effective. It was not until the several groups created a coalition called the United Freedom Movement (UFM) that effective agitation for improved conditions could be realized. The new coalition group staked out three areas in which they would concentrate their efforts: education, employment, and housing. Committees were formed to plan unified action programs in each of these areas.

The United Freedom Movement in Cleveland gained moral support from other protest and confrontation groups which formed and began campaigns for social change. One vigorous leader was Rabbi Arthur J. Lelyveld of Fairmount Temple in Beachwood. Although Rabbi Lelyveld had long been active in civil rights movements outside Cleveland and was a very eloquent speaker on the subject, his ethos was considerably enhanced when he returned from a Mississippi voter registration drive and appeared on Cleveland television. The rabbi came home a wounded veteran from that distant battle for civil rights, but with metaphors and images intact he awakened the avenging spirit of many Clevelanders.

The United Freedom Movement pressed for greater equality in employment and education. It protested discriminatory employment practices at the construction site of the new Mall Convention Center. The education committee of the UFM gained strength and confronted the Board of Education with the fact of segregation and the unfair practice of forcing ghetto children to attend schools in shifts because black neighborhood schools were overcrowded while schools in white areas had vacant spaces in their classrooms. When long negotiations between the UFM and the Board of Education appeared to be fruitless, UFM set up picket lines and demonstrations. In October of 1963 the Board of Education finally agreed to take steps towards integration of faculty, improvement in curriculum, and integration of black children in all-white schools. The Board of Education could hardly claim that it had been taken by surprise and was therefore unprepared to act, for these same demands had been pressed by a group calling itself SOS (Support Our Schools) long before the education committee of UFM began its crusade. As noted earlier, the Board of Education had been dragging its feet on these issues for nearly thirty years, and even at this time it continued to do so despite growing evidence that violence over the school issue was imminent.

Tensions mounted as the black community watched construction progress on two new schools which would be located geographically to prevent integration and further ghetto-ize their children. The UFM coalition through its various political action groups increased tensions by asserting that the Board of Education was acting in bad faith and had no intention of working towards integration of the city's schools. Paralleling the general pattern of confrontation, in this situation, too, disappointment turned into despair, anger into outrage, rhetoric into action—and the action produced a trend in the rhetoric of controversy which proved highly effective in the prevention of rational problem-solving.

The fuse which led to the series of explosive situations was lit on the morning of January 29, 1964, when pickets from the United Freedom Movement began moving towards the William H. Brett School located on Royal Avenue NE. A countermovement materialized, and the pickets were met by crowds of hostile whites. As the demonstrators moved on to Memorial School on East 152d Street, the hostility directed at them increased, but there were no reports of violent encounters between those picketing in protest and those protesting the picketing.

The following morning the pickets made ready to march to Murray Hill School, located in the heart of Cleveland's Italian settlement. A crowd of more than a thousand young white men and boys had gathered around the school site. A small band of Negro protesters moved towards the site. The white "defenders" of Murray Hill responded by smashing cars and throwing bottles and rocks at policemen, priests, newsmen—anybody who got in their way. The Negro pickets—the target for all this rage—delayed marching into the mob, hoping for some face-saving gesture from a meeting taking place at that same time between the Board of Education and the United Freedom Movement representatives. When it became obvious that help was not forthcoming, the would-be pickets had to withdraw from the scene while police held off the white mob.

The response of the Murray Hill mob provoked still more civil disobedience. The United Freedom Movement which until then had protested by means of peaceful picketing regrouped, determined to employ more aggressive tactics. On February 1, the *Plain Dealer* reported that forty-one people had staged an all-night sit-in at the Board of Education building. The night of February 3, sixty demonstrators camped out in a third-floor corridor. The next morning they blocked entrances and stairways with their bodies. Police were called in to remove them. Methods of removal allegedly employed by the police brought charges of brutality from the demonstrators. The encouragement which the

UFM had previously received from the local press disappeared, and a headline in the February 5 *Plain Dealer* charged: "Reds and 'Old Pro' Pickets Stir Negro Sit-Ins Here."

Though it is difficult to say with any degree of certainty why the local press and, subsequently, the readers of the local press withdrew their sympathy for the protesters, two possibilities come to mind. One is that the newspapers in Cleveland were far behind the times in their attitudes towards coverage of Negro news. That one-third of Cleveland's population was black was not reflected in the hiring practices of either the *Plain Dealer* or the *Cleveland Press*. In the early sixties there were but three black reporters on the staff of the *Cleveland Press* and only one, for a brief period, on the *Plain Dealer* staff. One city editor claimed that the news that came over his desk about Negroes was mostly unfavorable and, furthermore, subscribers gave them a lot of anti-Negro reaction when they printed stories about Negro concerns. Consequently, stories about Negroes did not appear frequently. Newsmen in Cleveland were, in turn, accused by the black community of ignoring what was going on in the inner city, of ineptly reporting an event in a historical context, of labeling Negroes, of rejecting Negro talent, and, moreover, of distorting the news. These accusations grew more vehement in the later sixties.

Of the two Cleveland dailies, the *Press* appeared more responsive to the Negro. As early as 1961 the *Press* decided to refrain from labeling Negroes. Unless a picture accompanied a story, there was no definite way of knowing whether a person was white or black. In the early sixties the *Press* ran a series on "blockbusting" with the definite purpose of showing that the deplorable feature of blockbusting was not that Negroes were, in this fashion, making an effort to break out of the ghetto, but that real estate brokers were exploiting and profiteering from the Negro's effort to move out of the ghetto. That series, though intended to portray the Negro favorably, nonetheless alienated many people. "It was not by design," stated one reporter, "that we hurt people, but in our zeal to expose we sometimes tar a lot of innocent people."

So it may have been that the *Plain Dealer*, in its zeal during the school crisis to expose the professional agitators who poach on worthy causes for their own selfish gain, succeeded in tarring a lot of innocent people.

However, responsible journalists should be aware of how the forces of persuasion interact to create a message greater than the sum of the words. The *ethos* of the source—in this case the respectability and reputation for integrity of the newspaper—adds credibility to the message. The *pathos* of the audience—its values, attitudes, beliefs, predispositions, and human capabilities of emotional and rational response to certain stimuli—determines the receptivity to and interpretation of the message. The force of the *logos*—the message itself—does not arise from a disembodied string of intelligible symbols, but from the appropriate manipulation of all the available symbols of communication to make the idea clear, vivid, and probable. The probability of an idea is not determined by mere logic but by the judgment of the audience based on its acceptance of the logic, its trust in the source, and its own experiences, beliefs, attitudes, and values. In this case, the story had behind it the ethos of the *Plain Dealer*, a staid newspaper not given to employing sensational bait-headlines. Some people in the reading audience, however, had already developed doubts and fears about the goals and motivations of the civil rights activists. There were also many people in Cleveland who had recently fled from lands where they had experienced Communist oppression. The effect of a story headlined by such emotionally loaded words as "Reds" and "'Old Pro' Pickets" upon these readers resulted in increased trust in the newspaper for serving their best interests by warning of impending danger and in decreased sympathy or total alienation from the Negro cause. The effect of the story upon the black readers and their white sympathizers was probably just the opposite—a decreased trust in the intelligence and goodwill of the newspaper and a strengthened dedication to the cause.

Violence and protest were not alien to either the foreign-born or native Americans in Cleveland. Only after twenty years of feuding did the Ohio City citizens on the west side of the Cuyahoga River agree to annexation to Cleveland. The first attempt to "bridge" together the two communities resulted in the famous Columbus Street Bridge-war of 1837. Nearly a thousand Ohio City citizens, armed with crowbars, axes, and the blessing of a Presbyterian minister, set out to destroy the bridge. They were matched by a similar mob from Cleveland who even had an old cannon in tow. Before the marshal and sheriff could halt the free-for-all, several men on both sides were wounded.

A hundred years later, in the 1930s, protesters who gathered outside the district relief offices to complain of inadequate food and clothing allowances were met with police clubbings and tear gas. Ethnic and neighborhood rivalries which ended in fisticuffs were common from the early days of immigration to the late 1940s.

But the invasion of the Board of Education was different. It was, first of all, not recognized as a local disturbance. Clevelanders were accustomed to settling their own differences as long as the boundaries were in sight. This time, the implications were broader. The action seemed to be part of a new *national* black movement. The *Plain Dealer* story even hinted that it might be part of an international conspiracy. Certainly, one headline cannot effect a complete change of attitude in a city, but on the other hand the insertion of an inflammatory suggestion at a time of crisis can do nothing to quiet fears nor open the door for rational deliberation.

In the two months following the sit-in, the decline in sympathy from the community at large served to weld the protest groups into a more unified whole, and the sides became more clearly defined. By April 4, 1964, the tactics employed by the United Freedom Movement became more dramatic, and the first tragedy occurred. Demonstrators at school construction sites in the Glenville area had taken to throwing themselves into excavation ditches and in front of the wheels of construction vehicles in order to halt construction. On April 7, Bruce Klunder, the Western Reserve campus minister, stepped behind a bulldozer. A young white woman, later identified as Beth Robinson, pregnant wife of Lewis Robinson (a member of the United Freedom Movement who was later a controversial figure in the Hough riots) threw herself in front of the bulldozer. Trying to avoid the woman's body, the driver of the bulldozer backed up and unknowingly crushed the prone body of Bruce Klunder.

The community was shocked. For the next three days massive picket lines formed at the Board of Education and City Hall, and the city hung on the edge of a race riot. The Reverend Charles Rawlings, the white minister involved in the early civil rights movement, said that "policemen were banging their clubs against garbage cans and walls indicating our heads were going to be next."

While the demonstrators gathered at City Hall, Mayor Ralph Locher, members of the Board of Education, and the negotiating committee of the United Freedom Movement were trying to resolve their differences. Judge John V. Corrigan was called to act as arbitrator. After two hours, an agreement was reached. The judge would impose a double injunction—on the one hand restraining the United Freedom Movement from any further picketing on the school sites (with the exception of the constitutional two or three pickets) and on the other hand restraining the school board from any further construction for the next six weeks which were to be a cooling-off period. During this time national experts would be brought in to Cleveland to study the situation and consult with leaders on both sides to determine recommendations for integrating the schools. Judge Corrigan said that the first temporary injunction and the ex-parte restraining order were issued in an attempt to forestall violence. He pulled the police out of the area and ordered the sheriff to "do all things necessary to accomplish the purpose of this order and to conserve and protect property on the premises." The police had previously been ordered to protect the workers but not to pursue agitators. Bricks had been thrown at the police who, in turn, could only stand and wait. Judge Corrigan's decision to remove the police possibly avoided confrontation.

At the official hearing Judge Corrigan offered a compromise. He asked that work be allowed to continue on the two school sites where contracts had been awarded but that work be delayed at the third school site until the merits of the case were investigated. Judge Corrigan further suggested that a committee of educational specialists be brought in to review the complaints and to recommend a course of action. Neither the Board of Education (which wished to appoint a review committee of its own) nor the United Freedom Movement committee would listen to compromise. Fourteen lawyers participated in the hearing.

Judge Corrigan said he saw merits to both sides of the case, but the issue of school construction was a minor one compared to the larger issue of equal educational opportunities and civil rights. The United Freedom Movement was trying to champion a cause, and the legal aspects of the case were of little importance to them. Frustrated by the lack of cooperation from all parties, Judge Corrigan turned to the law and revised the temporary injunction, maintaining the injunction against the school board. His objective was the cessation of hostilities and the avoidance of further violence. In this he succeeded. No further violence occurred until the Hough riots in 1966. The subsequent school boycott represented a nonviolent expression of unity among Cleveland's black citizenry.

Both newspapers headlined the scheduled school boycott on April 14, 1964, and in a special editorial plea, Louis B. Seltzer, editor of the *Cleveland Press*, urged "responsible Negro leaders" to restore reason. Seltzer was the best known and probably the most powerful man in Cleveland's mass communication field. As editor of the *Press* and editor in chief of the Scripps-Howard Newspapers of Ohio, his powers of persuasion in the community were legend. Some still refer to the election of Mayor Anthony Celebrezze as Seltzer's personal coup and the ultimate assertion of his power.

Since Cleveland television journalism was in its infancy at the beginning of the 1960s, the newspapers still held the position of primary opinion makers in the community. In general, the reporters' attitudes towards the black community were both liberal and sympathetic, but editorial policy, as previously noted, tended to be dictated by the reactions of the readers and the advertisers or, more accurately, the reactions *as perceived* by the editors. In the words of one editorial staff member, civil rights was not, in the 1960s, a very "sexy" topic for the majority of Clevelanders.

Louis Seltzer's appeal to "responsible" leaders resulted in a meeting at the Cedar YMCA. The Reverend Charles Rawlings, who attended the meeting, reported that a new mood expressed itself there. New leaders came forward but they did not act as Seltzer had expected. Instead of responding to his plea of "Don't boycott," the decision was made to endorse the boycott. Dr. Kenneth Clement, Jr., a Negro physician, emerged as a strong, fiery spokesman for the cause.

The school boycott was a tremendous show of strength and unity in the black community, with 85 percent of the school children remaining at home on the scheduled day. This display of unity was regarded by many as a prelude to the Stokes campaigns of 1965 and 1967. Negroes in Cleveland, like the whites, were also divided into haves and have-nots. Many were economically stable and had adequate political representation. In 1961 Cleveland had eight Negro councilmen—a percentage of seats (24.2 percent) which almost corresponded to their population strength. There were two Negroes on the school board. These Negroes, whom Louis Seltzer had labeled "responsible" leaders, during this boycott united briefly with the more militant members of the newest civil rights groups. This situation of uniting for a specific purpose was to recur throughout the decade of the sixties; however, the display of massive unity was generally not sustained after the initial effort, due mainly to the differences in ideology among Negroes (because of the age-old separation-integration conflict).

In 1964, however, a massive effort for unity to achieve political power began. The school boycott proved that it was possible to unite the entire black community. Rawlings made certain analyses which closely examined the potential for black voter-power. The impetus for the Cleveland voter registration drive in 1965 came from those black and white clergymen who had gone down to Mississippi for the same purpose. Political power was becoming the primary goal of the civil rights struggle in Cleveland, because most of the officials of the United Freedom Movement were also engaging in voter registration drives in other parts of the country. All over America the civil rights advocates were learning that black population figures were not accurate. They had been operating under the assumption that Cleveland's Negro population was between 20 and 25 percent, but evidence suggested that between 35 and 40 percent was the more accurate figure.[6]

THE HOUGH RIOTS

Between 1965 and 1967 several events took place that alerted the business community and effected an attitude change in the appraisal of Carl Stokes as candidate for mayor of a large city. In the early sixties prominent businessmen in Cleveland were members of the Fifty Club, the Union Club, the University Club, and the City Club—most of which excluded Negroes and, in some cases, Jews. They appeared quite secure in their exclusiveness. Yet, Leo Jackson, Negro councilman for many years and a man respected by the black and white community for his honesty, integrity, and idealism, claimed that the business community in 1967 was buying *security* in the form of a black mayor. If so, why did the business community feel it needed security in 1967 and not in 1965? Furthermore, was it merely security that was the decisive factor in the decision to support Carl Stokes in 1967?

Since that phrase "buying security in the form of a black mayor" became part of the rhetoric of the 1967 campaign, it is necessary to explore its validity before going on to other possible factors in the eventual defeat of the Locher administration. What happened in Cleveland between 1965 and 1967 was related to what was happening in the nation and, indeed, in the world during those years. The city riot is not just an American tragedy. One of the *universal* problems of city life is the community of the uninformed and the untalented within the larger community. These people, assigned the lowest paying jobs, know they are insignificant and unsuccessful, and sooner or later they rebel against the society that assigned them this role. It is not necessarily a racial problem. It is rather a violence stemming from *conditions* that cause eruptions in Russia, in Prague, in London, in Sudan, in Mauritania, in Kenya, and in Pakistan.

When frustration leads to violence, analysts are always quick to identify the most visible as the prime factor, that is, the factor which makes men feel different from each other socially, economically, or culturally. In America, especially, color is the most visible factor; therefore, racism is generalized to be the prime and root cause of all violence involving blacks living in white-dominated communities. Such generalizations are dangerous in their simplicity because they overlook the specific words and deeds which provoke this violence, in this place, at this time, by these persons. The general feeling of despair and suffering is the universal theme, but the assignment of individual roles and the playing out of the drama as it occurred in Cleveland's Hough area in 1966 bear tracing if the impact of the incident on the whole community is to be understood.

The first act could be set at the newly created JFK House (Jomo Freedom Kenyatta House), a recreation center for young blacks founded in 1964 by Lewis G. Robinson after he was fired from his job as a Cleveland housing inspector. Whatever the motives of the founder of the JFK House, it became popular as a gathering place for Negro youth in the Glenville area, and, though viewed with disfavor by some leaders in both the black and white communities, apparently no incident of consequence occurred to focus attention upon it until January of 1966.

According to Robinson's autobiography, *The Making of a Man*, an article in a neighborhood newspaper, the *Drummer*, of January, 1966, reported that on Wednesday, January 19, at 6:30 P.M. two white youths and their father were brutally beaten by five youths in an alleged robbery incident. According to a *Cleveland Press* account, the five *Negro* youths were demanding protection money from white youths. The next day police officers reportedly started picking up and questioning youths from the neighborhood, all of them Negro. Robinson wrote that on the Friday following the incident, Juvenile Officers John Smith and Charles McWhorter (also Negroes) entered the JFK House where a teen-age dance was in progress. Robinson was summoned to the scene by a youth and, according to the autobiography, parked his car behind the police vehicle. Recalling the event, Robinson said he got out of the car and addressed Officer Smith:

> Don't run over our kids just because two white kids have been beaten up. Hell, you never see the white policemen arrest white kids when black kids are beaten. It's just another nigger to them.[7]

Robinson contended that he had embarrassed the officers in the presence of witnesses, and they reacted by arresting him. "What for?" said Robinson. Smith, reportedly, said he would think of something and called for a paddy wagon.

Robinson and two others were held without charge in jail overnight. Two days later Robinson was again arrested, this time on a warrant signed by Officer McWhorter charging that on that previous Friday night Robinson had careened around the corner at a high rate of speed. (He was not cleared of this charge until well over a year later, in November, 1967).

The next day Robinson and a band of youths from the JFK House picketed the Fifth District Police Station protesting the treatment of the young people at the dance and the subsequent arrests of their leader and friends. The day after Robinson was arrested on the speeding charge, the group picketed the City Council meeting, at which time Negro

JFK House
Photograph courtesy of Lewis G. Robinson

Councilmen Leo Jackson and George Forbes praised the two black policemen (Smith and McWhorter) and said that a crackdown on numbers operators and sellers of marijuana was needed.

On February 5, the *Call and Post*, Cleveland's black weekly newspaper, carried an article by Bob Williams (presently employed by the *Cleveland Press*). Williams further explored the incident and reported another occurrence: "Last Christmas morning two Negro men were set upon by a gang of white hoodlums at the corner of St. Clair Avenue and East 79th Street." Williams wondered why this incident was not investigated in depth as was the incident in which white youths were attacked.

According to Robinson's account, all this time Glenville Councilman Leo Jackson kept saying, "I'm asking that something be done—a crash program if necessary to stem this general lawlessness. The city cannot progress if Glenville is going to hell." Robinson quoted Councilman Forbes, also from a black ward, as blaming the bombing of a record shop at East 113th and St. Clair on the numbers racketeers. Robinson felt both councilmen were dodging the basic issue—unequal law enforcement.

On February 11, 1966, the *Cleveland Press* deplored the fact that the militant JFK House had become the main gathering place for teenagers. The *Press* admitted the need for a place to dance and see friends and hear lectures on Negro history but felt that this need should be met by the Scouts, the churches, and school groups. On February 14 a publication called the *Militant*, distributed in the area, favorably described JFK House: "Lewis Robinson supported Carl Stokes for Mayor, ran as an Independent for City Council and came in a close second to the white incumbent. Donald Freeman, who was fired from his teaching position, teaches Afro-American history at the JFK House. JFK House is a meeting place for the Freedom Fighters, a militant civil rights organization."

JFK House was incurring financial difficulties during this time, and the Reverend Charles Rawlings, hearing of its dilemma, started a fund drive. He was supported in the drive by B. Kenneth McGee (who had helped in the 1965 Stokes campaign), Harold Weinstein, Hilbert Perry, and Mrs. Harley King—all of whom were identified as nonmilitant civil rights advocates. Rawlings said that $1,062 monthly was needed to pay Lewis Robinson and four members of the JFK House Board of Control, which included Harllel Jones, a city sanitation department employee who was to play a prominent role in Cleveland's racial history in the ensuing years.

The *Plain Dealer* denounced the fund drive, opposing the JFK House as a recreational center and suggesting instead that the youths gather at 8819 Wade Park Avenue where the Police Athletic League provided activities for youth. The editorial added, "The vesting of Robinson with the prestige of ministerial support and financial endowment gives him a stature to which nothing in his record entitles him."

Councilman Leo Jackson issued a statement supporting the *Plain Dealer's* editorial position that no one "in his right mind would support the irresponsible leadership of the JFK House." On May 7, even the *Call and Post* attacked the white leaders who were supporting the fund drive to reopen JFK House.

Despite an apparent lack of support from the established community leaders, Rawlings was successful in his fund drive, and the JFK House was reopened in May, 1966. The professionals offered support as well; psychologists and psychiatrists from Western Reserve University worked with Robinson's staff in group discussion sessions with teen groups.

Each person views and judges the phenomena of his life-world in his own unique way. In group life this fact of individual evaluation complicates the process of solving the very problems which prevent or deter the attainment of group goals. As philosopher and educator John Dewey pointed out, understanding the real nature of a problem and all its ramifications is half the solution. In group problem-solving, however, individuals, limited as they are to their own views of the world, must accept the existence of other views and work towards reaching *agreement* on the nature of the problem before deliberating the merits of solutions. If each member of the group insists on defining the problem in his own way, there can be no possible agreement on a solution. Conflict will result as each member becomes more defensive about the rightness of his definition. Eventually the defensiveness about one's definitions will extend to the whole self, and every assertion of a contrary opinion will be taken as an affront to the whole being. Unless the conflict can be resolved by compromise or arbitration, either the group will have to dissolve or fists will fly and the conflict will be settled by the victory of the physically strongest.

Obviously some kind of community problem existed in Cleveland in the mid-sixties which related to the social and recreational needs of black youths in the inner city. The symptoms of a social malady were acknowledged, but there was no attempt to make a realistic diagnosis before prescribing a palliative. Lewis Robinson provided a solution to the problem as he, personally, had defined it—the JFK House. Other members of the community rejected the solution and began to define the

Councilman Leo Jackson
Photograph by Odyssey Associates

Carl Stokes
Photograph courtesy
of the City of Cleveland

problem in their own ways, insisting that theirs was the right way. Soon other vocal members of the community advanced and extended the controversy over whose definition was right, and there followed a choosing-up of sides. All sides barricaded themselves behind their defenses. Even the most innocuous word or act was perceived as an attack or a threat. The situation was ripe for open conflict. Shouts of justification filled the air, but nowhere was there heard a murmur of compromise or conciliation.

Following the January, 1966, incident when a white father and his sons had been attacked by black youths, there were sporadic clashes between black and white youngsters in the Superior-Sowinski area. By late spring the gang fights in the Sowinski Park area occurred more often and more intensely. The white boys apparently claimed Sowinski Park and were ready to defend it against any black comers. Negro parents complained to the police and the mayor and asked that interracial police squads be assigned to Sowinski Park to insure equal law enforcement for both black and white. But apparently no direct action was taken at City Hall to reduce either the gang clashes or the mounting tensions.

While some black groups were pressing for more police activity to ward off a crisis situation, others were reportedly encouraging the black teen-age gangs into greater militancy and aggressiveness. One such group (allegedly working out of the JFK House) was trying to gain rapport with the young blacks and recruit them into the militant nationalist movement. Whether similar white groups were encouraging their youngsters to continue the warfare is not known, but it seems obvious that no one was actively trying to discourage the white gangs.

The first major incident occurred the night of June 22, 1966, when a white gang attacked two Negro youths. An angry crowd gathered at the corner of Ninetieth and Superior in protest. Police arrived and listened to the reports of the incident but allegedly refused to initiate an investigation. Infuriated blacks retaliated with several rock and bottle throwing incidents throughout the night.

The next evening there was a meeting of JFK House youths, their adult leaders (Harllel Jones, Charles S. Bey, and Lewis Robinson), and representatives of the Fifth District Police Station. The boys claimed they needed police protection. Robinson said the police asked for names and addresses of the white boys who were allegedly molesting them. Another source claimed the police excused themselves as too overworked and understaffed to investigate every incident. Whatever the police response to the situation may have been, it was not satisfactory to the representatives of the black groups, and there occurred another night of rock throwing and window smashing.

The following night a Negro boy was shot. The alleged assailants were two white men driving a blue Corvair who were somehow linked to the owner of a supermarket at Eighty-ninth and Superior. Police made no arrests on the basis of the information received, and the next night the supermarket was burned to the ground. The following day Mayor Locher met with residents of the area, heard their grievances, and promised to give them consideration. Peace was restored.

One month later the Hough riots broke out. The Cuyahoga County Grand Jury was impaneled to investigate the causes of the riots and bring forth indictments against probable perpetrators. The report of the foreman of the grand jury, Louis B. Seltzer, editor of the *Cleveland Press*, implicated several people, made accusations, and laid blame on several heads but formally indicted none. No real connection could be found between the Hough riots and either the JFK House or the people involved in the supermarket incident, but the grand jury report implied a positive connection. The same people had been seen in both areas; targets for destruction in both areas had been highly selective. This was indicative of prior specification of victims. The grand jury report linked Lewis Robinson with known Communists, and it stated that he had "pledged reciprocal support to and with the Communist Party of Ohio." The report implicated the JFK House as a rifle club and stated that speeches were made at the JFK House about Molotov cocktails: how to make them and how and when to throw them to obtain maximum effect. The report maintained that ". . . the outbreak of lawlessness and disorder was both organized, precipitated, and exploited by a relatively small group of trained and disciplined professionals at this business. They were aided and abetted, wittingly or otherwise, by misguided people of all ages and colors, many of whom are avowed believers in violence and extremism, and some of whom also are either members of or officers in the Communist Party."[8]

The findings of the grand jury caused considerable consternation in some parts of the community. A "citizens' hearing" was convened by several community organizations at Liberty Hill Baptist Church. On four consecutive evenings in August, 1966, twenty-six witnesses testified before and were questioned by five experienced and noted lawyers and by members of the panel who represented CORE, NAACP, Council of Churches, Negro Pastors Association, Hough Community Opportunity Board, the National Association of Social Workers, and the Wade Park Citizens Group. The panel brought forth its own report.

The "Report of the Panel Hearings on the Superior and Hough Disturbances" charged that the action of the grand jury was in direct violation of the Ohio Code which specifies that names of people suspected of subversive activity cannot be made public unless there is sufficient evidence for indictment or the consent of the state attorney is given. The citizens' report further stated that the "main thrust of the present Negro struggle is to become an integral part of the American economic system based on a philosophy of private property and incentive," and that the grand jury displayed "abysmal ignorance of American Negro history" when it believed that the Negro community could be stimulated by Communist outsiders. The report cited the grand jury's failure to give prominence to social conditions as a major cause of the riots.

The specific events leading to the outbreak of violence in Hough as described by the designated principal, Lewis Robinson, make both reports sound sanctimonious. Robinson stated that on July 18 he was at the JFK House watching his boys boxing when one of the girls came from upstairs and said very calmly that Harllel Jones was looking for him. "A boy is upstairs from Hough telling him [Jones] that a colored woman has just been shot on a bus on 79th Street." Robinson's immediate reaction was, "Superior and St. Clair again, those stupid-ass white kids!"[9] Several of the young boys wanted to go into the area, but Robinson told them, "Don't get involved and don't go off half-cocked." Jones himself then came in and stated that several boys on the street heard that two white men at the bar at East Seventy-ninth Street and Hough were holding guns on the black people and refused to give a black man a drink of water at the bar.

Robinson said he then ordered his boys to stay out of the Hough area, and he left for Hough, where he found a large crowd of about fifty people. Robinson related: "One of the brothers was saying, 'We've got to teach whitey a lesson. He come in here, steal and buy our women, proposition my mother, my sister, and my aunt, just because she's black and she lives on Hough. Now, this son of a bitch tonight refused to give a black man a glass of ice water to drink after spending his hard money for a goddamn fifth of wine.' "[10] (Another report said that the white manager of the bar told a Negro barmaid to "serve no niggers no damn water," and a sign was placed outside the door, reading No Water for Niggers.)

Robinson said the crowd was too emotional to be reached by reason. The brick throwing and looting began. Robinson described a drugstore at East Eighty-ninth Street:

> I stared at the front of the drugstore in disbelief. This store, equipped with heavy iron bars and grills, anchored in the brick wall to ward off burglars, was an unbelievable sight. Someone or ones with the new-found strength of Samson had peeled the iron bars away from the building. The place was looted.[11]

All the windows of the 79er Bar, where it all started, were broken and splintered. The side window facing Seventy-ninth Street had smoke marks where a Molotov cocktail had done its work. Robinson continued:

> For some people it was like a picnic, milling around, talking about the white man, laughing at the scared cops. . . .
>
> Through it all, a young black cop stood alone just east of the intersection near a beat car. Someone yelled, "Aren't you scared, blackie?"
>
> "Hell no," he answered, "I'm home!" The crowd roared with laughter. . . .
>
> That was Hough—a dirty grin with some teeth knocked out. We left the scene at 75th Street and headed south to Euclid Avenue. As we waited for the traffic light to change, I noticed a long line of more than two hundred people, mostly white, waiting for the next show to go on at Leo's Casino. I looked at the marquee to see who was the star attraction. It read, "The Supremes—Show Business' Most Successful Act!" What an incongruity. Black folks burning down Hough just two blocks away and hundreds of white people standing in the rain to see and hear and applaud three black women on stage.[12]

More teeth were knocked out as Hough continued to burn for three more days. But the cycle of controversy was spent. While the rumblings of discontent were noticed, there was a failure to come to agreement on the nature and realities of the problem. Nobody could say, "*This* is the problem. Now what shall we do about it?" Too many people insisted on the "rightness" of their own definitions, while the problem continued to rankle and irritate those who were helpless to cure it themselves.

The cycle began again. Recognition that a problem existed came from all quarters, again with little attempt to define what it was. The problem of the long, hot summer remained undefined, but it became obvious that a winter of discontent had set in.

An academic participant at a mass-media seminar on race relations put it in this way:

> The gut of the problem is that white people are in a state of shock caused by fear after that riot. That nigger at the bottom, who always knew his place, dares to tell us that he no longer buys the old dream. Now he says, "What's in it for me?" He doesn't realize that black people are supposed to tell it like it is by praying, singing, and marching. Instead he's throwing Molotov cocktails, bricks, and looting.

Fred Griffith of WEWS-TV expressed the stunned reaction of the city's news media:

> The Hough riots started the week I started here. I was over at the desk on the first night. One of our cameramen was pinned down behind his car, and he had the microphone to his little radio and he says, "Baby, this is war." And he kept saying it over and over again. He couldn't believe he was in it.

Given the information, the community found it difficult to evaluate the true situation. It is interesting to note that the citizens' panel composed of groups from the black community labeled the whole affair "Hough Disturbances." The grand jury called it "Hough Riots," and the media said, "Baby, this is war!" News films of those days in July, 1966, obtained from three local television stations, showed a surprising lack of violence. A professor at Western Reserve University, viewing the film clips, was heard to remark dryly that Cleveland had just not "made it" with a full-scale riot of the Watts and Detroit class.

But if there wasn't a first-class riot in 1966, the incident developed into one in 1967 as a result of the campaign rhetoric. Unquestionably the few days of rioting in Hough were the darkest period in Mayor Ralph Locher's administration. The Locher administration had already been under attack by the press for several years. When Locher had inherited the mayor's chair from Anthony Celebrezze who was appointed secretary of the U.S. Department of Health, Education, and Welfare in the Kennedy administration, Locher had also inherited Celebrezze's appointees and Cleveland's long-standing problems.

Although the Annual Report of 1959–60 for the city of Cleveland glowed with enthusiasm and accomplishment and Mayor Celebrezze's open letter stated that the "city's heartbeat is pulsing with a new tempo," the city was overextended on its renewal projects. Ralph Locher was certainly aware of the problems and weaknesses in his administration, and in December, 1965, he joined with the president of City Council in creating the Cleveland Little Hoover Commission to make in-depth studies of all city of Cleveland operations. The studies, made in cooperation with responsible city officials, were nineteen in number and contained six hundred recommendations.

Perhaps the best analysis of what was "wrong" with the Locher administration can be found in the "Chapla Report on Urban Renewal" published by the Cleveland Little Hoover Commission on November 16, 1966. Each separate report of progress, or lack of it, in urban renewal presented evidence that interdepartmental communication and cooperation at City Hall was almost nonexistent. Deadlines were rarely met, and the mayor's enforcement of deadlines was lax. In one instance, a request by the law director for a report was answered a year and a half later, but there was no indication that either the law director or the mayor pushed for compliance. In short, Ralph Locher, for all his honesty and integrity, was not demanding enough of his administration.

Thomas Vail of the *Plain Dealer* had been the first to endorse Locher in his bid for election in 1963, but by 1967 Vail had withdrawn his support. Said Vail, "It was my feeling that Locher had come to the end of his real usefulness as far as a leader in the community was concerned." Russell Kane, city editor of the *Plain Dealer*, thought members of the administration "had dug their own graves." Kane claimed, "When Locher refused to meet with the United Freedom Movement and said they couldn't shoot their way into his office—from then on he became more and more, not paranoid, but something like that—where he wouldn't talk to reporters."

Reporters, both local and out-of-town, became very harsh in their criticisms. A *Look* article of May 30, 1967, "You Can't Stop the Riot That's Coming," spoke of the failure at City Hall. John Skow, writing in the *Saturday Evening Post*, July 29, 1967, called Locher an "amiable and ineffective time-server," adding that he was "the last in a string of non-mayors." However, Skow, like most out-of-town writers, had obtained his information from local reporters and from certain personalities the reporters identified only as "colorful."[13] According to City Hall sources, Skow never interviewed Mayor Locher, but his article was accepted and made use of by Locher foes as if it were fact. Thus, with an unfriendly press, civil unrest in the inner city, and a poor image at City Hall, Ralph Locher became the focal point for Cleveland citizens who, after Hough, began to feel uncomfortable and began to seek out the "cause" of their discomfort.

Threatened by the recent turn of events, Clevelanders began to examine documents and records and to consult with those who had already determined causes and consequences. They studied the product—not the process—and they found it disturbing. While there is a certain justification in lingering over history for any study, it must be understood that records are static because they are final summations. From the records, one can arrive at certain generalizations and statistical analyses from which causes can be inferred, but the process is often more revealing than the product, for it shows the *interactions of people*. These interactions make the events meaningful.

From the general feeling of discomfort within the city, a controversy emerged between various citizens which became the first stage in what is now identified as a historical movement. If Clevelanders had decided during this first stage of the movement that the protest raised by various crusaders was not convincing, the debate would no doubt have ended. But the expressions of discontent were too widespread.

Ideas arise from all levels of life. They do not emerge full-blown. They evolve. They are uttered softly sometimes and vehemently at others. They are often reorganized and reinterpreted as they find their way into persuasive acts. They become more persistent as the avid search for solutions becomes more vocal and as the debate begins.

Though there were a number of citizens who decried the tendency for change, enough people were convinced during the first stage of this movement that there indeed existed a serious threat to their society. In the early spring of 1967 there arose an overwhelming desire for change. A growing number of Clevelanders were disturbed by the threatening social changes in their city and feared for the future. The desire for change propelled them into a search for new ways to solve problems and, ultimately, for new leadership. Ralph Locher, who had won in the past on the basis of his unchallenged honesty, was now constantly pictured as the man unable to cope with the urban crises which Clevelanders were now willing to admit existed.

CHAPTER 2

THE MOVEMENT FOR CHANGE

THE CLEVELAND primary campaign of 1967 had style in the classical sense; metaphors and other figurative language abounded in reference to the event. The television men called it a "big show," "an arena of talent." The newspapers referred to the Locher administration as a "crumbling dynasty." James Howard of Edward Howard and Company, a public relations firm, spoke of the conflict between the Aristotelian and Sophistic schools of rhetoric.[1] In the hands of the man on the street, a microphone became an invitation to oratorical heights. Clevelanders were also willing to listen, and the city became filled with the likes of Socrates, who once referred to himself as "a pining man who was frantic to hear speeches."

To study a campaign by looking at the speeches and the persuasive acts is to capture a particular moment in time. Unlike formal documents, a speech records a speaker's position at a particular moment—it reflects the influences brought to bear on him up to that moment and plants another seed of influence which will be acted upon by others. But a political campaign does not consist merely of formal speeches of candidates. It is a dynamic collection of communicative acts, each influenced by the combined constituents of speaker, listener, message, medium, and context—each creating a new relationship among the constituents of the acts which follow.

In an article entitled, "The Rhetoric of Historical Movements," Professor Leland Griffin identifies three phases inherent in any movement.[2] The first of these is a period of inception, which is a time when ideas begin to come alive or when some striking event occurs which creates a host of aggressor-rhetoricians.

Cleveland had gone through that first phase when the Hough riots occurred and when the black power movement gained momentum. An earlier "striking" event had occurred when Police Chief Richard Wagner testified before an Ohio House Committee in Columbus on June 7, 1965, in defense of capital punishment. Upholding the state's death penalty, Wagner said: "In Cleveland . . . we have people saying they intend to overthrow the government of the United States and, incidentally, shoot all the Caucasians. One of these groups is RAM (Revolutionary Action Movement)."[3] Many reporters later pinpointed the demise of the Locher administration to that brief moment when a man voiced his opinion about capital punishment and gave as support the name of a revolutionary group.

Civil rights groups demanded an explanation from Chief Wagner. They resented the implication that a Cleveland group was subversive. Many of the supporters of the United Freedom Movement said Wagner's comment was something they could use to their advantage. They claimed it was the same kind of rhetoric used in the grand jury report about the Hough riots which had so inflamed black citizens. While Chief Wagner was expressing his support of capital punishment and using as his motivation the many threats upon the lives of his policemen, his remarks reverberated through the corridors of City Hall during the period of the sit-in demonstrations. Chief Wagner's comment became the source of another argument in the fight for change which was to characterize the second phase of the historical movement.

The second phase, according to Professor Griffin, involves a period of rhetorical crisis when one of the opposing groups of rhetoricians succeeds in disturbing the balance between the groups which until then has existed in the mind of the collective audience. It was in this phase of rhetorical crisis that the citizens of Cleveland decided to take the initial step and select the men who would lead them on to the final stage—one of consummation. The deliberative writing and speaking, the planning and counselling which would lead to the solving of problems could not begin until the leaders and spokesmen had been chosen.

The search for spokesmen began in the spring of 1967.

Seth Taft, grandson of a President, appeared to claim the Republican nomination in the early spring, but the press and the public came to look, and looking, withdrew. The Republican one-man primary race stirred little sporting interest. The first man to be wooed by businessmen for the leading role in the real contest, the Democratic primary, was Frank Celeste—an energetic sixty-year-old man, former suburban mayor (Lakewood), president of the Ohio Council of Churches, practicing lawyer, and president and director of National Housing Consultants, Inc. Then James V. Stanton, thirty-five year-old president of City Council, was pressed by friends to consider the mayor's role. Several others were also considered, among them Charles Vanik, the Democratic congressman from the Twenty-first District. Then, unexpectedly, a man came forth to *apply* for the job.

On the filing date, July 5, Carl B. Stokes, who had this time gathered sixty thousand Independent signatures on petitions which would enable him to bypass the primary, decided instead to file in the Democratic primary. This move surprised some politicians and caused Common Pleas Judge Frank D. Celebrezze to abandon his own plans for filing in the Democratic primary. He didn't like the odds presented by such a crowded starting lineup. Frank P. Celeste filed his petitions. James Stanton's nominating petitions did not contain the required master petition, which is the first petition taken out upon declaring one's intention to run. It is notarized and copies are then made of the original petition. Both the original and copies must be filed. Stanton was attending a funeral at the time of filing and Councilman George White, who later became a judge, went back to Stanton's office and found the master petition, This simple act of kindness almost cost White his council seat, as it was interpreted as an anti-Stokes act. Carl Stokes had not concerned himself with filing a master petition. Were it not for Deputy Director of Elections Joseph P. Mull, who caught the error, Frank Celeste would have been the only legitimate Democratic contender against the incumbent for the office of mayor. Incumbent Mayor Ralph Locher filed his petitions properly. At that point James Stanton decided the race was too crowded and, predicting accurately that the contest would be between Carl Stokes and Ralph Locher, he withdrew.

In order to analyze the rhetoric within this phase of the movement it is necessary to distinguish two classes of rhetoricians: aggressor-orators and mediators who gather around them the events of the day, shape them, reshape them, and hurl them forth to effect change upon the world; and defender-orators and mediators who resist change and defend existing ideas and institutions. The term "mediator" here includes newspapers, news magazines, radio and television newscasts or documentaries, press services, trade magazines, corporate house organs, or any other agencies which interpret acts and events *for* an audience.

Aristotle described the art of rhetoric as the faculty of finding all the available means of persuasion in a given case. The result of the rhetorician's application of this art is the manifestation of the communicator's choices of what, among the myriad utterances, will be most persuasive with this audience at this time in this context. Even the most studious and prudent application of the art of rhetoric by a speaker does not guarantee that he will persuade his audience unless the credibility of the speaker (ethos), the values and predispositions of the audience—human capabilities of emotional and rational response to certain stimuli (pathos), and the message itself (logos) interlock in the right combination. In a political campaign the persuasive purpose of any rhetorician is to elicit the specific responsive act from each registered voter of marking an "X" beside his name on the ballot.

As the period of rhetorical crisis drew near there appeared three aggressor-orators and one defender-orator ready to engage in decisive verbal combat. But before the public speaking could begin, the candidates and their advisers had to sift ideas, plan, write, rewrite, and revise. Even the best-laid plans were subject to revisions as the candidates began to confront each other and their publics.

Ralph Locher, the single defender, had as his campaign manager Bronis J. Klementowicz, the law director of Cleveland. Called the "Silver Falcon" because of the steel-gray shock of hair that fell heavily over his brow and dark, penetrating eyes that could send sparks in all directions, Klementowicz's trademarks were his cigarette holder and his quick wit. "This is a very cosmopolitan city," he would explain to visitors. "I'm Polish myself." Putting on his overcoat after one interview was finished, he said, "I got this seven years ago from a guy named Levy. Changed his name to get the Jewish trade. He really was Polish." Locher, the only candidate who did not hire a public relations firm, drew assistance from Klementowicz, his staff, the Democratic party, and the people at the ward level.

Frank Celeste employed C. Robert (Bob) Carr as his campaign and advertising manager. Carr left a well-paying job in public relations to work full time in the campaign. He later claimed he never had the opportunity for the creativity he anticipated.

Carl Stokes prevailed upon Alexander Ostrow, veteran ex-newspaperman (*Cleveland Press*) and prolific ghostwriter, to take over his public relations job. Ostrow, his office floors sagging from the newspapers piled almost to the ceiling, his desk cluttered with scripts containing both fact and fiction, was to be the center of much controversy. Directing Stokes's political campaign this time was Dr. Kenneth Clement, Jr., a courageous civil rights defender who later became disillusioned with the Stokes regime.

There were also many women gathered around Carl Stokes, all dedicated and devoted to the man and/or the cause. Geraldine Williams, perhaps the most prominent, handled the secretarial duties of the organization. She said of her experience:

> Well, '67 was going to be a slick professional campaign. When Carl decided to run he called all the old workers and told us that

> the campaign was to be run by Ostrow and Company. Both Ken McGee and I said, "Give us a chance, Carl; you know we learned enough in the last campaign to run this one." He said that this one has got to be different, and nothing will ever be like '65 again.

John C. Little, a young man who sounded and acted as if he were fresh out of college, and Dr. Louis Masotti, a political scientist from Case Western Reserve University, offered to research material for Stokes's speeches. Eventually Masotti and Ostrow were to disagree, and Masotti withdrew from the campaign. Masotti was later to reassert himself, however, in the first major crisis of the Stokes administration.

Seth Taft, unchallenged in the Republican primary, nonetheless marshalled a young and impressive campaign force very early. William Silverman, Jr., vice-president of the Edward Howard and Company advertising agency, was assigned the job of public relations manager. A slightly built young man, he occupied an office that was in direct contrast to Ostrow's—neat to the point of sterility. There were no drawers in his desk, no papers on the floor. A large window gave light. Silverman was young, but there was no room for fantasy. Silverman, too, would become a figure of controversy in the Stokes administration.

Robert Bennett, a young, stocky man with a drawl, was the campaign manager for Seth Taft. He gathered his "school chums" to work for Taft and ran a modern campaign complete with graphs and charts, poll-taking and vote-pulling studies.

There were other men behind the scenes with the power of influence and money, the necessary political angels. Important among this group were Cyrus Eaton, James and John Carney (vice-chairmen of the County Democratic Committee), Ralph Besse (chairman of the Board of the Cleveland Electric Illuminating Company), John W. Reavis (of Jones, Day, Cockley, and Reavis law firm where Seth Taft was employed), Howard Metzenbaum (of APCOA, a parking-lot company), and Albert Porter (chairman of the Cuyahoga County Democratic Committee). Included here were also the images of President Lyndon B. Johnson and the national Democratic party powers. Richard Maher of the *Press* stated in an article dated December 23, 1969, "It was put to Stokes bluntly: 'Run as a Democrat and we'll help you.' "

There are many other forms of power which figure in a political campaign: press, money, numbers, geographic location, organization, knowledge, etc. The old politicians claimed three forms were needed to win an election: money, newspapers, and organization. In the 1967 campaign the "newcomers" were adding different concepts derived from sociological studies and political science reports. There was conflict within the campaign organizations between ideologies, between youth and age, between grassroots politicians and those they called "ivy-leaguers." The ivy-leaguers were not necessarily identified by the cut of their coats. They were, however, generally young, interested in audience analysis studies and structured campaign scheduling; they were also generally unable to be compassionate towards the old-time precinct committeeman who was ready to move on feelings rather than figures.

As the momentum grew and the voices of the city became more audible, the mediators visibly entered the race, sometimes merely to present but more often to persuade. The influence of Thomas Boardman, editor in chief of the *Cleveland Press*, and Thomas Vail, Jr., editor and publisher of the *Cleveland Plain Dealer*, was reflected in varying degrees by the reporters themselves. James Naughton of the *Plain Dealer*, an intense young man sincerely dedicated to change, and Richard Maher, respected veteran political reporter of the *Press*, led the way.

Eventually the eager voters, frantic to hear speeches, also decided to engage in the rhetoric. Encouraged by the mediators, they became adept at being interviewed, accustomed to the newspaperman's pencil and the television lights. Of these eager 326,003 registered voters, 34,000 were Republicans, the remainder Democrats and Independents.

The planning stage of the campaign to persuade the voters actually began months before the filing date for most of the candidates. For Frank Celeste, perhaps it had started years before. Celeste said that Louis Seltzer had been after him for years to run and, finally, when a change was needed in Cleveland, Seltzer and several other influential Clevelanders came to him. Celeste said: "First Seltzer. And then they had me meet with Tom Boardman and Tom Vail, both of whom pledged their support. What really made me make the decision was when Jack Reavis came out to see me. It was the first time he had been on the west side. He said he had never been on 'the gold coast.' He sat in the chair over there and outlined what they would do. They thought they could deliver the newspapers; they thought they could deliver the funds. Also I met with Albert Porter and he indicated, and the indications were—up until the night Locher had filed—that the party was going to endorse me."

Celeste had promises, promises, promises. Upon them he built his campaign strategy. Carr, his campaign manager, said that while fortified with these promises he conducted a survey by telephone of four hundred Clevelanders asking about their preference for mayor, pitting Celeste against Locher, Taft against Locher, and Stokes against

Locher. Carr said that Celeste ran better than any of the others and claimed that people who did not even know who Celeste was said they would prefer him to Locher. However, the survey did not test the lineup that finally developed: Stokes, Locher, Celeste.

Frank Celeste formed a strategy committee composed of Don Carmichael, Richard Celeste, Sidney Spector, and Robert Carr. They came up with thirteen housing "issues":

1. Enforce housing code to "clean up Cleveland."
2. Establish a "traffic court" procedure to process housing violations.
3. Set up "community rehabilitation" boards to encourage neighborhood improvements.
4. Provide tax relief for homeowners who rehabilitate their properties.
5. Seek financial help for new home builders.
6. Appoint a task force to study means of lowering building costs.
7. Encourage steps to make home-building profitable for industry.
8. Provide temporary homes for families relocated by development projects.
9. Encourage developers to employ good architectural design.
10. Set up a fund to encourage neighborhood family businesses.
11. Computerize housing information to facilitate efficient flow.
12. Provide mechanisms for "get-involved" loans of personnel among various housing and development agencies.
13. Appoint a "deputy mayor" for community development.[4]

Frank Celeste was a builder. He was selling his construction experience in housing and neighborhood renewal. Unfortunately, in 1967, nobody seemed to be interested in the housing crisis which was to become such an issue in 1969 and 1970.

Celeste also detailed a program to improve public safety. He promised to:

1. Insure that citizens throughout the city receive *equal protection* and that the law be *enforced equally* in all neighborhoods.
2. Revamp the police procedure to guarantee that legitimate complaints be acted upon promptly and not be ignored or rebuffed.

3. Open the doors at Police Headquarters *outward* by beefing up the police-community relations program.
4. Build respect for law enforcement officers by strengthening their self-respect through better pay, improved professional training and sounder promotion policies.
5. Wipe out inefficiencies in the Police Department by reorganizing and streamlining lines of responsibility and authority.
6. Establish a new police communications system to permit flexibility in the use of patrol cars and speed up responses to calls.
7. Increase the number of police cars on patrol by reducing the number of men assigned to each car from two to one.
8. Hire civilians to do clerical work, car repairs, receive bail and guard prisoners, thus releasing more professional police for active law enforcement.
9. Recruit and examine applicants for the police force on a year-round basis rather than periodically.
10. Use available federal funds to provide police training both in the department and at cooperating universities.
11. Improve street lighting throughout the city.
12. Institute a riot-duty training program for all police officers.[5]

Celeste recognized the major problem areas, many of which were to crop up later, but his audience at this time did not seem interested in problem-solving. A political campaign is not the time for deliberative rhetoric where issues are debated. What usually passes for an "issue" in a campaign is really no more than an affirmation of a generally held value. At real "issue" are alternative choices of action to reach an accepted goal. Thus, with pollution, the issue is not *whether* we should have pollution, but what is the best method of eliminating pollution. A candidate who says he is "against pollution" is not "coming out on the issue" but merely endorsing a value. Once queried about whether he thought corruption would be an issue in the campaign, former Ohio Governor Mike DiSalle said he supposed so but couldn't imagine who would take the "pro" side.

Accustomed to thinking in solidified categories, the politicians and the voters failed to recognize that Frank Celeste was proposing specific courses of action to resolve two basic community problems. He was raising genuine issues which could be debated. Klementowicz, Locher's campaign manager, reflected this mistaken notion of issues when he commented: "In a campaign you can't have more than two issues. If you've got three you have too many, and he [Celeste] had a baker's dozen."

But both Celeste and Klementowicz missed the point. There is only one issue in a campaign: Which *candidate* will best serve the needs of the constituency? The voter does not vote on the ways and means a candidate proposes for solving problems, but on the candidate himself. What a candidate says, favors, and proposes gives the voters reasons for choosing one candidate over the other, but the vote itself is an expression of confidence that, given the chance, *this candidate* will act more prudently on specific matters than his opponents.

Celeste presented himself as a knowledgeable problem-solver in two areas—urban renewal and law enforcement—but he became bogged down with specifics and plans. The voters were looking for reasons to trust him; he was confusing them with details of matters they weren't being asked to decide. No speaker could explain and elaborate on the many proposals contained in Celeste's position papers because a candidate's schedule calls for him to meet with many people briefly rather than few people in depth. Celeste should have narrowed his ideas into a short presentation suitable for a variety of audiences.

Mediators covering campaigns often fail to recognize that a candidate meets with segments of his total audience and that, except for a few adaptive utterances to meet the specific audience on a specific occasion, he must redeliver the same message many times. A reporter may have to attend the meetings in Wards Seven, Eleven, and Thirteen, but it is highly unlikely that the members of the three ward clubs will travel to each other's domains. So the candidate repeats his one message to three separate audiences. Bob Harper of WKYC-TV covered Celeste every night of the primary campaign and observed that he was giving the same speech. He took film clips from several performances and compared them—on the air. He noted that Celeste was repeating the same speech over and over again. According to Martin Haag, the news editor of WKYC-TV, this editorial comment by Harper prompted Celeste to write a new speech. It also demonstrates how effectively a mediator can insert himself into the campaign as a persuasive force.

The assignment of one news reporter to the same candidate over an extended period of time can work either to the advantage or disadvantage of the candidate and the public. The reporter's conscious or unconscious attitude towards the candidate cannot be entirely erased from his reporting. The reporter thus becomes a rhetorical force in the campaign not only as he addresses the voting public but as his style of coverage affects the behavior of the candidate.

By the time the actual campaign was under way Celeste was not a serious contender. The moment Carl Stokes stepped on stage, the spotlight shifted and never returned to Celeste except for two brief moments: when rumors began that he intended to withdraw, and when a columnist accused him of being a "spoiler." However, Celeste's presence in the campaign cannot be ignored. His words and the reports of his campaign activities did reach primary and secondary audiences, those who heard him and those who heard what he had said to his immediate audience. Celeste's stand on his issues and his modus operandi affected the behavior of the other candidates. He campaigned harder and longer and more hours than the other candidates. Carr said that after a full day of campaigning, Celeste made as many as five meetings an evening and went to bars and restaurants after the regular meetings. On most occasions Celeste approached his audience with, "Hi, I'm Frank Celeste, and I'm running for mayor." After some brief remarks he answered questions.

Celeste told his audiences that there was only one candidate who had "proven-successful experience" as a *mayor* and that if it weren't for the fact that Carl Stokes was black, he wouldn't even have been considered. He stated on one occasion: "The election of a choice of mayor is far overshadowed by the race problem. This race has degenerated into whether we pick a Negro or an anti-Negro candidate."[6] He asserted that he was the mayor for all the people and spoke of finances, safety in the streets, and housing. He said, "Housing is horrible—50,000 units out of 255,000 are substandard. The Hough area is atrocious. I went to a house where sixteen kids were trying to sleep in two rooms, vying with the rats for a place to lie." He claimed that if *either* Stokes or Locher were elected, "one-half of the town will be sullen and mutinous and the other half unhappy."[7]

But no one was paying any attention to Celeste, and his manager sadly admitted that they were crying in the wilderness. "Those thirteen planks were sharp points. We couldn't even get the *PD* [*Plain Dealer*] to come to our press conferences. The money dropped away as the hope of winning dropped away. Volunteers did not volunteer." With his support dwindling away, Celeste was dealt a further blow by Milt Widder, columnist for the *Press* who, on July 10, wrote:

> In spite of all the flak about the "Washington high up" pressures for Carl Stokes' mayoral candidacy, the real man pushing for Stokes in the nation's capital is Robert Weaver, the new cabinet member. The talk in the capital persists that Weaver is keeping

> tight reins on Frank Celeste's candidacy in the Democratic primary and insists on Celeste staying in the race—to help the Stokes cause. Weaver can easily wield this pressure because he controls lots of housing and urban renewal money. Celeste and one of his principal backers, Don Carmichael, are in the housing business.[8]

Frank Celeste made no rebuttal to Widder. Locher's campaign manager, Klementowicz, remarked that there were certain things in politics which must be denied. Milt Widder had said rather bluntly that Frank Celeste was not a true candidate, that he was a spoiler, and, according to Klementowicz: "When you're accused of that kind of business you have got to, what they call in the law of rape, 'raise the hue and cry.' You can't delay it and a month later say you've been raped. Nobody's going to believe it. You've been outraged, and you've got to do it forthwith. Well, he didn't."

According to Celeste, he didn't raise the hue and cry because he followed a rule throughout his public service that he would never try to be an editor of the newspapers. However, when a newspaper said he was going to get out of the race, Celeste called a news conference and in no uncertain terms stated that he would not withdraw.

So he stayed, and he campaigned. This sixty-year-old man with such boundless energy nonetheless realized from the moment Carl Stokes entered the primary that for himself the chances of victory were nil. Later he said:

> Well, to be perfectly candid about it, I didn't think I had a chance. . . . I think this was a time in history when a Negro had to be mayor. There was no question in my mind that history was in the making, and all the guilt feelings of the churches and civic groups and everybody *rose up*, rose up at this particular time to support Carl Stokes. Of course, Stokes is a very eloquent, articulate, rambling sort of speaker who appeals to the masses and is a demagogue type, but very persuasive.

Frank Celeste debated Carl Stokes many times on the west side but finally quit because Stokes would filibuster in the question-and-answer periods to a maddening degree. Carr stated that Stokes would talk 90 percent of the time, and on one occasion Frank Celeste lost his temper and "jumped on Carl for doing all the talking about being a dropout and making a big comeback and Frank pointed out that he'd stayed in school and he had been a kid living in poverty, too, and had worked in the steel mills for thirteen hours a night on Friday, Saturday, and Sunday while he was in high school. . . . Well, he tried to make the point that you didn't have to be a dropout. Well, of course, everyone jumped up and said, 'Well, yeah—but *he* wasn't a Negro.' "

At all these early west side debates with Celeste, more than thirty in all, the audiences really came to see Carl Stokes. According to Mayor Locher's manager, Klementowicz, these debates hurt the mayor, too, because Celeste was giving Stokes a platform on the west side that Stokes could not, at that time, otherwise have obtained. Besides which, remarked Klementowicz, "Everytime he [Celeste] debated Stokes, Stokes made him look bad."

Carl Stokes needed those west side votes to win. The principal task of any politician is to attract that audience which is in the "middle," because the "middle" generally decides the election. However, he must not alienate those who are predisposed to vote for him while he is wooing those who are more critical.

The "middle" audience for Carl Stokes resided on the near west side. The solid bloc of Negro votes on the east side was for him. He knew he had only to be sure that they would vote, and he appeared on the east side constantly to reinforce favorable attitudes. But voter registration was really the key factor there. When Carl Stokes crossed that "polluted Cuyahoga" and began his odyssey to the west side, he was aided in his quest for votes by that political mystique known as *charisma.* "Let's face it, he is a beautiful man," remarked Vail, publisher of the *Plain Dealer.* Michael D. Roberts, a reporter also with the *Plain Dealer*, described the candidate: "Carl B. Stokes, his insignia—an expanse of French cuff; his charm—a syrupy but engaging agent."

"Charm" was a word that would take on a negative connotation later in the campaign. A psychiatrist, Dr. Raymond Headlee, claims that people who flaunt their favorite political candidate because he has the political mystique known as charisma are doing him no favor by calling attention to it. Headlee says that "a man who must have power but can't get it through exercise of actual ability or learning does it through charisma."[9] As the campaign progressed, attaching the label of "charming man" to Carl Stokes did nothing to enhance his own contention that he was intellectually equipped to handle the office of mayor of Cleveland.

But during those early primary debates, Carl Stokes's west side audiences enjoyed being charmed, although they were extremely critical

Seth Taft
Photograph by Ralph Marshall

Mayor Ralph Locher
Photograph courtesy
of Ralph Locher

at the inception of each speech. After all, Stokes was an east sider besides being a Negro.

The near west side, an area bounded by West Twenty-fifth Street on the east, West Eighty-fifth Street on the west, Lake Erie on the north, and Walworth Run on the south, grew up separately from Cleveland. It had its own political identity as Ohio City. There exists today a group on the west side which calls itself the Ohio City Association and is seeking to restore the area to its original grandeur. It will be recalled that in 1854 this area had been annexed to Cleveland only after twenty years of feuding and occasional fisticuffs between settlers who seemed to be separated by more than the Cuyahoga River. It is frequently said in City Hall that psychologically the marriage of the two cities has never been consummated.

In 1854 the inhabitants of the near west side were upper-middle- and upper-class, and the architecture—the grand homes of the Franklin Circle area—rivaled Euclid Avenue. But as the industrial valley of Cleveland expanded, immigrants from Ireland, England, Germany, and Hungary settled in the area. The wealthier people began to move further west and south, and the mansions, deserted, became private schools and nursing homes. Population changes and deterioration began before World War II. As the war workers arrived, the larger homes were converted to rooming houses. Two-family dwellings became three- and four-family tenements.

After World War II, the west side middle class began its exodus to the adjoining suburbs of Lakewood, Rocky River, Parma, and Brookpark. Into the near west side came two new kinds of immigrants—the American Appalachian whites and the Puerto Ricans. While the common bonds of language, culture, religion, and racial characteristics provided the Puerto Ricans with a certain kind of strength and unity, the Appalachian whites who moved to the northern industrial city were American immigrants without a cohesive sociological background.

Carl Stokes seemed to understand his west side audiences. If one can believe Dr. Headlee's further claim that the charismatic person has the capability to understand people psychologically—their flaws, their needs and their strengths, so that these can be harnessed, avoided, or neutralized—then Carl Stokes was the epitome of the charismatic individual during this time, and his charm was indeed opening doors. Word spread that he was an orator, and as an added feature, he was a Negro.

Besides the Celeste-Stokes debates, Stokes spoke extemporaneously on many other occasions on the west side. Churches welcomed him for speaking engagements after the evident success of his initial appearance on the west side. His informal speaking was emotional, graphic, rambling, illogical, and ungrammatical. But he was personally persuasive. On those occasions when he used scripts he deviated slightly, usually to establish rapport—to gather in someone, to point out a familiar face, etc.

Writing on the nature of campaign oratory, Professors James H. McBath and Walter R. Fisher observe that campaign persuasion is not at all like legal persuasion which demands that every statement be logically defensible.[10] Facts and arguments are not necessarily found in political communication; on those occasions when one does discover them, they are not usually valid, relevant, or sound. Nor does anyone expect them to be, though occasionally a candidate, such as Adlai Stevenson, deviates from the pattern and presents a campaign program by speaking intelligently to the people. But Stevenson, the man, apparently didn't come through his highly literate speeches as a man to be trusted with the office, in spite of his relevant facts, inferences, and arguments.

Buffon, the eighteenth-century naturalist, posited that "style is the man himself." What the man *is* comes through in his choices of language, and the product speaks of the man. Of all the candidates, Stokes seemed to sense the importance of style in his speaking. He did not strive for a "literate" quality in his prepared speeches. But Stokes had a good writer who *implemented* (a word Stokes loved to use) his style and made it palatable to the many Cleveland political audiences. Stokes commented on this:

> We started out with Al Ostrow writing the general structure of the campaign. Then we met in a group, defined, agreed upon the general structure, agreed upon the number of issues we were going to enunciate [another word Carl Stokes used often], and then we began implementing. Ostrow took all the old speeches I had done, and for about a month he just followed me on the campaign while I was speaking extemporaneously—taking notes—and then he started writing the speeches. From that point on, it was essentially good for the three—Clement, Ostrow, and myself.

Ostrow confirmed what Stokes said and stated further that he tried to pattern the speeches to fit Carl Stokes. "All I was doing was taking thoughts and ideas and putting them into words that fitted Carl Stokes," he said.

There were really two Stokes campaigns in the primary. For the most part, Carl Stokes spoke extemporaneously on the east side unless the occasion called for a more formal presentation (as occurred later in the campaign in the telecast debates with Taft). On the east side the slogan was "Vote for Carl Stokes because he is a Negro." On the west side it was "Don't vote for the Negro; vote for the man." At Ostrow's office, the story was told about an elderly Negro man, confused by the slogans, who commented: "I'm not voting for Carl Stokes because he is a Negro. I'm voting for him because I'm a Negro." One young idealistic campaigner from Case Western Reserve University said that she quit the Stokes campaign because she thought Carl Stokes changed his speech much too radically when speaking to his "own" people. "It was dishonest," she said.

The simple fact was that Carl Stokes adapted to his audience, and they responded in kind. He said: "I draw something from an audience. I get a kind of sustenance." He told one reporter that it was like going to church. People revitalized him. He said that whenever he was at a "lulling" point, he would go before a group of people and the tussle with the audience gave him the kind of boost that any other person would get by going to church.

Stokes moved gracefully. Seth Taft's public relations man, William Silverman, advised Taft to view a tape of the Celeste-Taft-Stokes debates. Silverman observed that Carl Stokes was obviously on stage even when he was not at the podium. Ostrow described it as a remarkable facility for getting words, ideas, fixed in his mind and adapting a combination of a prepared speech and ad libs to a specific audience. While Stokes never needed help on delivery, Ostrow was sometimes bothered by his pronunciation: "There was one word in his pronunciation that has always intrigued me—afraid. Did you ever notice? It comes out *afred*."

Like Celeste, Carl Stokes's role in the primary was that of an aggressor-orator. Though Stokes claimed the basic unstated issue was race, his general purpose in speaking was to establish his goodwill and to attack the administration. Capitalizing on the voter's desire for *change* was his thematic technique.

One example of Carl Stokes's appeal for votes on the predominantly white west side occurred on September 28, 1967, at Saint Ignatius High School, where he appeared on the same platform with Seth Taft. After Stokes was introduced by Father James Kirby, he rose, smiled, moved to the podium, and began:

> Ladies and gentlemen, it is my hope that after you go to the polls next Tuesday, I'll be able to be back with you again. I hope

> that after November seventh we'll be able to return and ask you specifically what it is that you want us to do for you and not to you.

It seemed apparent to Carl Stokes that this was a feeble start, and he paused, regrouped, and began again to establish his goodwill and intelligence—his *rightful image* according to newer terminologists:

> I was informed by a television team that came to me from the Huntley and Brinkley show and they, uh,—I guess we have some kind of interest around the country—and I don't think that this young man had done his homework because the first question he asked me was, "You are a rather unusual fellow to be in the position you are because you're not known as a Negro leader." "What do you mean?" He says, "Well," he says, "you're sort of atypical—that whatever leadership you might have had in the community has not been in the Negro militant but rather coming from all sources across the community."

With one brief stroke Carl Stokes emphasized his national reputation as a man with general appeal and popularity and as one clearly disassociated from any militant black movement. Going further he stated:

> Well, this was the best testimony in his questions because as I go around the city this here is one thing that I tried to demonstrate in my services as a legislator, in my participation in the city and community life, and in my candidacy for mayor, and that is you, whomever you're going to be elected, cannot be a mayor for the white people. Whomever is going to be elected has to be a mayor for the people of the city of Cleveland without favoring one or the other.

The audience applauded at this point. The "whomever" Stokes referred to was in error, but his delivery was good and his message clear enough. He worked to relieve fear and doubt by talking about the black power extremists and the advocates of white power. "I don't believe in either of them," he said. Then, pointing to a man in the audience, he said:

> I believe in this gentleman over here who said a little while ago that the way this area right here came to be, the way the city of

> Cleveland developed into what it is, and in fact what the Western Reserve, what the state of Ohio, what the United States has been, that because of the fact we have taken all kinds of people from all cultures, all languages, all religions, all races, all nationalities, and taking the best of them and filtered them into the world, and in fact this is why if Cleveland is going to continue to go forward at any pace, reversing the trend which has been part of the city down over the past twenty to twenty-five years—and I say twenty to twenty-five years because you can't give Ralph Locher all the blame for everything that's happening in the town now—much as I'd like to but I can't—this would be giving him too much credit that just in five years he could bring us to where we are now.

This long, involved sentence, with its use of numerous phrases and the piling of images to inevitably lead to a glorification of the "American way" and an attack on the Locher administration, exemplifies the style which caused Stokes's opponents to complain that he always spoke in generalities and was apt to go on and on and on.

Carl Stokes next spoke of his record as a state representative, the Locher administration's failure with urban renewal, and went on to make his first "if elected" promise: "To find the best man who has any concept of city planning and urban renewal and of community development that we could find in the United States, and we would bring that man in, and the criteria that must be followed in each of the neighborhoods to be affected has been set out in which the government is going to step in and do something about it."

Despite a discernible ambiguity, he barged on. Citizen participation was his solution to the renewal problem. He stated that he did not have a problem with people. He was willing to meet with anyone. He attacked Locher for not meeting with Martin Luther King and stated that it would be just as wrong if he (Stokes) had refused to see Governor Wallace.[11] Launching into a personal experience, he said, "I'll tell you what I did three years ago." He confessed to sharing breakfast with George Wallace. He said, "I understand George Wallace just like I understand Martin Luther King—just as I approach this campaign coming to ask your support, so I go to every area of the city." Then he entertained his audience with a couple of stories of strong police enforcement by an old Negro policeman named Jack Jones who single-handedly captured a band of criminals on Murray Hill. Stokes promised the same kind of law enforcement that Jack Jones delivered. He promised to put the policemen back on the street, to change police methods.

When Carl Stokes's time was up, the audience responded appreciatively. He brought back from his odyssey to the west side the sound of applause. Although one phase of the campaign had ended, his rhetoric was not completed when the applause died down. He again rearranged it and faced another audience.

Carl Stokes's rhetorical primary campaign was climaxed by a paid television appearance the night before election. It was a speech about a dream—an American dream of an exciting city filled with bright-eyed youngsters, "where human beings of all ancestry live together in harmony, where people swim and picnic in a clean lake and parks, where industry flourishes, higher education, scientific research, and culture in the 'brain capital' of the world. A renaissance in Cleveland where police officer and citizen share in a dream brought about by a new administration."[12]

Though running unopposed, Seth Taft also appeared on the platform at Saint Ignatius the same night as Carl Stokes. While the writer for Carl Stokes wrote for Carl Stokes and not for himself, William Silverman, Taft's chief speech writer, explained: "Seth and I are a great deal alike, as far as we think about things, and this is an advantage if you're a public relations man. It was possible for me to write something for myself, and it would be the same kind of material that he would write for himself."

The method of preparing Seth Taft's speeches was more involved and produced quite a different result. The Stokes speeches were created by Ostrow who dictated a stream of words, which were seldom reworded, as fast as his secretary could take them down; the Seth Taft speeches relied upon a research firm that supplied statistical and factual information as a basis for "Position Papers." These, in turn, were written into speeches by Barbara Schoonover and William Silverman, Jr. Some attempt was made to use "smaller words," but the speeches still sounded like written reports and lacked even the smallest measure of eloquence.

"At the beginning," said Seth Taft, "I divided the campaign up into four areas: (1) unemployment, (2) housing, (3) police protection, and (4) unresponsiveness of City Hall. These are the issues that I talked about from early April until the eighth of November and didn't change at all when it turned out that Stokes was my opposition." On the issue of race, Seth Taft said, "I was talking about the problem of race relations. Some people were talking about the problem of the color of the two candidates."

The overt issues became less important after the campaign was limited to the two men, Carl Stokes and Seth Taft, because as Taft stated:

> Our views in general were pretty close in terms of what the needs were and what had to be done. They were important in another respect in that in the Stokes campaign there was an either subconscious or conscious effort to take advantage of people's embarrassment about being white and voting for a white candidate. Somehow they were a bigot if they didn't vote for Carl Stokes. Now he never quite put it that way, but "Do Cleveland Proud," for example, was a subtle playing on that issue. . . . And, of course, it was a double campaign because over in the Negro part of the city the ministers and the newspaper editors and everybody else were saying, "Vote color," and over in the white community Stokes was saying, "No, don't vote color—consider a person on his qualifications, not on account of his color."

Taft analyzed his initial rhetorical task in the primary campaign in this way: "Taking off on the present administration and presenting what I affirmatively believed in and just carefully taking notes on what they [Carl Stokes and Frank Celeste] were saying."

Taft appeared on numerous occasions on the west side with Frank Celeste and Carl Stokes. Ralph Locher, the defender-rhetorician, never appeared with the three. He was busy at Democratic ward meetings where the podium was denied to the other candidates. Frank Celeste, however, attended ward meetings, and at times would be permitted to speak for a few minutes. He could not, of course, attack the endorsed candidate.

When Taft appeared with the Democratic rivals at Saint Ignatius High School (September 28, 1967) he looked long, lean, rumpled, and tired. After Carl Stokes's dramatic presentation, he rose politely, acknowledged the men seated on the platform, and turned to the audience.

Seth Taft had also done his homework. He knew about the urban renewal problems of the area, the unemployment problems, the racial tensions. The speech he gave was similar to many he would give all over the city. It was filled with information such as, "There are 160,000 housing units in the city of which 60,000 are substandard. The most recent Bureau of Labor Statistics ten-city study on employment rates show that Cleveland had the worst double standard of employment of the cities checked."[13] Taft had statistics for everyone. He told the Fire Fighters that of the thirty-seven fire stations in use, only twelve were less than a quarter century old and 54 percent of them were more than a half a

Thomas Vail,
editor and publisher
of the Cleveland *Plain Dealer*
Photograph by the Cleveland *Plain Deale*

Thomas Boardman,
editor of the *Cleveland Press*
Photograph by the *Cleveland Press*

century old. He mentioned the fire station at West Third and St. Clair that was 115 years old. He spoke of unemployment and said that in Cleveland's Negro ghetto there were 22,000 men and women who had never held steady jobs.

Taft's speech at Saint Ignatius followed the same pattern of progression used by Stokes. But though Taft said that it was a real pleasure to have a chance to speak with the people, he did not establish his ethos vividly. There was no imagery in the simple statement that "I'm running for mayor because after twenty years of working on urban renewal, housing, community problems, welfare, race relations problems, I have come up against a blank wall—City Hall." Seth Taft's attack on Ralph Locher was gentlemanly:

> Now, when Ralph Locher announced he was running for reelection in June of this year, he said this was Cleveland's proudest period. And one of the things he pointed to was the fact that we had low unemployment, under 3 percent—hardly anyone except the lame, the old, and the blind would appear unemployed. The fact is that, in the poor neighborhoods of our city, unemployment is over 15 percent.

Taft spoke of urban renewal plans that had worked in other cities and of the manner in which South Bend, Indiana, solved its unemployment problem. Facts and statistics were used to combine evidence and argument in an organized manner, producing a type of legalistic rhetoric which operated under rules of rationality. There was validity, relevance, and soundness in the speech that evening—a kind of deliberative rhetoric appropriate for a time when men are seeking solutions to problems. It was not, however, campaign rhetoric and, while the audience listened respectfully, the response was not as enthusiastic as that given to Stokes.

Silverman, Taft's public relations man, attributed the lack of audience-interest to Taft's delivery and said, "Well, he was a lousy speaker. He got better as he went along."

Taft did improve his delivery. During the middle of the summer he obtained advice on public speaking from a number of people, including Professor Vincent Klein of John Carroll University. Professor Klein held three consultations with Taft during the last stages of the primary and prior to the general election campaign. Professor Klein first observed Taft's performances on radio and television and spent an evening at the Glenville Community Center where Taft was campaigning. He said: "I was looking for something. There was some comment about his high voice. Personally, I did not react unfavorably to his voice on radio and television. But live—in an audience—I was aware of hypernasality. Laymen would say just too high a voice." After taking an informal poll of eleven people, Professor Klein found that Taft's high voice did not bother those interviewed even though it did bother the professional advisers very much. "I was personally impressed with the man's ethos—everything he said he supported," added Professor Klein.

The professor met with Seth Taft and, using a basic three-monosyllabic exercise that singers use for producing resonance and voice placement, explained that there were three palatal placement areas and tried to let his pupil distinguish between them. Klein went into the characteristics of the English language, explaining that it was a "frontal" type of language. "It dances on your lips and you can see the person forming the sounds," he told Taft, further explaining that midwesterners have a tendency towards nasality.

During the general election campaign when the Stokes-Taft debates were broadcast, Professor Klein tried to make Taft aware of two audiences—the one in the hall and the one tuning in at home. Klein emphasized techniques: "In your desire to dramatize something, don't walk off the microphone," he said and commented on voice placement, explained vocal variety and elements of pacing. He warned Taft that in the emotional involvement of the moment Stokes displayed an abundance of energy and often too much bombast. He advised Taft to retain the contrast—the deliberate, poised air. While Professor Klein advised Seth Taft about composition, he did not attempt to evaluate content, although he did mention that it was advisable to limit oneself so that the audience was immediately aware of the central theme. "The surprising thing, as I look back on it, was how much the two of us accomplished in a very short time," said Professor Klein. Reflecting on his impression of Seth Taft, he said: "He dropped over casually dressed—delightful time. To me he looked like [John] Kennedy coming through the yard."

Seth Taft also looked like Kennedy on billboards. It wasn't planned—the picture just happened. The resemblance was a happy circumstance. Just as Carl Stokes took on the image of the great conciliator by using the "I had a dream" theme of Martin Luther King, so Seth Taft, by a photographic fluke, took on the image of a youthful idealist crossing from the old Taft conservatism to the new Taft liberalism.

But at Saint Ignatius, at Glenville, at the numerous Celeste-Taft-Stokes so-called debates, which were really only joint appearances, Seth Taft still delivered his facts and figures in a nasal, monotonous

Martin Luther King and Carl Stokes
Photograph courtesy of the *Call and Post*

manner. The very fact that he ran unopposed made him the least active of the four candidates in the primary. He needed only to make himself heard attacking Ralph Locher, make his face familiar to the public, then sit back and wait for the primary to end.

Locher, however, could not afford to sit back and wait his turn. He needed to win only the primary to be assured of election. But the image of City Hall hurt him. Attacks were leveled at the Locher administration, but no one attacked Locher the man. "No one can attack a Ralph Locher," said Stokes. Locher himself observed:

> I don't know if they honestly felt that I was that, uh, high principled or whether it was blaming with faint praise. I didn't feel flattered by it. You see, they had access to poll-takers. They had the Madison Avenue boys conducting the campaign, which we never had done and didn't have the money to do. They might have found it was an effective way to attack someone—"Nice guy, but . . ."

Two major speeches were written for Locher—the speech before the City Club on September 22, 1967, and the speech at the annual Democratic Steer Roast. The ideas in Locher's extemporaneous speeches are contained in the literature known as the "Locher Letters."

Information for the "Locher Letters" came from the various departments in City Hall. This information was correlated and given form by Bronis Klementowicz, Daniel O'Loughlin, Andrew Sarisky, James Gorman, and Mayor Locher himself. Although the "Locher Letters" were somewhat like the Taft "Position Papers," they contrasted with the Taft papers in having more originality and style. They were designed to persuade the reader rather than merely provide data.

There were twenty-nine letters in which City Hall, water, rubbish collection, Erieview (the downtown urban renewal program), manpower development, water sports recreation, street maintenance, law enforcement, safety, and human relations were discussed in a defense of the Locher administration. The "Locher Letters" took in every angle, but Locher said: "I told Klem, 'You are going to be so late with these letters that they'll all be thrown in the maelstrom.' So here were these thoughtful letters instead of being ready early weren't ready until the eleventh hour."

As a defender-rhetorician, Locher stood by his record in his public appearances, but, without newspaper support, few people heard or read his well-structured supportive defense. However, political argument does not rely on legal rigor for acceptance. Locher would not alter his style to meet the rhetorical challenge. "People wanted him to get angry, and he's too much of a gentleman for that," said his campaign manager Klementowicz. As far back as 1963 reporters tried to persuade Ralph Locher to change his self-image. A *Plain Dealer* reporter urged him to be more forceful, angrier, asserting that he needed to destroy the "mousy" image obtained during his apprenticeship with Frank Lausche.

Essentially, Ralph Locher had two speeches—a formal defense of his administration and an informal speech he repeated with some variation at ward meetings, picnics, and in private meeting halls. He used these speeches everywhere. Klementowicz said:

> We had entries everyplace because the mayor was campaigning from three arenas. One, he was campaigning just because he was mayor; two, he was campaigning as mayor at ceremonial functions because he makes a good appearance; and three, he was campaigning on a political stump. He comes across. People wanted him to get more angry, which we tried to get him to do, but he wouldn't get angry unless he felt angry. He was a gentleman. Locher is good in eyeball-to-eyeball conversation. He will go to a banquet, talk, shake hands. On a personal basis he comes across better than anybody else does. We always sent him to those places. He made fifteen-sixteen [appearances] on Saturday and Sunday. He would walk around, and everyone was glad to see him.

At a Ward Four meeting at Sixtieth and Lorain on September 30, the hall was filled with Democrats. People were seated around small tables or standing along the walls. A center aisle had been cleared. Ward leaders were present. Music came from somewhere. People stood up and cheered—a leader was approaching. Ralph Locher and James Stanton (the Ward Four councilman) strode the length of the hall amid cheers, shaking hands and acknowledging salutes.

Amid the commotion, Stanton approached the microphone and said:

> I'm not going to believe any newspaper polls. I'm not going to believe any propaganda about who's going to win the election. I'm going to believe what's resulting on October 3, and I believe that the results will show that Mayor Locher will be elected for two more years.

There was wild applause. The sight of Ralph Locher, neatly dressed in a dark blue suit, white handkerchief in his breast pocket, brought forth cheers and then immediately afterwards a respectful silence. Locher was more impressive "live" than on television. The mayor began by thanking Stanton and the members of the Fourth Ward; then he told a joke:

> Thank you very much, Jim Stanton, and the officers of the Fourth Ward Democratic body. As I was driving over here this evening, ah, Irwin Silbert, who drove me here, told me an anecdote that I feel I must share with you. . . . He was telling me about the fellow who came home early one day and, ah, smelled cigar smoke in the house, and that immediately alarmed him, of course. So he started searching around, being the trusting soul that all of us husbands are, and he started walking around and, ah, searching, and finally he came to the bathroom and there he observed the shower curtain, and he pulled the curtain back and there was the man smoking a cigar. And the husband said, "What are you doing here?" And the fella said, "Why voting, of course." If that didn't go over too well, you can blame Irwin Silbert.

Locher proceeded to draw the audience more firmly together by praising their efforts in helping the city, thanking them for voting against the repeal of the city tax, and for sustaining Stanton and the City Council. He went on to cite what his administration had accomplished. First, his administration added 234 policemen and twenty scooters for better mobility on the beat, a helicopter, and a computer. He said:

> One of my opponents says, "Let's get rid of a police chief who is known for his honesty and integrity and for his lifetime fight against crime, racketeering, and gamblers." Ladies and gentlemen, if Chief Wagner is fired, it will be open season in Cleveland for every lousy thief and every hoodlum.

Second, he stated that his administration had combined rubbish and garbage collections. Third, his administration had waged war on air and water pollution for the first time in Cleveland. Fourth, also for the first time, mercury street lights were installed on every single residential street in the city.

Then Locher reversed tactics; he attacked his opponents. In simple and vivid language, Ralph Locher spoke of a new crisis:

There are those selfish interests in the city of Cleveland that want to defeat your mayor, and they are being aided and abetted by those from the outside—Washington, D.C., and from New York City and elsewhere. And they've met in concert, and they're working behind the scenes. And they don't care who wins so long as Ralph Locher is defeated, because Ralph Locher, ladies and gentlemen, has stood up to them, and has said, "No, the Municipal Light Plant is not for sale." And Ralph Locher has not been intimidated by subtle threats of violence and riots, because Ralph S. Locher and his police division have kept the peace.

And then they have a troika. They got three horses running under the same banner, and they don't care which one wins, so long as *this* fella gets beat, because he's the only one of the four who is not for sale. There's a wagonload of money coming from New York City. Just last week the non-carpetbagger candidate, Mr. Liquidator [Stokes], was in New York City in a spacious apartment—a sunken apartment—and there he slumped into an easy chair and said, "What a relief to be out of Cleveland." Those are not my words. They're his words from the *New York Times.* Why would anybody who wants to be your mayor feel it's a relief to be out of his home town? He's there to collect money and every dollar he gets, and every thousand dollar bill (and it will take many, many thousand dollar bills to pay for this campaign that he's waging)—every one is tainted and labeled. And, ladies and gentlemen, New York City will never win an election as long as you support Ralph Locher. Neither will Washington, D.C., or anyone else. . . . Besides that wagonload of gold I described has come $175,000 from the Ford Foundation for the aid of CORE and for the aid of having voters register. Not one nickel came to the Fourth Ward. Not one nickel came to most wards. But many, many thousands of dollars went to certain wards on a restricted, limited basis in this city. Ladies and gentlemen, that's wrong, and I'm 100 percent against that kind of self-elevating of one section of town and pitting it against another section of town. What do you think of that?

Ladies and gentlemen, the biggest single shareholder in the CEI [Cleveland Electric Illuminating Company] is the client of one of my opponents [Stokes], so what does he say? "I'm going to sell one of your largest assets—the Municipal Light Plant," which contributes $1,693,000 to the general fund of the city of Cleve-

> land. It makes it possible for Jim Stanton and your other fine councilmen to appropriate enough money that the equivalent of 290 policemen a year, or 2 Fifth District police stations, or 6 swimming pools, or 290 firemen—that's what our Municipal Light Plant pays into our general fund each and every year. And he says, "Let's sell it!" And when you say, "Let's sell it," you mean, "Let's give it away," because the minute that's sold, what happens to your rates? Your yardstick is gone. They raise the rates from the CEI to pay off the city of Cleveland. You're paying for that giveaway. Ladies and gentlemen, in conclusion, the Municipal Light Plant, so long as I am your mayor, will never be for sale. City Hall is not for sale! And Ralph Locher is not for sale!

This was Ralph Locher delivering a partisan speech to partisan sympathizers. His audiences in the ward meetings were generally composed of party loyalists who responded to their party leader with applause and shouts of "You tell them, Mayor!" Locher said, "I thought I was well received." He was especially well received at Murray Hill, scene of the 1965 Cleveland disturbance, where he was given eighteen separate rounds of roof-raising cheers during a five-minute speech.

Locher delivered his speeches in an emphatic but almost static manner. His voice was loud, and he emphasized almost every word. He shouted phrases like "Ralph Locher is not for sale!" and punctuated them with outstretched hand gestures. In response, his audiences exhibited religious fervor that the other candidates had not been able to elicit from the crowds. It was old-time politics of a grassroots, stump-speaking variety. It had style, form, and emotion. Afterwards Locher said, "We were victims of the time. You can't win in this time of great conflict, especially when there is an appealing Negro running."

While this may have been true, it cannot be denied that Locher's campaign strategy was to avoid rather than to confront his competition. He spoke primarily to ward meetings where he alone, as the party candidate, had access to the platform. Stokes's, Celeste's, and Taft's attacks were made before one audience, and Locher's rebuttal was made to another. Locher spoke mainly to those who already supported him, and he allowed Stokes to go after the doubtful and uncommitted virtually unchallenged. This would seem to indicate that the Locher forces placed too much importance on party endorsement as a factor in winning a primary election.

The only confrontation between Locher and Stokes was contrived by the electronic medium. WKYC-TV took film clips from a speech by

Carl Stokes and from Ralph Locher's City Club speech and simulated a debate. Many politicians and citizens considered Ralph Locher the winner of the staged encounter. Earlier, in 1965 when Locher appeared at the City Club for an actual debate with Carl Stokes, Ralph J. Perk, and Ralph A. McAllister, the *Plain Dealer* noted: "Mayor Ralph Locher and Carl Stokes were generally regarded as having been the sharpest, County Auditor Ralph J. Perk and Ralph A. McAllister as the weakest." Locher was not frightened about facing Carl Stokes, the orator, but merely considered it poor strategy to give his opponent a platform.

Klementowicz said that the Locher campaign was based on action. "We wanted people to see what we had accomplished and thus gain confidence in the city's future. We weren't just talking. We were doing something." But an important issue was the safety of the city, and the mercury street lights could light the way only if people were unafraid to walk down the street. The charge was leveled at Mayor Locher that he did not listen to all the voices of the city, that he was polarized. Taft accused him of not listening to the Inner-City Action Committee, of listening only to those groups who agreed with his policies. Locher was accused of not listening to Martin Luther King, to CORE, to the voices of dissent.

When he was questioned about these accusations, he replied: "I tried to be fair—fair but firm." He did not like the methods employed by various dissident groups, particularly the emotional rhetoric groups and the sit-ins. He wanted others to act in as orderly a fashion as possible. He did not like threats. The motto he had hung on his office quoted Benjamin Franklin: "Those who give up on essential liberty and purchase a little temporary safety deserve neither liberty nor safety."

Ralph Locher's speech before the City Club on September 22, 1967, was the "best defense of his administration"—according to Ostrow, Stokes's public relations manager. Richard R. Campbell, an editor of the *Cleveland Press*, introduced Locher as a man who liked beer and ball games and who had "lived in an integrated neighborhood before it was fashionable."

Before an audience of prominent businessmen and inquiring citizens, both Democrats and Republicans, Locher did indeed give a speech that answered the challenges made by his opponents and firmly defended his administration. He began by saying that Cleveland had suffered under slanderous attacks and downright lies; he accused the media of deciding that Cleveland was a "doomed city, destined for oblivion." However, he said that perhaps these attackers had done Cleveland a favor for "they brought about in Cleveland a renewed awareness. They made the people fighting mad."

Locher then spoke of the great construction boom of the past five years, of the $571 million in new construction, of the additional housing inspectors and policemen. As for urban renewal, he said, "We have ripped apart the Urban Renewal Department and have a Community Renewal Department." He listed its accomplishments. "How can you look and not see?" he asked of the audience and quoted Shakespeare:

> What a strange repose is this
> To sleep with eyes wide open.

Contending that his opponents just hadn't been around—"two of them have been commuters"—he disposed of Frank Celeste as a small-time mayor and Seth Taft as a man who "doesn't have a record." As for Carl Stokes, the mayor labeled him "Mr. Liquidator"—a reference again to Stokes's plan to sell the Municipal Light Plant, Shaker Lakes, and Garfield Park. Spending considerable time attacking Stokes, Locher said one must be a mayor seven days a week, twenty-four hours a day, and that no man can run the city of Cleveland from a plush apartment in New York or even Washington, D.C. He attacked Stokes's record as a legislator: "He has missed 54 percent of roll calls."

Then Locher proceeded to defend the men of his cabinet whom Stokes had attacked. He cited the fact that Chief Wagner had been mentioned as a candidate to head the FBI. Quoting articles in which Carl Stokes first praised the policemen in a Cleveland newspaper and then blamed them in the national press, Locher questioned the duality of opinion. He further quoted Carl Stokes as saying: "The riots we had were an immediate result of the action of the city administration, and if you reelect Ralph Locher, I'll guarantee that the city will be plunged once again into economic waste of human life." Commenting upon this, Ralph Locher said, "I am shocked that a man has resorted to racial blackmail." Furthermore, he said that Carl Stokes owed an apology to Bronis Klementowicz for calling him a racist. The mayor cited Klementowicz as a "man who has served his country and his city."

As for the racial issue, Locher said: "The fact that a man is a Negro does not *disqualify* him from running for office of mayor, but by the same token neither does it *qualify* him. This is my first and my last word on this subject."

The speech very neatly covered every attack made upon his administration. His own attack upon Carl Stokes was methodical and clear. He used Stokes's own words as evidence.

Ralph Locher went over that speech three or four times, revising, editing, and rewriting. James Gorman made the original draft, but Locher himself turned it into the final speech. It had a style appropriate to the man and the occasion. He began and ended with a plea that citizens open their eyes to what was taking place about them. The attack upon his opponents was swift and to the point. He said nothing of himself personally but "stood on his record." He was firm, stoic.

Ostrow was right. It was Ralph Locher's best effort. Ostrow was also correct in observing that the papers did not report the speech accurately. They did quote, however, Ralph Locher's single reference to the race issue.

The old theory of winning elections called for money, organization, and *newspapers*. Locher did not have the support of a single newspaper, which, according to Klementowicz, hurt deeply. He said, "It hurt us because it gave the Stokes camp respectability which it didn't have at the time." Carl Stokes admitted that the word "respectability" aptly described the service rendered him by the *Plain Dealer* endorsement. Frank Celeste expressed disappointment at the lack of coverage he received. Seth Taft thought the way he was "buried in the primary" was not fair coverage. Ralph Locher said that he did not want to be a bad loser; he would rather not complain. He was more irritated by what he considered one television station's bias than by the newspaper coverage.

It will be recalled that there were two major dailies, the *Plain Dealer* and the *Cleveland Press*. By 1967 the venerable editor Louis B. Seltzer was no longer the *Press*; however, a portion, at least, of the political power the *Press* had enjoyed under his leadership still remained. The citizens of Cleveland hadn't entirely forgotten the newspaper under Louis Seltzer's reign as "kingmaker." The stories of his editorial power may have become exaggerated with the passing of time, but most of them are good enough to be true. One of the favorites is that Mr. Seltzer held court at 8:30 A.M. each day at the *Press* offices at East Sixth and Superior, where he was surrounded by editors, politicans, and aspiring politicians. It is undoubtedly true that candidates or would-be candidates for every important office in the city, county, and sometimes even the state did come to the *Press* offices seeking endorsement. The screening sessions with candidates usually included, in addition to Mr. Seltzer, Richard Maher, Richard R. Campbell, and Norman Shaw. The present editor, Thomas Boardman, had often been consulted. Final choices were, however, left to Louis Seltzer. Belief that Seltzer's endorsement was as good as victory itself has already been cited in connection with the election of Anthony Celebrezze to the office of mayor. The City Hall reporter for the powerful *Press*, Paul Lilley, had been credited by political gossips as Mayor Celebrezze's brains. Many readers believed Seltzer wrote every word which appeared in his paper. Speaking to a group of graduate students at Case Western Reserve University in 1969, Mr. Seltzer said that from the number of telephone calls he used to receive in the middle of the night, he could well believe that his readers held him personally accountable for every word.

Whether Louis Seltzer exercised all the power attributed to him is speculative, but that he was in a position of power is undeniable. Until recently, the *Press* had the largest circulation of any daily paper in the state. Seltzer was dean of the Scripps-Howard editors in Ohio, had complete autonomy on the treatment of local issues, and more than once bucked Scripps-Howard editorial policy on national issues. His endorsement for public office would have been important to any candidate. Reportedly the only man who ever declined Louis Seltzer's offer of stardom was Seth Taft. Not only did he not solicit the *Press* endorsement of his candidacy in the 1963 mayoral race, but when Louis Seltzer printed an editorial endorsing Taft as the most likely Republican candidate, the unconsulted favorite publicly replied, "No, thanks."

About the time Louis Seltzer retired from his editorship of the *Press*, the *Plain Dealer*, which had been less of a crusading paper and by no means as influential in political campaigning, inherited a new editor and publisher, Thomas Vail, Jr. In 1963 Thomas Vail scooped the *Press* and endorsed Ralph Locher and then actively campaigned to dethrone Council President Jack Russell, in favor of the young rebel James V. Stanton. The roles of the two newspapers seemingly reversed. Thomas Boardman, new editor in chief of the *Press*, said, "I don't believe that the role of an editor is to summon the candidates for political office to the throne room." Vail, however, did not seem averse to the practice.

There are interesting differences in the atmosphere of the two offices and the personalities of the men who occupy them. Robert Carr, Celeste's manager, said, "It's a kind of situation where you walk right into his [Boardman's] office without a great deal of fanfare, whereas with Tom Vail, it's almost like seeing General de Gaulle."

To test this statement both men were called for appointments for interviews near the end of the general campaign in 1967. It was easy to speak with Boardman directly; the appointment was made for the following afternoon. There was little difficulty in finding his office. Boardman, on first impression, had a clear, smooth head topping a thin, interesting face with almost delicate features. He was in shirt sleeves; the office was airy and bright. Boardman was fastidious but casual, a strange combination that was comfortable, though an awareness of authority was ever present.

Vail was not as easy to reach. It took several phone calls, lengthy explanations to two male secretaries, and finally a referral to Thomas Guthrie, assistant publisher. Guthrie, a charming Scotsman, was interesting, informative, and inquisitive. This pre-interview was stimulating, and at its end he finally said, "You ought to see Tom Vail." He then made the appointment immediately.

Vail looked like a boy who had grayed prematurely. Unlike Klementowicz who had prominent steel-gray hair, Vail had fine white strands framing his youthful face. His clothes were stylish, his office dimly lit and impressive, the furniture heavy.

Vail said, "Ask me anything at all you want; you don't have to worry about this. I'm not sensitive." Yet there was a sensitive area, and it manifested itself when the national press was discussed. Vail's response was, "I've never read so much baloney in all my life, and on election night—and we went alone without any party support for him [Stokes] or other newspaper support and elected him—and not one member of the national press asked to talk to me about it."

That the *Plain Dealer's* early endorsement gave Carl Stokes respectability, Stokes readily agreed was true. Vail's irritation with the national press was understandable, as he felt the *Plain Dealer* had not received the recognition it deserved for its early commitment to the support of a Negro for mayor of a large city.

He explained why he first considered endorsing Frank Celeste:

> Now, the question about Celeste. Well, when the election began to form up during the year, I talked to Celeste in some enthusiastic way because it was my feeling that Locher had come to the end of his real usefulness. And we were all desperately looking for alternatives because elections are not just those of who's the best man, but who are the available men.

Because of the very nature of campaigning, those who apply for office are not necessarily those who qualify for the positions but, rather, those who qualify as campaigners. A campaigner must not be averse to risking his whole self in a rhetorical battle where the weapons all carry emotional warheads. He must be able to face realistically situations which are ethos-enhancing and ethos-demeaning without letting his perception of self become too distorted. Perhaps for this reason most candidates need to surround themselves with image-builders and flatterers to serve as buffers for some very bad moments when a man's ethos is challenged and threatened with destruction. Vail's words about trying to select the best "available men" are generally true of all political campaigns because of the enormity of the personal risk involved.

With regard to Seth Taft, whose image seemed to be that of a man not interested in the emotional side of the rhetorical engagement but who had nevertheless entered the political arena, Vail stated that he was not crazy about people, who at the age of forty-four, having been lawyers all their lives, having lived in the suburbs, suddenly saying, "Well, I want to run for mayor." Vail stressed that by the time he decided upon Stokes, Stanton had voluntarily withdrawn from the race; Celeste, who had been operating for two or three months, was not proving effective; extensive conversations with Locher had not been encouraging. Vail further verbalized the thoughts of the community and what gave them verve and cohesiveness—there was the idea of being in on a movement: "We had the man, and we had the moment." In politics, timing is, after all, an essential ingredient of success.

Vail of the *Plain Dealer* rushed in where Boardman of the *Press* hesitated to tread. The endorsement of the *Press* for Stokes came later. While Vail and Boardman were the key men in the newspaper medium, the reporters and columnists who covered the primary could not be ignored, for not only did their writings become an important factor in the campaign, but their methods of coverage affected the behavior of the candidates. A survey by the Edward Howard agency recorded the column-inches given to each candidate by newspapers between March 22 and July 5, the official filing date. The summary showed that Carl Stokes led the candidates in total coverage. He received a total of 469 column-inches, followed by Taft with 384, Stanton with 281, Celeste with 204, and Locher with 168. From these statistics it is evident that Taft was not entirely overlooked by the newspapers, despite his monopoly of the Republican nomination. However, Carl Stokes, from April 5 through the general election, actually led all candidates in every area of news coverage. In editorial and comment coverage, Stokes buried his opposition. Space alone was not significant; phrases such as these added magnitude to the column-inch:

> Stokes has a candor rare among Cleveland politicians, obviously articulate. . . . Stokes is loyal. . . . Stokes, a personable, energetic, imaginative candidate. . . . He has a magnetic personality. . . . He has a driving capacity. . . . On the municipal level, Carl Stokes

> would have the same compulsion to succeed as did John F. Kennedy as a precedent-setter in the White House. . . . He has the innovator's courage and the lawmaker's experience.

The candidates' responses to the methods and coverage of the newsmakers varied. Celeste said that James Naughton, Cleveland *Plain Dealer* reporter, troubled him because he felt Naughton was oversold on Stokes. He observed shrewdly that Vail wanted a winner and when Vail saw what was happening, he just decided to go with the winner. Klementowicz, Locher's manager, said, "The newspapers left the impression of nice, honest guys, the caretaker government, no imagination, no drive. We almost overcame it. If we had had a newspaper that would print the 'Locher Letters' . . ." Locher himself remarked:

> I had no commitment from either paper, I'm frank to say. And I knew they had attacked me unmercifully for several years. I don't know of anything I had done that the papers might have taken umbrage at. I am opposed to CATV [Community Antenna Television] proposals that they introduced in the council—both papers you know. They had divided up the city into two sections, and each paper was to have a monopoly on community antenna television.

Ostrow's statement was, "It seems to me that the media magnified and pounced on anything with an element of controversy in it. And what all the candidates were saying on basic issues was completely submerged. Ralph Locher got the worst deal."

The newspapers, while not always fair, were not cruel. An underground campaign, replete with its own literature, played an important role. The "whispering campaign," the accusations and name-calling done by some of the candidates and/or their advisers, did not receive much amplification in the two major papers although it reached into the electronic media.

Frank Celeste's campaign against Ralph Locher included a series of campaign leaflets entitled "Inside Reports." One of the "Inside Reports" cited an alleged conversation overheard at a First Ward meeting: "Locher for the umpteenth time shouted, 'Ralph Locher is not for sale.' And a woman under her breath muttered, 'Who'd want to buy him?' "

The "Democratic Letters," which appeared on County Democratic Committee letterhead, made such allegations as the following:

> Stokes points to a spotless record as a public servant, but there is

> documented proof that shows another side of Stokes. As a probation officer Stokes was suspended without pay for getting classified information about himself by impersonating someone else on the phone. As Ohio Liquor Department investigator he quit under a cloud of suspicion. A Cincinnati permit holder accused Stokes of soliciting money. Stokes quit without answering to charges and departed for the University of Minnesota.[14]

The "Democratic Letters" were disowned by the Locher camp. "They only hurt us," said Klementowicz. While the disavowal was not universally accepted, Locher had a convincing record of avoiding gutter tactics.

The contents of this and other "Democratic Letters" gained currency on the west side particularly. Finally one night on WGAR-radio, phone-in questions concerning these accusations were put to Carl Stokes. According to the *Plain Dealer*, "He handled them well." Other issues of the "Democratic Letters" mentioned the fact that Stokes bought a home for his mother in Shaker Heights and implied he would live there rather than in Cleveland; that he was not invited to the platform of the Democratic Steer Roast because he hadn't paid his party dues for two years; and that, if Stokes were elected, Martin Luther King, in effect, would run Cleveland.

Just as damaging as the County Democratic Committee's slurs was the small newspaper called *Comment*, put out on the east side by the League of Non-Partisan Voters. This was the same organization, composed mainly of black citizens, which had backed Stokes in 1965 but endorsed Seth Taft in 1967. The August 24, 1967, issue of *Comment* printed Stokes's record as state representative in the 107th General Assembly (January 2 to July 20, 1967):

> Thirty-two bills were introduced of which nine were either indefinitely postponed (dead) or are dying in Committee, seven were introduced for publicity, seven were not to be printed. . . . Of thirty-two bills introduced, Stokes, a third-term legislator, has not been able to get a single bill made into law. Grade: Zero.

The same issue of *Comment* further accused Stokes of being "a wolf in sheep's clothing where Negroes' interests are at stake."

Never printed, but certainly whispered about, were Carl Stokes's divorces. Vail said, "I think that if there are circumstances in a divorce that do reflect on the moral position of the person, that would weigh on my mind. I did not feel that it had done so at this particular race."

Silverman said, "He was divorced. Now this is a fact. So what?" This aspect of the underground campaign apparently never surfaced, even on the radio call-in programs where the callers could remain anonymous.

Carl Stokes's personalized attacks were mainly aimed at Klementowicz. Stokes said, "He was made to order. You can't attack a Ralph Locher." Ostrow thought even the name sounded sinister. Though most politicians concede that during a campaign they take name-calling in stride, the consensus was that the Stokes organization went overboard in its treatment of Klementowicz. Ostrow wrote many speeches in which he called Klementowicz a "sly, scheming, wheeling and dealing law director" and attached adjectives like "vicious" and "devious" to his name. Carl Stokes went further and called Klementowicz a "racist, degenerate, evil man." In one speech Stokes said: "Richard Wagner [Chief of Police] will go because he cannot run a decent police department. Bronis Klementowicz will go, too, because he has led a lifetime of hate and built a government around it."[15] Ralph Locher repeatedly asked Klementowicz not to answer the charges.

The radio stations were the prime carriers of these whispering campaign issues through the audience call-in programs, and on a number of occasions Carl Stokes defended himself on the air with admirable coolness and facility. Bronis Klementowicz and Chief Richard Wagner never had the opportunity, though it is doubtful that they would have answered. Newsmen could not reach Chief Wagner, and Klementowicz was loyal to Ralph Locher's wishes not to become involved. It was Locher's desire that the men in his administration make no effort to answer charges leveled at them. In this way he felt the issue would remain a minor one. Locher spoke of Wagner's honesty and good works, but he did not answer Carl Stokes's strong criticisms of Klementowicz. He did not want the papers to "play it up."

Sustained exposure by the media can seriously affect a candidate's image in many unexpected ways. Celeste was continuously pictured by the *Plain Dealer* as a man interested in eating first, campaigning second. For example, one columnist depicted him in this way: "Celeste likes eating—six times he remarked, 'I really like ice cream and strawberries.' . . . Whenever a new customer arrived Celeste put down his fork and jumped up and introduced himself. . . . He spent the afternoon going from door to door before leaving for the Ippolito dinner."

While television didn't play the important role in the primary that it was to play in the general election, it did perform a function earlier in the race. It introduced the candidates to the public. It assisted in the creation of campaign personalities. Most of the exposure received by the candidates was on news programs, which meant that the candidates' images were created in time spots ranging from about thirty-five seconds to probably no more than two minutes.

Before examining particular roles played by the news broadcasters, it is important to understand the nature of the broadcasting service in the Cleveland metropolitan area. In 1967 the Cleveland area stood eleventh in the nation in population; it was the ninth largest television market. Although every station—commercial and noncommercial—is charged by Congress through the Communications Act of 1934 with the responsibility of serving the public interest, convenience, and necessity of its primary area of coverage, not one commercial television, AM radio station, or the two daily newspapers in the Cleveland area is locally owned. This fact has considerable bearing on the service rendered by any one of the broadcast outlets. It would be naive to assume that any of these large parent-companies—in some cases conglomerates—are in business for the primary purpose of engaging in a public service. Programming policies of any given local station are determined far less by the needs of the community than by whether the ledger will show a profit. To a large measure, the profit potential of a television station is dependent on the popularity of programs fed to it from its network affiliate. Since very, very few non-news programs originate locally, it is important that each station maintain a competitive news service which will attract a large share of the local audience. In 1967 there were only three commercial television stations, and each had its own unique news service personality.

WKYC-TV, Channel 3, is one of the five stations owned and operated by the National Broadcasting Company. Personnel assignments and transfers are determined by the parent company, resulting in great turnover in staff. In 1967 WKYC-TV had its fourth news director in three years. Its news department employed by far the largest staff of any television station in Cleveland—about forty-five persons in 1967. Newsmen at the station seem to take a great deal of pride in their status of "NBC" and do not consider themselves just local reporters. One reporter at a competing station said, "There is a certain amount of snobbery at WKYC."

WJW-TV, Channel 8, is owned by the Storer Broadcasting Company and is affiliated with the CBS network. WJW tries, with some success, to project the image of a station more integrally involved in the life of the community. Certainly when its popular "City Cameraman," Doug Adair, lent his support to a 1968 appeal for clothing for disadvantaged children, the community response was overwhelming.[16]

WEWS-TV, Channel 5, is owned by the Scripps-Howard newspaper chain and is affiliated with the ABC network. WEWS is more adventurous in its approach to local programming and is the only station that presents local talent to any extent. Its news department has a more dramatic flair than its competitors. The anchor man, John Hambrick, has a drama background which comes through in his presentation of the news. He is known for having the most communicative eyebrows in town. Special reporter Dorothy Fuldheim admits she likes the dramatic and wishes to present her story in a colorful way. As will be seen in the next chapter, the feeling of WEWS for the dramatic moment had a definite impact on the campaign.

Ironically, of the three stations, WKYC, which prides itself on being more objective because of its network orientation, was the most criticized during the primary for biased reporting. Rebecca Bell, a newsgirl who, like most of her coworkers, came from out of state, was the target of much of the criticism. The station news editor admitted that she made a name for herself by asking Ralph Locher "sharp questions." Locher thought she was not fair. Rebecca Bell was admittedly a Carl Stokes fan. She so irritated Ralph Locher that she was influential in creating an unsympathetic image of him. "He changed the minute those cameras rolled," said one of his staff. When Klementowicz complained to Martin Haag, WKYC news director, Haag assured him that there was "no calculated move to hurt Locher." Apparently the only time Ralph Locher acted less than the gentleman he is occurred because of Rebecca Bell's persistent badgering. The story goes that after one speaking occasion she followed Locher to his waiting car. Locher ignored her questions, but she would not relent. After Locher got inside the car, Rebecca Bell thrust her face and microphone through the open window. As the mayor started to roll up the window he demanded that Rebecca Bell remove her microphone and suggested an appropriate place for its disposition.

Dorothy Fuldheim of WEWS-TV presented Ralph Locher in another light. The difference in his response was amazing. He was a relaxed man in an interview she conducted in an informal way. Ralph Locher said, "She [Fuldheim] was sympathetic." Dorothy Fuldheim said that she tried always to bring out the best in her guests no matter what party they belonged to. (The exception came in 1970 when she literally threw the book at Yippie leader Jerry Rubin and refused to continue the interview.)

Martin Haag of WKYC-TV thought that his station created more activity on the part of the candidates because the candidates became more conscious of television exposure and actively sought it. Because Taft was unopposed in the primary, Martin Haag did not assign a reporter to him; however, reporters were assigned to the others. Bob Harper covered Frank Celeste; Rebecca Bell covered Ralph Locher; Fred Briggs covered Carl Stokes. Haag said that he was conscious of the inherent danger in having the same reporter with a candidate too long: "A couple of times in the primary, when we were getting criticism, I took a close look at the scripts to assure myself that we weren't bending over backwards to nominate Carl Stokes."

But television is not just words in a script. The visual element and the whole context of the television presentation can create an impact which words do not reveal. Much concern has been voiced in the past decade about the influence of television on politics. Some critics feel the influence is not always good. A professional politician who has worked out details for several nominating conventions claims that all spontaneity has gone out of the conventions which are now run by television.[17] Television is purported to have destroyed the debate that generally goes on in conventions. Robert MacNeil said in *Harper's* that television is responsible for a sort of political star-cult that supports individuals instead of parties: "People now feel loyalties to individuals rather than to parties, so we have personalities like the Kennedys rising."[18]

One of the strongest criticisms is that television is making it possible for only the rich and the handsome to run for office. It is estimated that in most cases about 60 percent of campaign cost is for television time. The stations demand cash on the line—in advance. Gene Wycoff, television writer and producer, says in his book, *The Image Candidates* (MacMillan, 1968), that television has turned campaign coverage into a theatrical experience. News programs add to the illusion that the campaign is a "political drama" and that the candidates are players who will be judged as dramatic characters. In such a situation, he feels, the glamourous candidate tends to win. Every man carries a makeup kit, and the major candidates have a specialist to provide the right kind of paint job.

Such critics apparently ignore the history of political image-making before the advent of television. Otherwise they would be less tempted to assert that technology has suddenly thrust upon the electorate not a new medium for image-making, but image-making itself. Abraham Lincoln used every medium then available to him to create the proper image of himself in the months between his defeat by Stephen A. Douglas in 1858 and his appearance at the presidential nominating convention in 1860. He even purchased a German language newspaper in order to project his image to that element of the Midwest electorate.[19] Contrary to some opinions, Lincoln had made himself very well known throughout the North and had obtained second-ballot commitments from almost every delegation. That Lincoln did not campaign for himself once he had been nominated was not unusual. Stephen A. Douglas was the first presidential candidate ever to take to the stump for himself. Lincoln let the party and newspaper publisher Horace Greeley take over his public relations during the campaign.

One of the great masters of political image-making was Cleveland's own Mark Hanna. Realizing the weak image his candidate, William McKinley, projected in public appearances, Hanna confined McKinley to his front porch. The aura of the shy, reluctant candidate inviting the world to his doorstep is not far removed from that created by the staged television presentation of the candidate in his parlor with a loving family and loyal friends or the film clip of the candidate, resplendent in an open-collared white shirt, sleeves rolled up, meeting the blue-shirted worker while a cultured voice assures the public of the candidate's warmth and sincerity.

It has ever been the case that campaign managers design a style of campaign that will allow the candidate to present himself to the public in the best possible way. Whatever methods and media the candidate manages best are the ones utilized to the greatest degree, at least by intelligent managers. When a candidate is lacking in presentational skills, he is tutored. In another age, when oral communication was virtually the only means by which a politician could assert his leadership abilities, the study of rhetoric was a central part of education. Indeed, the most famous teachers of rhetoric attracted students from far distant places. Cicero left his native Rome to seek the instruction and counsel from Apollonius of Rhodes.

The emergence of public relations firms who purport to be all-knowing in selling any given candidate via the television screen have in reality fared no better than image-makers in other years using other media. The five major firms dealing in television image-making in 1970, for example, could claim no more than 50 percent success for their candidate-clients.

However, the danger of image distortion does not arise as much from the television appearances which are planned and produced by a staff of professionals as from the image which is mediated by television news reporters, editors, and on-camera personalities. Staged political broadcasts are *programs* which can be deliberately tuned out in favor of another program in the same time slot. Political reports are news items within the context of a program the viewer has already deliberately chosen for viewing. The distortion in newscasts is not necessarily and probably not usually deliberate, but that is irrelevant. It occurs, and that is a fact. The audience listening to a candidate speak for ten to twenty minutes picks up many cues from the context and the totality of the speaker's presentation. The audience selects certain factors about the man and his ideas from the total experience of the speaker-listener confrontation. The television audience does not have access to the total experience. The viewer is shown a picture of the candidate taken at a particular angle during a few isolated seconds of his total presentation. The totality of the communicative event has been mediated by the reporter or cameraman's choice of what is significant at the time and by the news editor's choice of what is significant enough to be shown. The event is further mediated by the interpretation placed on it by the reporter's words—usually limited to a hundred words or less. By its very nature, television mediates reality. One can see no more than the camera's angle of view permits, and the more magnified any one object in the environment becomes as a result of camera manipulation, the less information about the total reality of the event is transmitted to the viewer. When this natural limitation of television is increased by the interposition of value judgments of one or more persons, the chances for distortion are also increased. Self-righteous claims of television newsmen notwithstanding, the television viewer has available to him only what the program producers want him to see. And that is an alarming fact.

In the Cleveland primary campaign of 1967 there was clearly a "show biz" quality about the coverage despite the denials of some television reporters. Dramatic highlights of events were featured. Some of this highlighting tended to crucify the candidates—some actually enhanced. As if to reinforce the beliefs of the political television critics, the handsome man with the attractive wife and the biggest bankroll did win.

Charges were made that the broadcast newsmen just didn't have good political judgment. Ostrow claimed that the newsman's purpose was to pick up something controversial rather than to convey the stands of the candidates on what should have been the issues. However, Boardman of the *Press* said that television helped to develop the personalities of the candidates, which, he felt, was a real public service. He felt the newspapers handled the depth of the campaign, and the television medium handled the personalities. These two services in tandem helped to inform the public.

An interesting part of American politics is that the voter demands to be wooed and catered to by the candidates. He must have the information and arguments laid on him. The candidate must reach out, using every means at his disposal, to pull in, to seduce every vote. So the candidates, the image-makers, and the mediators dutifully oblige.

Since television time must be paid for in advance, Ralph Locher and Frank Celeste, the candidates with the least financial backing, did little television advertising. However, Carl Stokes spent $27,000 on television alone during the primary campaign—almost as much as Ralph Locher's entire primary expenses of $38,000. More important, Carl Stokes managed the television medium to his advantage. Frank Celeste did not seem spontaneous on television and, as reported, Ralph Locher became a different person when the cameras rolled.

In his paid broadcasts, Carl Stokes dealt in universal truths, elaborated on the American dream, and spoke of his hopes for the future. Media analysts have written that television encourages such generalities. One scholar in the field of communications wrote that since television is so costly, political candidates must "husband the minutes and use as much of their allotted time as possible, even at the risk of making oversimplified presentations."[20] Another reported that television has been discussed as "an intimate medium wherein complex policy matters are watered down to simple alternatives and where the search for 'truth' becomes a search for 'trust.' "[21] But that would be true of political campaigning even without television, because the voter's choice is not between 'truth' and 'falsity' but between this candidate or that. Thus, a campaign is, inherently, a search for 'trust.'

What Carl Stokes needed most was the trust of the white voters of Cleveland. By the end of the primary he seemed to be developing a rapport with the television audiences which the other candidates lacked. Discussing his reaction to Carl Stokes on television, Professor Klein of John Carroll University said that by the end of the primary he was not thinking of Carl Stokes as a Negro candidate, but merely Carl Stokes as a man running for mayor of a city. "I did not see a black man," he said. "I saw Carl Stokes as a human being, and to me this was a tremendous observation."

Television enabled the people of Cleveland to become accustomed to seeing Carl Stokes as more than merely black; the fact that he was black simply added a further dimension to the campaign. What was happening locally soon became a part of what was happening nationally as the network cameras began to focus on the event. On the national scene the picture of an articulate, handsome Negro running for the office of mayor in a major American city was news.

The color of the candidates' skins influenced the reporters and rhetoric of the campaign and was particularly a part of the informal conversations throughout the city. William Silverman, Taft's public relations man, contended:

> In order to win we had to clear the conscience of a white voter who felt that it was the time for a Negro. This was a pretty big issue and Carl was aware of this. How blunt can you get: "Do Cleveland Proud"—by electing a Negro.

Seth Taft's comment was:

> In the Stokes campaign there was either a subconscious or conscious effort to take advantage of people's embarrassment about being white and voting for a white candidate. Somehow they were a bigot if they didn't vote for Carl Stokes. Now he never quite put it that way, but "Do Cleveland Proud," for example, was a subtle playing on that issue—that you can't really prove that you're a person who looks at problems without colored glasses unless you vote for Stokes; otherwise you haven't proved you're free of prejudice.

Bronis Klementowicz, the main target of Carl Stokes's attack on racists (though Stokes also included County Democratic Chairman Albert Porter and Police Chief Wagner) came through with the following analysis of why he personally wrote nothing about race into the "Locher Letters" and why Locher himself did not bring up the issue even though forced to answer remarks made by other candidates:

> We didn't look at it as a racial issue. Supposing we had won and we had raised the racial issue. The split at City Hall would have been worse. We're not going to go out and campaign that way. After all, they're a third of the town and growing. We considered them as a bloc of votes, no different than an Irish bloc or a Polish bloc. And if anybody asks me, on all kinds of levels, I just tell them they [the blacks] caught up with the Cosmos and the Irish, that's all. They're voting for their own, and for that I give them credit. Supposing they were all Lithuanians and white. Would you call that Lithuanian racism? So we operated on that basis. Whatever racial prejudices were in the race, those took care of themselves naturally.

Not only do large ethnic groups still maintain their identity, but the

Cleveland Cosmopolitan Congress (colloquially, the "Cosmos") enabled the various nationality groups to band together into a cooperative association for the purpose of exerting a unified front. So the remark of Bronis Klementowicz, "They [the Cleveland Negroes] caught up with the Cosmos," illustrates the thrust for power by a subordinate group, the same thrust used by minority groups since the beginning of American history. Interestingly enough, in 1970 the Ford Foundation offered money to those professors who wished to research the various ethnic cultures in America, and there has been revived, recently, a feeling of pride in ethnic heritage.

Carl Stokes's reaction to the racial aspect of the campaign was to support the theory that the black political movement was just another phase in American history. "You have to be aware of the history of this country," he said. "Everything that I know and understand about this country meant that a Carl Stokes was going to get elected because a La Guardia got elected, because a Cermak [Chicago] got elected, because a Fitzgerald in Boston got elected. The histories parallel."

The heavy Negro vote was due, in part, to Martin Luther King, Jr., who visited Cleveland to aid in a registration drive, and to a grant from the Ford Foundation to the Cleveland Chapter of CORE. This grant has since raised some serious questions about the participation of tax-exempt foundations in efforts which would result in the election of a particular candidate. The money that poured in from the foundation and from private business, said one politician, was to insure a safe summer and a safe mayor. The threat of violence was implied, and it was answered in the campaign by the candidates—both in formal speeches and informal interviews.

Locher said in a speech at the Eighth Ward meeting on September 30 that he would not be intimidated by subtle threats of violence and riots. In an interview, he said that one of his opponents used racial blackmail by saying that riots would be the result if Locher were reelected. Carl Stokes made repeated mention of Locher's "internationally documented record of fumbling and failures, . . . failures that divided us into anger, hatred, discords—failures that have made Cleveland one of the most disrupted and troubled cities in America."

The candidates reminded the citizens over and over again of the previous summer's riots. Frank Celeste promised to train Cleveland police for riot duty. Seth Taft said that it was reasonably clear that a lot of people expected some action, and William Silverman quoted Stokes as saying flatly: "If I'm not elected there will be riots." Frank Celeste said he had spent a lot of time on the west side, and a lot of people told him that they were going to vote for Stokes to see if he "can't stop the riots."

There is no way of determining if the threat of violence influenced the voting, but it assuredly influenced the rhetoric. The 1966 riots were still a vivid memory. Cleveland was still thinking riots and talking riots, and the politicians used the fear of riots as campaign fodder. Martin Haag, WKYC-TV news director at the time, reported that when he arrived in May his predecessor informed him that the network would probably be calling upon him to produce an instant special—a documentary—should Cleveland have riots, and a budget had already been set up for it. "Some film had already been pulled from the Hough riots in 1966 and since the national press was talking about Cleveland, it was a foregone conclusion that Cleveland would have a riot again."

And according to the late Whitney M. Young, Jr. (at that time national director of the Urban League), "Cleveland Negroes didn't riot last summer [1967] because they were anticipating a reward that Carl Stokes would be elected mayor."[22]

Without doubt, the fear of violence was in the city.

The *apparent* solution to the problem of violence lay in the hands of the politicians. Only one politician offered a visible solution. It was a part of his ethos and a source of his emotional proof. He was black. While all others offered some means of suppressing violence, such as better police, better human relations, more jobs, etc., Carl Stokes seemed to be a solution in himself. Fear and other emotions furnish their own logic, and the rhetoric of the campaign was directed to the emotions rather than to cold reason.

The overt rhetoric of the primary campaign came from the four candidates: the articulate Carl Stokes who desired to "enunciate" his ideas; the dry, self-conscious Seth Taft whose job was to watch and gather material; the dogged Frank Celeste who persisted even when he knew he couldn't win; the defensive Ralph Locher who desperately attempted to vindicate his administration and to dodge the criticisms of an angry press. What the candidates said made news, and the news of what was said created more rhetoric. Commenting on the quality of the primary race, Thomas Boardman of the *Press* said: "People were more interested in it than they had been in the kind of humdrum races that went on in earlier years. Everybody had an opinion. That's right. And they were perfectly willing to express it."

Aristotle said in his *Rhetoric*, "All men . . . endeavor to criticize or uphold an argument, to defend themselves or to accuse." In Cleveland the citizens became a part of the movement for change, joining the politicians, becoming aggressor-rhetoricians and defender-rhetoricians. Campaign rhetoric is always generated at several levels. Behind the candidate are his paid public relations men and his political "pros." But the true apostles are the volunteers. They are the ones who carry the gospel to the neighborhood, to the doorstep. They are the gut-level rhetoricians.

The two candidates who most aggressively advocated change—Stokes and Taft—attracted the younger crowd of volunteers. Thomas Vail said that the group of interns at the *Plain Dealer* who were in the eighteen- to twenty-two-year-old category were strongly in favor of Stokes. Suburban youths joined the Stokes organization and were very vocal. Polls taken at schools favored either Taft or Stokes to the complete exclusion of Celeste or Locher. Volunteers for Stokes in the primary had more "zeal" according to Klementowicz. Carl Stokes learned to use young people in his campaign; he said later that their lack of logic never bothered him. In subsequent campaigns he was to organize not only college students but junior high and high school students as well.

Old and young alike were involved. Newsmen were constantly querying the public. More surveys were taken than in any previous mayoral contest. On September 30, just before primary election day, the *Plain Dealer* poll showed Locher edging into the lead by 6 percent.

On Tuesday, October 3, 1967, the sun shone brightly on all three Democratic contenders for the mayoral nomination. More people were to vote in the 1967 primary than in any other mayoral race in Cleveland's history. The next day the *Plain Dealer* summarized the results:

> When the ballots were counted Stokes had 52.5% of the votes—he had defeated Locher by a plurality of 18,000 votes. Celeste was the man in the middle, getting only 4% of the votes, the lowest of any mayoral candidate in recent Cleveland history.

Earlier the suggestion was made to look at the campaign in Leland Griffin's framework of the historical movement, which is composed of three phases, the first phase being the period of inception when ideas become alive. The 1967 primary campaign fulfilled all the requirements of the second phase—the period of rhetorical crisis with its aggressor- and defender-rhetoricians. But the primary election certainly did not result in the third phase—the period of consummation. Instead, a *second* period of rhetorical crisis began. The Griffin formula breaks down here because at the outset of the general election campaign there was no defender-rhetorician. Both the contenders had been aggressors in the same cause. The day after the primary election, the two candidates were left with no focal point of attack. Stokes could not be held responsible for the Locher administration nor for the policies of the Cuyahoga County Democratic party. He had denounced and had been denounced by both. Taft was champion of a party which had seldom even made a good showing in Cleveland. As aggressor-rhetoricians in the primary campaign, both Stokes and Taft had attacked the Locher administration and both had advocated measures to improve living conditions, security, and community relations.

Though it was evident that those who had decried the status quo had convinced a strong section of society that a change was needed at City Hall, the time had not yet arrived for counsel and advice, for planning and deliberative debate. The period of rhetorical crisis was to continue; the period of ethos-enhancing rhetoric was to continue. The candidates had still to manifest their character, their intelligence, and their goodwill towards the audience through specific acts. If a candidate wishes his audience to perceive him as a man of integrity, he must first know something of the moral value system of his audience, so that he can speak and behave in a manner that will reveal the characteristics of the "good man" as defined by the audience. Similarly, the man must communicate through his speech that he is sufficiently knowledgeable or intelligent to inspire confidence in his ability to handle the job, to make good judgments. The audience determines from this listening experience what constitutes the signs of goodwill on the part of the speaker. The man, as communicator, must understand and manifest these signs if he is to create the impression that he recognizes and is concerned with the needs and interests of his audience.

Carl Stokes and Seth Taft considered the ethos factor crucial in the campaign. Not only did they make a deliberate effort to enhance their images by their acts, they hired public relations men to help them analyze the public's standards and adapt their presentations of self to meet those standards.

The problem that emerged at the beginning of the general campaign was that both men tried to achieve the same image—youthful, aggressive, dedicated to change. Also, practically all the suggested programs for community improvement presented by the two aggressor-rhetoricians looked alike. The two challengers began tilting at windmills because no defender-rhetorician existed who could articulate a clear alternative choice. But choice for the Cleveland voter was imperative. Therefore it was necessary that one of the aggressors force the other to assume the role of defender. Midway in the general election campaign the roles were decided and the battle resumed.

CHAPTER 3

CRISIS AND CONSUMMATION

"WHEN WE'RE TALKING about political campaigns," said Martin Haag, news editor of WKYC-TV in 1967, "we're talking about appearance." Haag thought that Taft, with his slender build, high voice, and family name came across in the beginning of the campaign as an ineffectual "do-gooder." He added: "In print Taft came across as rather colorless. TV was responsible for the tightness of the race."

The second phase of the rhetorical crisis was played out before the television cameras in a series of debates. There was, of course, a continuation of typical campaign tactics during the month between the primary and the general election, but the most crucial events were the televised Stokes-Taft debates. Although these may not have been debates in the academic sense of the word, a proposition, nonetheless, was formulated on which the two speakers took opposite sides on the resolution: That the voters of Cleveland should select Carl Stokes as their mayor. A debate proposition is stated in terms of the alternative requiring the greatest degree of change from the status quo, so that in one respect Taft was relegated to a defender-role from the beginning.

During the primary, Carl Stokes had several times challenged Ralph Locher to debate, but to no avail. Now Seth Taft rose to challenge Carl Stokes. Stokes accepted the challenge, and speculation ran high as to why he did so. A number of politicians guessed that Stokes thought he could project better on television than could Taft. The *Plain Dealer* quoted a Taft aide as saying that Stokes really thought he could "cream" Taft on television.

Carl Stokes wanted to become as familiar as humanly possible in a large, sprawling community; this was impossible in ward meetings, street club meetings, and rallies. He said: "You have to reach these people by the medium. Television was unparalleled in this regard because—when you read a story in a newspaper you can't get the flavor of a person—TV lets you become almost on a one-to-one relationship with each other." The politicians, he said, all told him not to give Seth Taft a platform, but he felt that the uniqueness of a Stokes victory had "overtones and some realities about it that made the day afterward more important than the actual victory day. You have to win right." Stokes did not fear the contact. "My power was in an identification with needs and the ability to articulate them," he said.

Fred Griffith of WEWS-TV news sent telegrams to Seth Taft and Carl Stokes, and he immediately received a reply from Taft saying, "I have approached Carl Stokes and asked him to let us have the prime-time debate." Griffith offered prime time—*any* time, he told the candidates. Carl Stokes responded by saying, "We're willing to have two debates." Two debates were proposed, one on the predominantly black east side and one on the predominantly white west side.

Griffith said: "We told our director to keep the camera mobile, keep it moving, give us reaction, give us faces, scan the audience. To our amazement no one else did [employ these techniques]. It was great show-biz. I think if you had set up two cameras and set up a one-shot of the guy as he talked it would have been bad. We told our director to keep it fluid. We didn't know what to expect, so we said, 'Do your best to keep it visually interesting if it's going to be verbally dull.' "

The Edward Howard agency, on behalf of Seth Taft, sent out the following publicity release to all media, but not one of them carried it. The document is intrinsically interesting as a chronicle of how such encounters come about, but its terms and how they were arrived at are also important to understanding the debates and their role in the campaign:

> We have reached an agreement with Carl Stokes as a result of my having challenged him to a series of debates. There will be two debates plus the traditional City Club meeting at the end of the campaign. The first debate will be at an East Side location on Monday, October 16; the other will be on the West Side on Wednesday, October 18. Both will be two hours long, from 8 to 10 P.M.
>
> These were terms laid down by Carl Stokes' representatives on the virtual "take it or leave it" basis.
>
> I had asked that there be four debates on specific subjects so people could understand exactly how each candidate stood. And, if he liked, Stokes could propose the subjects or if he liked newsmen could pick the subjects.
>
> This was refused.
>
> I had asked that time-honored procedures be followed so that each

candidate could be guaranteed equal time during the critical question and answer period.

This was refused.

I had asked that there be the same impartial moderator for all debates.

That was modified. I pick a moderator for one debate; he picks the other.

I had asked that the debates be held either in one central location downtown or in all parts of the city.

This was refused. We will hold one debate on the East Side, one on the West Side.

I had asked that questions be put in writing to avoid people in the audience standing up and making speeches.

This was refused.

I had asked that requests of three TV stations to hold the debates live, during prime time at a period not to exceed an hour, be honored so that everyone in the city could hear all that was said.

This was refused. At first no time limit was offered; then they finally agreed that each debate would not exceed two hours.

I had asked that the debates be held starting next week so voters would have optimum time to think over what they had heard.

This was refused.

To be perfectly honest with you, I don't think Carl Stokes wants to debate the issues of the city. Well, debate we will, even on these terms. Never before have the people of Cleveland needed so much to know specifically what the candidates will do to correct the city's most pressing problems. I think they are crime, unresponsive city hall, deteriorating neighborhoods and unemployment, adding up to a crisis in human relations.

On the appointed night the east side's Alexander Hamilton Junior High School auditorium was filled. Nearly six hundred Clevelanders packed themselves in to hear the mayoral candidates. The night was hot. Hugh Danaceau and Dave Buckel of WEWS-TV chatted before the camera while a troublesome sound system was doctored. "I talked to

Taft today," said Danaceau. "He and Carl Stokes will be talking to those few thousands who haven't made up their minds." Both candidates were sharply aware that the live audience in the auditorium was primary in fact, but not in importance.

The moderator chosen for the evening was the former *Press* editor, Louis B. Seltzer. It was the first time many Clevelanders had seen Seltzer in person, despite the fact that for years his name had been a household word. Very precisely he outlined the rules: a twenty-minute presentation by each candidate, followed by five minutes of rebuttal or amplification; and a period for questions from the audience. A toss of a coin gave Seth Taft the first twenty minutes—not really an advantage in this intellectual sport called debate.

After acknowledging Louis Seltzer, Carl Stokes, and his audience, Taft said, "These debates are the beginning of a highly educational process for the people of Cleveland. I think that the very process of holding these debates is proof that *Cleveland* will win this fall." Then, turning to his script, Taft stated the central theme of his speech: Who can best handle the problems of a large city? He depicted Carl Stokes as a man with powers of persuasion and himself as a man capable of tackling the city's problems, a man of words against a man of action. Although he stated that both qualities were needed, he persisted in the dichotomy:

> During the weeks ahead, the voters will have ample opportunity to decide for themselves which of us best combines these qualities. I will continue to deal in specifics and my opponent, I suspect, will continue to persuade.

As a further tactic to discredit his opponent, Taft posed three questions to Stokes:

1. How many outsiders are behind your campaign, and what are their motives?
2. How about those compromises after the primary? You backed down on Bert Porter, Muny Light, and Shaker Lakes. Will Chief Wagner be next? Then what's left?[1]
3. Do you intend to present a program? Or don't you think the people would understand?

Not waiting for a response, Taft proceeded to answer the questions himself, citing Stokes's outside support from Washington, San Francisco, and New York and then illuminating and amplifying the nature of the compromises. Finally he ridiculed Stokes's use of ambiguous phrases in talking about programs. This last served as the transition into what Taft considered his best selling point—his specific program to help solve the problem of an unresponsive City Hall which had at its root the larger problem of human relations.

Taft explained his system of "branch city halls" in detail, complete with graphs and charts.[2] He touched briefly upon the subjects of air pollution and police protection, then returned to attacking the credibility of his opponent.

"Persuasiveness" as Taft interpreted it took on a derogatory meaning—deception and doubletalk. Taft said Carl Stokes was a fast talker, a doubletalker, and specifically illustrated his point with examples.

> First, you joked in a speech to the Fraternal Order of Police about how you were stopped for speeding and, because the policeman knew you, he didn't give you a ticket. Then you said, when you were questioned about it on the Alan Douglas radio show, that it demonstrated your ability to work with the police force.

Taft's conclusion restated the request for specific answers to his questions and promised he would insist upon a response "if I have to send you a letter a day to get answers." (Seth Taft was a compulsive letter writer, a faculty that would haunt him in a later debate.)

There was little color in the speech, a minimum of adjectives. He adhered closely to his script, reading it in a careful manner. He obviously attempted to vary his pitch and tone, but was in no way conversational. His delivery was stilted.

Taft's strategy seemed to be twofold: to discredit Stokes by stigmatizing him as a "persuader"—a trickster of no substance—and to establish himself, by contrast, as a plain talker who not only had a specific program, but was astute enough to recognize that his opponent did not. He further attempted to enhance his own image as a man of substance and integrity by assuming the burden, for the voter, of forcing Stokes to show his hand.

William Silverman, Taft's speech writer, revealed one of his assumptions about the audience when he said, "We had to reduce it to little words." There was also an apparent assumption that perceptible honesty is directly proportional to plainness of style. That the audience may have drawn other inferences from Taft's choice of words did not appear to have occurred to Taft or Silverman. For example, an audience looking for language cues which would indicate warmth, liveliness, quick-wittedness, and sympathy would have inferred from the speech that Seth Taft was somewhat lacking in these qualities.

Warning an audience that one's opponent will try to trick them with fancy words is an ancient rhetorical ploy, but one which can easily backfire. The opponent so characterized has only to adopt a down-to-earth style in order to refute the charge. (And Stokes did, in fact, make such an attempt.) The first speaker in a debate always risks his own credibility if he attempts to define or characterize his opponent, for the opponent need not argue against the characterization. He has only to behave contrary to the definition. Another inherent disadvantage in being the first speaker is that one's opponent has the opportunity to scrutinize the audience and analyze its responses. Perceiving an audience's dissatisfaction with the substance or method of the first speaker, the second can alter or adapt his presentation to satisfy the needs of the audience.

It would appear at first glance that Seth Taft had misread his rhetorical challenge. First, he was facing a predominantly Negro audience whose choice of a mayor was unlikely to be made on the basis of either a humble or an ornate style. Any audience puts its own interests first. To reach the audience before him, Taft should have outlined the effectiveness of his program in terms of the specific problems and values of that audience. He should certainly have recognized that an attack upon the integrity of a black man before a black audience was bound to be met with coolness, if not hostility. However, when there is a larger audience to be reached than the immediate one, the classic considerations may not prevail. In the television audience there were undoubtedly people, black and white, who were looking either to make a choice or to be given justification for a choice already made. It is conceivable that Seth Taft knew that reaching his immediate primary audience was hopeless, and so adapted his presentation to the secondary, television audience; however, his own testimony (page 86) indicates that he had not as yet come to understand the nature of the rhetorical challenge nor the most effective method of coping with it.

After Seth Taft sat down, Louis B. Seltzer congratulated the audience upon its good manners. (Throughout the Stokes-Taft confrontations, Seltzer attempted to impose silence and "good manners" on the audiences, as if they were unruly school children.) Seltzer then introduced Carl Stokes.

Stokes first introduced his wife and his mother. These introductions became standard during the confrontations. Not to be outdone, Seth Taft in a later debate shyly, almost giggling, followed suit by introducing his wife and family.

While Seth Taft had told the audience in two simple statements that they were participating in an educational event, Carl Stokes amplified that event into a "true town meeting," into "something that could only happen in America." He referred to the audience as judge and jury witnessing a contest between "the grandson of a slave and the grandson of a president."

Stokes's central theme was identical to Taft's: Who can best serve at Cleveland's helm? Taft had said the contest was between a man of words and a man of action. Stokes presented it as a choice between a man who would act "boldly, courageously, and successfully," and a man isolated in committee meetings, the creator of documents "doomed to gather dust in unconsulted filing cabinets"—between a man who had experienced life and a man protected from life by wealth. Stokes softened the claims about his own ability by admitting (as he was to do on many other occasions) that he was not a superman. "My wife will be the first to tell you," he quipped.

Stokes claimed that because of the time limit he could not tell all that he planned to do for the people as mayor. He offered, however, a "new belief" in people, a spirit of adventure, a spirit of dedication. He said that the city needed leadership and Carl Stokes could supply it. He vowed he would abolish discourtesy from City Hall by reminding the employees that they work for the citizens. Stokes said he would improve the police department by a simple process of reassigning personnel.

With four pages of his prepared text left, Carl Stokes ran out of time. Claiming he wished to abide by the rules but didn't care if his opponent ran overtime because "he needs as much opportunity as he can get," Carl Stokes sat down amid much applause.

Carl Stokes's attack implied that Taft was attuned only to the remote security of his suburban Pepper Pike, that he didn't understand hunger and need. In comparison, he presented himself as tough, understanding human beings of all walks of life, as particularly attuned to the audience because, like them, he had no suburban haven to escape to and must work with the people to make the city safe. He claimed to have been already tested in the legislative arena and in the arena of life. Stokes made no reference to Taft's charge that he was merely a man of words, nor did he answer Taft's three initial questions regarding outside financial support, his compromises with the Democratic party, and his failure to present substantial programs to the voters.

Taft was correct when he said that his opponent dealt in personalities, but then that was the prime issue in the proposition: That the voters of Cleveland should select Carl Stokes as their mayor. Stokes asserted that he was the toughest, strongest contender, and he acted out the role. His adaptation to the immediate audience was evident in his identification with hunger, courage, inner-city problems, and unemployment. He claimed to have experienced everything the audience had experienced and that his interest was not purely academic. Carl Stokes was appealing to the long-suffering and disadvantaged citizens of Cleveland (and to those who sympathized with their plight) whether present or at home, so both audiences could be accommodated by the same speech.

For Seth Taft the first debate was a disaster. The predominantly black audience cheered mainly for Carl Stokes whose delivery was fiery, whose style was vivacious, who identified with his immediate audience and their needs, who stressed his own humble beginnings as opposed to Taft's aristocratic background. Stokes's reasoning was reminiscent of the vice-presidential inaugural speech of Andrew Johnson (March 4, 1861) who identified himself as a plebian and who said he was proud to be a plebian, for "the people are the source of all power." Carl Stokes approached the audience as a poor boy—a plebian. "Carl Stokes," said James Naughton, *Plain Dealer* political writer, "is streetwise." Taft prepared a case without accounting for the jury. He admitted as much later when he said, "My law practice is not a debating-type law practice. I'm not a trial lawyer, so it's a long time since I've done a lot of vigorous debating."

Taft workers who attended the debate were depressed. It was generally conceded that Stokes had won the evening. However, this first televised debate, in addition to presenting the candidates' images to the public, also presented the audience with images of the electorate. WEWS had used its cameras to go out into the audience. "Keep it fluid, keep it moving," Fred Griffith told his men, insisting on reactions, faces, drama. The next day the Taft people began to sense a different reaction to the event. Robert Bennett, Taft's campaign manager, said they were flooded with phone calls. While many calls were complimentary to Taft's performance, most of the people reacted to the audience. The live audience was in a campaigning mood. Many people held signs, a few beat drums, and many wore costumelike attire. The people were enthusiastic, at times cheered wildly, and exhibited disapproval verbally and visually. It was not an unusual political audience, but the television cameras amplified the emotional atmosphere for the home viewers who were not *part of the scene.* The television audience did not respond to the emotional level of the predominantly black audience in the same way they would have responded to a live audience. Watching television they could be detached, not caught up in the fervor of the moment, and they were quick to criticize. Bennett said, "We got calls like 'Did you see that audience? They were like madmen. We can't let them get hold of our city.' " Bennett believed that the Stokes people subsequently made an effort to keep what he referred to as the "tom-tom beaters" (those who actually brought drums to the meetings) in the background. Ostrow also was concerned that the television cameras were picking out black members of the audience who would satisfy predetermined stereotypes.

The reaction of a secondary audience to a primary audience that identifies with a candidate can in turn reflect upon the candidate. There are many communication models which concern themselves with the interpreter's role in the communication process. It would be interesting to find one that considers an audience's reaction to another audience's reaction. Of course, this phenomenon is the direct result of the presence of television and the director's desire for action, for what is visually interesting. Fred Griffith's dicta probably did more to present the viewers with the totality of the event than a more restrictive staging could have done. By shifting their attention, as any normal participant in the audience would have done, the cameramen were able to take the home viewers inside the event. But it must be remembered that the decision to shift attention and the selection of a focal point was not made *by* the audience but *for* the audience by the mediators.

The general campaign began to take form. The candidates had begun to characterize each other as polar opposites: rich-poor, academic-streetwise, man of words-man of action. The audience may have added colorful-drab. But as yet, nobody had polarized black-white, at least not in public.

Carl Stokes selected the site of the second debate, the west side's John Marshall High School. By the time the debate began, the auditorium was filled with nearly eleven hundred people (mostly white), some lining the hallway aisles. Hugh Danaceau and Dave Buckel of WEWS-TV were again at their microphones. Danaceau, called by many the best of Cleveland's television journalists, had worked as a newspaper reporter before entering the field of electronic journalism in 1953. The two men set the stage for the viewing public, and their remarks were at once suggestive and prophetic. Whether the remarks by the two reporters, particularly those by Danaceau, prepared the audience for what was to come or helped to create an atmosphere of anticipation, curiosity, or expectation is questionable. But no one could have planned a more appropriate "warm-up" for the show which was to follow. Danaceau mentioned that each candidate was getting a little tired and a little edgy. He said, "Monday night each candidate lost his temper at least once, and we may find that to be true tonight." He warned the viewers that many questions coming from members of the audience were planted and designed to "get the goat" of the man to whom the question was directed.

Louis B. Seltzer, again the moderator and timekeeper, stepped to the podium and said, "May I ask for complete, absolute silence while we start the debate. I'm going to ask the police to remove anyone who doesn't allow this show—this debate—to go on in complete silence."

Seth Taft began the second debate. This time either his voice was pitched lower or the technicians had performed some electronic feat that brought out more bass tones. The television audience, in any event, was hearing a more pleasant sounding Seth Taft. He asked for the help of the audience, specifically that they listen to him and understand the problem which he would detail for them. The problem was that of deteriorating neighborhoods, or the broader topic of housing. But before embarking upon the specifics of his plan, Taft took time out to reply to Carl Stokes's attack on him Monday night, stating that he didn't think Stokes knew what tough really was. "I'm afraid Mr. Stokes confused toughness with belligerence. I'm afraid Mr. Stokes confused strength with bravado. I'm afraid Mr. Stokes confused courage with being cocky." Each line was punctuated with loud applause. The repetition was effective. The cadence lent force to the words. He climaxed it all with, "I'm afraid Mr. Stokes never noticed the fact that in any situation the men who are strongest and toughest are the ones who have to do the least talking [Applause], the least talking about just how tough they really are."

Seth Taft's attack in this debate was more forceful, more direct, and not quite so polite. Before Carl Stokes even rose to deliver his remarks, Taft had established a stronger image for himself. Shouts of "Bravo! Bravo!" echoed and reechoed in the auditorium when Taft finished. The audience was predominantly a Taft audience, according to the newspapers, but the speech presented a tougher Taft. In the first debate Carl Stokes attempted to emasculate Seth Taft, to portray an ineffectual do-gooder unable to cope with reality. He almost succeeded. The first-debate Taft could not have convincingly mouthed claims about his strength and toughness.

But a political campaign does not consist of a collection of discrete events; it is an event in process. It is an ongoing series of actions and reactions which creates new relationships and interactions among the participants at different points in time. It was, as Hugh Danaceau had told the audience earlier, "late in the game"; the way in which Carl

Stokes could filibuster at length when he didn't want to answer a question had begun to weary audiences. The standard appeals had been rehearsed so often that listeners could almost recite with Stokes the stories of his poverty-ridden childhood, of the depression days when he and his brother trudged from a fatherless home to where surplus food was handed out, of the way his mother had scrubbed floors. The images of Stokes-then dimmed as the picture of Stokes-now became more familiar. Audiences could see that it had been some time since Carl Stokes had been hungry. His suits looked better than Seth Taft's. It was known that he sent his children to private schools. The economic gap between the two candidates appeared narrower. Now Taft was growing tougher, developing calluses on the soft spots. The two candidates were growing more alike when there should have been a marked emphasis on their differences.

Louis Seltzer congratulated the audience for their good manners while listening to Seth Taft. "I hope you will do similarly for Mr. Stokes," he added before making the introduction. The boos and cheers were about equally divided. Chants of "We want Carl!" "We want Seth!" began. When the audience settled down Carl Stokes introduced his wife, addressed a few complimentary remarks to Louis Seltzer, and spoke of Cleveland's great achievements of the past. He presented his central theme: Carl Stokes is the best man to serve Cleveland as mayor. He listed his qualifications, professional record, civic responsibilities, and his ability to work with people.

There remained, after that, only the necessity of discrediting his opponent. In the first debate he had depicted Taft as a weakling. In the second debate he charged that Seth Taft had no faith in the people. For the audience, the language Carl Stokes used to discredit his opponent was highly offensive but also highly effective in literally changing the whole complexion of the campaign, and it succeeded in turning his opponent into a defender-rhetorician!

> The question before you, the voters of Cleveland, is quite simple: Which of the candidates do you believe—do you honestly believe—is best prepared to do all the things that have to be done? [Shouts. Pleas by moderator for quiet.] Thanks. And I appreciate the feelings, but we have to get along with our talks. Which of us is best suited by training, job experience and actual living experiences, personality, understanding of human beings, the ability to win cooperation from all the thousands of people whose help we will need?

Well, I'm going to be brutally frank with you and equally frank with Seth Taft.

The personal analysis of Seth Taft—and the analysis of many competent political analysts—is that Seth Taft may win the November 7 election, but for only one reason.

That reason is that his skin happens to be white.

[Prolonged booing.]

Seth Taft has pretended to bypass this so-called black-white issue. In fact, he had his public relations firm, Ed Howard and Company, pin up a so-called Bill of Rights.

But, in practically every public utterance he has made during this campaign, he not so subtly points out that, quote, Carl Stokes has more experience than Seth Taft at being a Negro (which is true), but Seth Taft has more experience at being a white man. Unquote.

This is so remindful to me, ladies and gentlemen, of 1960 when Richard Nixon punctuated his campaign against John F. Kennedy, a Catholic, and when at every point Nixon would say with similar references that people should not vote against Kennedy because he is a Catholic.

Now, if this is not some kind of subtle appeal to race prejudice, then why does he continually bring this up. *Just be quiet a minute!* On October 3, the voters of this city clearly demonstrated by their votes in the Democratic primary election that they are more concerned about a man's ideas and ability than they are with the color of his skin. So that has been resolved in this city. But that very demonstration by the electorate is the very thing that has frightened Seth Taft in his desperateness to become mayor.

Just a minute! Listen! Just let me finish! If you don't agree with me when I get through, that's what you have ballot boxes for! Because he never *believed*—as I did and do—that the white Cleveland electorate would vote for a person who happened to be a Negro.

Seth Taft, Seth Taft, let me say for all in this listening audience, is not a racist. He is not a bigot. But he does not believe that the people of Cleveland can rise above this issue. He believes that any white candidate—*I'll finish it, Mr. Seltzer*—would beat Carl Stokes in the general election.

> Do you know how I know this is true?
>
> Because Seth Taft told me!
>
> He not only said this to me in two conferences which he requested at my office, but he also repeated it in two subsequent conferences separately with my brother Louis Stokes, relative to this same subject.

Seth Taft's rebuttal showed a man awakened to his task. The reluctant orator disappeared, and in his place rose a confident, inspired debater. Taft's extemporaneous answer is recorded here in its entirety.

> *Well, well, well. It seems the race issue is with us.* I was charged at Carl Stokes's campaign-opening with bringing up the race issue by telling my workers that race was not a factor in this race. As far as I'm concerned it is not. It was not in the Democratic primary, as Carl Stokes pointed out. He won by the votes of fourteen thousand white voters who voted for him. Now it appears that if I say something on this subject, it's racism. If Carl Stokes says something about it, it's fair play.
>
> [Holds up advertisement.] "Don't Vote for a Negro—Vote for a Man," said Carl Stokes in full page ads this summer. After the primary the theme changed, "Let's Do Cleveland Proud." May I take a moment to explain that advertisement. What is it that Cleveland has done that it may be proud of? [Voice from audience: "Vote for a Negro!"] You are exactly right in the audience—nominating a Negro, and it says now you've done yourself proud by nominating one, do yourself proud by electing one! *That* is talking about race. It is impossible to ignore the fact in this city that there is feeling on the subject of race. I have not brought it up—not once in these debates—and I had no intention of bringing it up. But I resent the notion that the reverse is true. That Carl Stokes can talk about it, but nobody else can. Now he's made a reference tonight; he's made a reference before to Pepper Pike. Yes, I have lived in Pepper Pike. I don't defend that community. There's plenty of bigotry there and plenty of bigotry in Cleveland. But I'm a citizen of Cleveland—I've complied with the law—and for twenty years. Now Carl Stokes and his brother bought a house in 1961 at 3130 Albion Road in Shaker Heights. In 1967 the house was transferred over to his brother Lou, and his brother lives there now. On September 12, 1967, Carl Stokes bought another house

> in Shaker Heights at 3718 Lindholm Road. He said this house was for his mother. It has *four* bedrooms. Carl Stokes said he was a fine legislator. [L. Seltzer: "I will add one minute to Mr. Taft's time for prolonged disturbance.] Carl Stokes during the last two sessions introduced only three bills in two sessions. I don't call that a very impressive record.

More important than what was said in the second debate was what was heard and how the message was decoded. Who did the decoding was a vital issue to the rhetoric which ensued in the weeks to follow. James Naughton, *Plain Dealer* political writer, thought the audience at home responded more to the reporters' interpretation than to what went on in the debate. He said he went home after writing the story and watched the debate on television at 11:30 that night. He added, "I was amazed that it didn't come across nearly as dramatic as sitting in that audience." Vail asserted that when he had the tape played for him he was not at all shocked by either Stokes's or Taft's words. Norman Wagy, news editor of WJW-TV, however, heard it on the radio and remarked, "My wife happened to come through the bedroom just as this thing came on. Then she stood there with her mouth open and, you know, we both just couldn't believe our ears."

The impact of the words without the visual element was obviously direct and forceful in Mr. Wagy's case. The radio listener must make all his inferences from language and voice cues, so it was natural that Mr. and Mrs. Wagy would have found the language much more striking. But that the audience at John Marshall perceived the insult immediately upon its being spoken is rather remarkable. Up to that point the emphasis had been positive—"Do Cleveland Proud," "Don't Vote for a Negro; Vote for a Man." Now Carl Stokes was saying that if Seth Taft happened to win it would be only because he had white skin.

If one rereads the excerpt, it can be seen that Stokes actually said the "political analysts" were the ones making the statement about Taft. It appears that he was even attributing the accusation to Taft himself. But Stokes's syntax was too complex in the explanatory sentence. Sandwiched between "I'm going to be brutally frank with you . . ." and "That reason is that his skin happens to be white," the explanatory sentence was lost. Perhaps, at that point, if Stokes had countered the reaction with "But I don't believe that. I believe that the people of Cleveland can rise above this issue," the moment would have been saved. However, by sticking to his prepared text, Stokes compounded the insult by seeming to accuse Seth Taft of being the number-one bigot. By the time he reached the sentence disestablishing Taft as a racist or bigot, the damage had been done. The disclaimer was not believable, especially since it was followed by a statement further implicating Taft.

Seth Taft was not a man who could be attacked on those grounds. Taft's devotion to liberal reforms through the years made his record appear more politically liberal than Stokes's. Taft had reached out to the more militant element of the black community. He had addressed more CORE meetings than had Stokes. Taft's children were known to have devoted much of their time to helping inner-city young people. Carl Stokes had called Albert Porter and others in his own party racists, and the reaction had been minimal. But Seth Taft's image had begun to firm up. Martin Haag said, "He's Mr. Nice Guy, U.S.A." Taft tried awfully hard to play "fair." He even fired two volunteer workers for bringing up the racial issue. "That's going pretty far," said one old-timer in politics, "when you fire your volunteers."

The day following the debate, twenty-five Stokes workers had breakfast together and unanimously agreed that Carl Stokes had blundered. Dr. Kenneth Clement, Stokes's own campaign manager, told reporters that he wished there were a third write-in candidate he could vote for. He said, "If he performs like he did last night for the next two weeks, he'll lose. . . . He did it against my advice. . . . Maybe all that booing helped him a little, but, you know, I'm interested in more than Carl Stokes. I'm concerned with what sort of social situation we will have in this city after the election."[3]

If Dr. Clement was so appalled, who made the decision to bring up the black-white question? In an interview with Stokes, he said he was fully responsible for that decision. "The basic unstated issue was race," he said firmly. A *Washington Post* story (October 29) quoted Ostrow as saying that the occasion was worth ten thousand votes in the Negro community. "They thought he had already won, and they weren't planning to come out again. Sure, everybody is moaning and groaning today. But we won through calculated risks before. It's the only way to go."

Rhetorically, the risk was that Carl Stokes converted Seth Taft into a defender-rhetorician in this second debate. When Carl Stokes said to the electorate that if Seth Taft won the election it would be only because he was a white man, he transformed Taft from a contender for a prize to a defender of a cause. Stokes made it possible for liberal-minded people to vote for a white man and still preserve their self-respect, for the liberal would not condone race as a criterion. Had Taft forced Stokes to defend his race instead of his ability, it is conceivable that

Stokes would have cornered every liberal vote. But since Taft had assiduously avoided bringing race into his attacks on the personality and programs of Stokes, the attempt to identify Taft as a racist candidate backfired. In the minds of many, Taft became the symbol of high-minded idealism, purity of purpose, and thoughtful practicality. Instead of coming on like a hero and a champion of harmony and goodwill, Stokes began to look like a villain. He now was obliged to reestablish for himself the kind of image he had helped to create for Taft. He was helped in his task by Taft when the latter, not fully appreciating his advantage, began taking on the characteristics of an aggressor and almost reversed the roles again.

Meanwhile, the media perpetuated the issue. The *Plain Dealer* banner in the morning-after paper read: "Suddenly GOP Here Hums Taft Victory Song." Taft also kept the issue alive. On October 31 he wrote Stokes a letter, enclosing the *Washington Post* article which revealed the "unfortunate mistake" to be a "calculated strategy." Reminding Stokes that on two occasions Taft had fired his own volunteers for using "the question of race in a manner which I thought was improper," Taft urged Stokes to ask for Ostrow's resignation. The incident of the second debate was not forgotten. What Carl Stokes said on that night did affect his campaign adversely and what Seth Taft answered was likewise instrumental in helping Taft's own campaign. But in both cases, the news media firmed up the images and kept them before the public. James Naughton said, "Those who were there were much more emphatically impressed, and the television newscasters—really shocked with the impact—indicated that shock subconsciously in what they wrote and what they said in front of the cameras."

On the night following the John Marshall incident, Stokes and Taft engaged in another debate. Since it was not televised, few reporters considered the encounter important, but the event was significant, and it revealed a heightened sensitivity on the part of candidates and audience alike.

It was at this debate, held at Saint John's College in downtown Cleveland, that James Howard of the Edward Howard agency remarked, "Stokes is a good speaker and a poor orator in the classical sense of the word. Taft is a poor speaker and a good orator—good orator in the sense of having some substance to it. I think, as a result, Stokes is suffering from exposure. I think it's impossible to keep up that emotional pitch."

The moderator at the Saint John's debate tried to create a more relaxed atmosphere that night. He showed how similar the two candidates were, citing their profession, armed forces training, civic activities, ages, and the fact that both men had lost an election by a hair's breadth—Seth Taft in 1962 for the Ohio senate seat and Carl Stokes in 1965 for the mayor's office. "Despite what you heard on Monday and Wednesday, both have a great deal of respect for each other," he concluded. Each speaker was charged by the moderator with the task of giving the audience his program for revitalizing Cleveland.

Stokes's program included the reassignment of policemen and the installation of a computer to help solve the problems of crime in the streets. The housing problem he would solve by "cutting red tape" to allow private groups to get on with their projects. Concerning jobs, Stokes said, "I talked with the [U.S.] secretary of labor last week, and we agreed it was the responsibility of private industry to provide on-the-job training."

Taft's program included citizen participation in government, the establishment of a new housing development in Warrensville Township,[4] increased revenues from the parking fees at Burke Lakefront Airport, and crime control. On the last issue Taft proved that he was learning a strategy of debate; a straight-line attack on an opponent's plan will often serve better than self-defense. Taft took apart Stokes's plan for taking three hundred policemen away from their present assignments and putting them on patrol.[5] He also charged that the computer Stokes claimed he would install in the police department was due to go into operation on January 1 anyhow and would do one job—record stolen license plate numbers on a chart.

The mood was pleasant, cordial, and constructive until microphones were sent out into the audience for questions. A stocky man rose and asked whether it was true that Carl Stokes hated Jews because his mother had been a cleaning woman for Jews. A rustling of robes behind indicated the discomfiture of the nuns. Dirty politics had invaded the sanctity of the cathedral. Carl Stokes was advised that he need not answer the question, but he slowly came to the microphone and in a voice at once soft and filled with emotion spoke of his donations to the state of Israel and his willingness to answer every question, even those asked by misguided people. When he was finished the audience was silent. They had witnessed a poignant performance.

Perhaps no political strategist would have planted such a question, for by this time in the campaign it was evident that low blows or anything looked upon as "not fair" added points to the recipient. And this question certainly worked to Carl Stokes's advantage at a time when Taft was cornering all the "underdog" sympathy, because audiences still regarded Stokes's attack on Taft during the previous night's debate as unfair. In order that Stokes regain some of that sympathy, the audience had to perceive that *he* had been attacked unfairly. Not only did the question evoke such a response from the Saint John's audience, but it provided Protestant Stokes with an opportunity to defend Jews to a Catholic audience. He was the new ecumenical spirit personified.

It was at the Saint John's College appearance that Carl Stokes was asked to evaluate himself as a speaker. After the debate a number of people on stage gathered in a circle around Stokes to wish him well. The question actually created an opportunity for Stokes to defend himself as a man of intelligence and integrity. He said:

> The only thing I can say about myself, as a speaker, is this, and that is that you're persuasive when you're personally convinced and when you're really speaking from your heart and when you're speaking from information. And this way, you see, anyone who went back to 1965 or went back to 1960 and took any statement of mine have never been able to find my having contradicted myself, because I never say anything about which I don't have first the kind of information upon which I have made a judgment and, subsequently, placed it within my entire framework of the approach to government that I have. As long as you do that, as long as you don't worry about pleasing people, then in politics you never have to worry about being contradicted as, of course, my colleague was tonight.

After the Saint John's appearance Seth Taft said, "Every time Stokes faces me I pick up strength, because people are seeing through his charm-school act." Taft was starting to look like a fighter. He was beginning to act like a politician. "Sure. He got his feet wet and, furthermore, he liked it," said Dan W. Duffy, Democratic party official. No longer afraid of confrontation, Taft's strategy was to take the offensive. His public relations man got busy and started sending out challenges via the news media. Taft claimed that Stokes was avoiding him. In one press release Taft spelled it out again:

> Carl Stokes has been ducking me ever since last Wednesday's debate. His decision makers have told him he can't lose—providing he can avoid answering the questions I ask. They know every time Stokes faces me I pick up strength, because people are seeing through his charm-school act.

> Except for the traditional City Club debate on November 4, which he can't duck, the only joint appearances he accepts are safe ones with his ground rules saying I cannot question him or comment on his answers.
>
> He ducked out of eight neighborhood meetings where the people asked for joint appearances. In each case he said either he wouldn't come at all, or would come only before or after I spoke.
>
> The people want debates and he's turning them down . . . like tonight when he maneuvered to avoid me at the Goodrich Sterling Neighborhood Center. The people asked for a debate, and I accepted. Stokes refused. I'll speak at six-thirty, and I'll wait for Stokes to show. And I'll have a question or two to ask him.[6]

The television medium played up Taft's remarks about more confrontation. On October 25, Taft said he'd be at the Goodrich Center and urged everybody in town to tell his opponent to meet him there. The news media were there in force hoping for another sensational clash. The two men were scheduled to speak that night at different times and, instead of sticking around to confront his opponent, Taft left. The *Plain Dealer* later reported:

> That night Taft spoke first at the Goodrich Center and then left, just as Stokes began to speak. Stokes quickly called him on it. "I regret Mr. Taft is no longer here. He said he would come early so we could be together. What was the first thing he did? Go out the door."[7]

Taft's departure that night was a signal to the Stokes forces to reassess their campaign strategy. Ostrow felt that it was at this point that the Stokes forces gained the offensive again. "For a week Taft had been steadily rising, growing. We were concerned, and Carl was preparing for a real effort. The way Taft was talking we thought it might come at Goodrich. It didn't. After that we knew Seth Taft was finished."

Stokes agreed to a third televised debate as the first step in the new offensive. The Taft forces apparently did not detect the strategy, for they conceded to all Stokes's demands about time and format. The event was scheduled for the afternoon of October 28 at the Public Auditorium Music Hall. Taft supporters had wanted an evening performance, but, again, it was the Stokes organization that selected the site and the time. The afternoon time slot may have been significant for several reasons.

First, WEWS-TV was committed to carrying the Notre Dame–Michigan football game, a television event which would naturally draw off scores of viewers. This meant that another station would have to carry the debate. At WEWS-TV Fred Griffith's directions to his staff to pick up audience reactions had caused some embarrassment to the Stokes people. The station thus chosen to carry the debate was WKYC-TV. There is no evidence that the change in visual style was deliberate, but the difference was obvious. WKYC focused its cameras only on the speakers.

Another significant factor related to the time slot was that neither side anticipated attracting the "uncommitted." In the experience of the political managers, the curious do not come out as readily in the afternoon as do the dedicated. "The audience at the third debate was split—50 percent for Stokes and 50 percent for Taft," said Bennett, Taft's campaign manager.

Another concession made by the Taft people was the choice of moderator. In the first debate, according to Bennett, Ostrow had selected Louis Seltzer. The Taft people then asked Seltzer to moderate the second debate so that "all things would be equal." However, in the third debate, Carl Stokes did not want Louis Seltzer. School Superintendent Paul W. Briggs was chosen to act as moderator. The performance of Paul Briggs did make a difference in the conduct of the debate. A *Plain Dealer* editorial commented:

> His calm, firm conduct of the moderator's role kept demonstrations from interrupting the program. He did not hesitate to cut short questions which became speeches in support of one or the other candidate, nor to rule out questions which in his judgment were out of order.[8]

It would seem that every precaution was taken to insure that the third debate would be as controlled and emotionless as possible. For the television audience, according to the newspapers, it was also as dull and colorless as possible. The *Plain Dealer*, in a Sunday supplement article which appeared a month after the election, summarized the event in critical terms:

> Within an atmosphere of palpitating interest, the third debate, the great rubber match and the confrontation all awaited, was held. It turned out to be nothing more than a ritualistic performance that saw Taft turn attacker, riddling Stokes with personal barbs, only to see his opponent ignore them, drop five pages of

> similar material from his prepared speech, and discuss his program inch by inch, point by point, trying to defeat the accusation that he had no real program. . . . It was evident, though, that Stokes was employing a new strategy. He was trying to appear more humble, trying to assume a quiet, defensive position in contrast to the bold, attacking manner he had exhibited in the earlier debates. He apparently had taken the advice of those, who, before the general election campaign began, had said: "If Stokes loses this election it won't be because Seth Taft beat him; it'll be because Stokes beat himself."[9]

Actually, in a review of the complete texts of all the campaign speeches, the switches in strategy were not all that dramatic. Stokes had gradually grown more cautious and expository, probably in response to both Taft's technique and to the audiences' response at the second debate. At the same time, Taft had grown less pedantic and more willing to engage Stokes on his own terms. It is perhaps more realistic to say that the third debate revealed the evolutionary stage at which the two candidates had arrived.

If the campaign is viewed only in terms of the four televised debates, then the "change" remarked upon in the third debate becomes a more prominent feature. When the debates are put into their proper perspective they indicate certain milestones in the race where the candidate's pacing, stride, and progress can be assessed. Each candidate had stumbled in the early stages of the race. Each had to change his strategy enough to overcome his own disadvantage and reduce his opponent's advantage, but neither changed his course altogether. However, most spectators care little about how a race is run until the contenders come into the final stretch. Political writer James Naughton made these observations in an interview after it was all over:

> The charge was that he [Stokes] wasn't offering concrete platforms as to what he would do if elected mayor. In the last *two* debates the roles were almost completely reversed. Stokes talked almost entirely of programs and what he would do if elected mayor; now he would say, "If so fortunate as to be elected mayor." And Taft began sniping at Stokes, and I think that this hurt Taft because a lot of people really don't pay that much attention to a campaign until the last couple of weeks. Most people do make up their minds in advance and then reinforce their opinions based on what they see in a debate. But there are some, a sizable number, who

> are perhaps not convinced until the last days of the campaign. . . . Taft was riding the crest of that second debate and, at the tail end of the election, when Stokes began talking programs at length and began pointing out areas where Taft's housing project in Warrensville Heights was legally impossible at this time—when he began concentrating on programs and issues—he began to win back some of the people who were disturbed at John Marshall.

Naughton's analysis is interesting, though not shared by William Silverman who constructed an elaborate chart to show how Seth Taft gained steadily from the very first debate and did not taper off near the end of the campaign. Rather, Silverman felt that had the election gone one more week Taft would have won. This view was shared by the other primary candidates and their advisers as well.

The image of Seth Taft, the man, had become stronger and clearer to the public. Taft's speeches indicate that he was saying the same things at the end of the campaign that he had said at the beginning, but he was saying them in a firmer, more confident, way. Taft became more relaxed and seemed to enjoy his role. Bennett, Taft's campaign manager, said, "The biggest factor against him was that he was unproven." Carl Stokes never gave up on that factor. In the third debate Stokes hit as hard at Taft's "ivory tower" approach as he had in the first debate: "This is no time to entrust our city to a man who participated in planning everything that did not happen. There is no time for on-the-job training."

Carl Stokes agreed that he and Ostrow had decided to change his style but not the content of his speeches:

> If you listen to the way I talk really—usually Ostrow wrote the way I talk—and what happened was we talked about the issues, but neither my way of speech nor the way our speeches were written singled these things out clear and simple and sweet to people because they were always put into a context and you'd have to go in there and understand and separate; but if you wanted to make it very short and sweet you'd have to take it out of there. We didn't set it out for them.
>
> Well, they [Taft's people] began using the very good strategy of capitalizing on this in many ways. Unfortunately, many of the things we would say to people were more professorial, sort of, in a way. It's our style. But, one thing that Ostrow and I understood was that we had to strip away so much of what we were saying and set it out for easy consumption for people, and so that's what

> you started seeing in the latter part of the campaign. We were really—everything we were saying in the more simplistic way we had been saying all during the campaign, but people were responding. I guess it's true [that they] responded more to the *impact* of what we were saying than what they really understood. So we turned around and started giving it to them in bite-size chunks. You had to. You had a very smart attack upon us and the newspapers were picking it up, so we figured it's the only thing to do.

From Carl Stokes's remarks, it would seem that Taft's constant criticism followed by newspaper evaluations led to a change in his style of presentation. The role of the newsmen as interpreters and mediators is reminiscent of the remark attributed to Woodrow Wilson that he didn't realize what his platform was until a newspaperman pointed it out to him.

If there was any reversion to type—that is, any attempt to recapture the images the candidates had projected earlier in the campaign—this occurred during the presentations Stokes made on November 1 and Taft made on November 2 at Cleveland State University. Stokes was completely charming, the consummate showman. Taft was plainspoken and pleasantly academic. The students generally agreed that although Stokes "didn't say anything, really," they enjoyed his performance. They respected Taft for respecting them; he treated them like voters.

For more than half a century it has been traditional that the candidates for mayor of Cleveland appear and present their final arguments before the City Club members at the Friday luncheon meeting in the club headquarters at 712 Vincent Avenue NE. The City Club, formed in 1912 by followers of Tom Johnson and the progressive politics of Teddy Roosevelt, has as its credo:

> I hail and harbor and hear men of every belief and party; for within my portals prejudice grows less and bias dwindles. I have a forum as wholly uncensored as it is rigidly impartial. "Freedom of Speech" is graven about my rostrum; and beside it, "Fairness of Speech." . . . I am accessible to men of all sides—literally and figuratively—for I am located in the heart of a city. Spiritually and geographically, I am the city's club—the City Club.

In one respect prejudice has not grown less nor bias dwindled within the portals of the City Club; women are still barred from participation. The only way for a woman to gain entry is by temporary "appointment" to the staff of a local television crew.[10]

The City Club schedules a forum each Friday for oratory that is mainly political in nature. The format includes remarks by a guest speaker followed by a question-and-answer period in which the assembled members and guests participate. Many politicians invited to the podium have flatly refused to participate in the question-answer period. The late Governor Vic Donahey at first refused to appear. Finally he reluctantly took the podium long enough to give his address, then promptly bolted the room before the first question could be hurled at him. In 1928, when U.S. Senator Charles Curtis, the GOP vice-presidential candidate, found out that questions were involved in the forum, he shouted: "I won't do it!" The late Senator Robert A. Taft, however, accepted the challenge and was the first City Club orator to be aired on radio. Many old-timers believe that this 1938 debate helped him to victory.[11]

In 1965 Ralph Locher, Carl Stokes, Ralph Perk, and Ralph McAllister appeared before the City Club as mayoral candidates. Richard Campbell, moderator for the 1967 Taft-Stokes City Club debate, remembered the 1965 debate. He said, "Locher was as forceful as I had ever heard him, and Carl Stokes was so relaxed, so in good humor, and so charming."

Many in the audience at the 1965 debate did not feel that Carl Stokes posed any real threat, that he was merely another one of the many candidates opposing Ralph Locher. Fred Vierow, secretary of the City Club, believed, however, that the 1965 debate did much to boost Carl Stokes as a man capable of handling himself at a podium.

On November 3, 1967, Carl Stokes and Seth Taft met at the Hotel Sheraton Cleveland where the City Club had chosen to stage the debate in order to accommodate a larger audience. There the candidates offered what were essentially their final arguments. The audience was composed of the business and professional men who were City Club members and of representatives of both partisan groups. Moderator Campbell recalled:

> At the November 4 debate, besides the professional men who were members, there were quite a few partisan tables. An attempt was made to pack the house by one of the partisans who wanted to buy five tables, but the City Club officials tried to accommodate both camps equally and did not allow this to happen. The audience was sprinkled with City Club members and heavily made up with partisans.

Stokes, the first speaker, concentrated on the question: Which candidate is best qualified to provide the dynamic leadership our community needs in this hour of crisis? There was no time, he again said, for "on-the-job training." He added, "I respectfully submit that I have the know-how. I have the experience." In support of that claim, Stokes listed his credentials, mentioned his legislative career, his love for the city, and his awareness of the problems which beset the city. Stokes's plans for the future included an inaugural ball which would raise funds for clothing needy children, a county transit board, a look into police-community relations, the immediate audit of books and accounts of the city,[12] a reduction of the tax burden on the small homeowners, and the creation of new jobs. He promised to bring about "a spiritual and physical renaissance." Stokes waged no attack on his opponent but concentrated on building his own ethos and making clear that he had plans. Stokes did not elaborate on his methodology or the ways and means of accomplishing his goals.

Taft, too, put the man before the plans, saying, "This is important, every bit as important as plans and programs—because to a very great extent the destiny of the city is in the hands of a single man." In his own defense Taft cited not only his ability to make plans but his ability to stand the heat and pressure of a campaign. He said he had "passed this test of exposure without conflicting promises, without misunderstandings, without pressures from those whose interests are not the interests of the citizens of the city." The next five hundred or so words were devoted to an attack on Stokes. He claimed that Stokes was not qualified because he was an absentee landlord, an absentee Democrat, and an absentee legislator. "How can a man who does not comply with the housing laws for property he owns and rents be expected to enforce the same laws in Cleveland?" Taft then elaborated only one of his plans—the branch city halls—because to him that seemed the answer to Cleveland's larger problem of human relations.

After the initial presentation each candidate was given a ten-minute rebuttal. Then the question-answer period began. Richard Campbell recalled: "We had mikes set up so that anybody could come to a microphone. For some reason the questions at the beginning of the question-and-answer period were all directed to Seth Taft." At one point Carl Stokes became so angry that he informed Campbell that unless his people got to the microphones he would leave the room. In an effort at appeasement Campbell had to break in and request that the questions be alternated so that each candidate had equal time.

Stokes was particularly effective in this final debate in attacking specific fallacies in Taft's programs. Using a plat map of the area where

Taft planned to build new housing, Stokes showed that the city-owned land was separated from the city itself by parts of Shaker Heights and Warrensville Heights. He put the final hex on Taft's plan by citing the section of the Ohio Revised Code which states that land can be annexed to a city only if it is adjacent to the city.

Stokes's final thrust came at the very end of the debate. In answer to a question about his record as a legislator, Stokes pulled out a letter and, waving it like a red flag, said:

> Very quickly, I've just been told that I have thirty seconds. Folks, you know that I have not only been endorsed by every leading newspaper and the Democratic party, but I'm going to give you what I think is the best attestation of Carl Stokes's service in the legislature was—I have here—Seth has mentioned he began his campaign in April—[Campbell: Our time is up. We're off the air. We thank you all. I'm sorry about the air. Now, we'll let Carl finish his answer.] I'll finish my answer for our people here. The attestation that I have of the way that I have tried to serve the people of the city of Cleveland is furnished best, I think, by Seth Taft himself. And Seth, I'll hand to you the letter that you yourself wrote me on June 7, 1967, and I read it to the audience here on June 8, 1967. "Dear Carl: The reports I hear of your performance in Columbus are excellent, and I congratulate you on the job. With best regards, Seth Taft."

Richard Campbell thought the impact would be lost because the scheduled broadcast time had run out, but one television station stayed on the air long enough to televise the incident. The newspapers highlighted it; a picture of William Silverman's face and the utter dejection he revealed was printed for all to see.

Bronis Klementowicz said later:

> That's why I never write letters. I only send condolences, and then Dorothy and I both sign them—because you and I know it [Taft's letter] was just sent as a letter. But the tough part about the letter was he [Taft] wasn't talking about it from his personal observation—he was talking about the reputation Stokes has got on the street. You see, this is like a character witness in a divorce. . . . If you come up and say you're a character witness for Mrs. X but also say that people you know say that she has a fine reputation as a mother and she has been done wrong, you actually testify to inadmissible evidence, hearsay. So he [Taft] says what he hears on

the street is good about Stokes. This is what is so damaging about it. Now, if he said so personally—but it was rumor that he reported and Stokes said, "Well, it's true."

Some of the wisest political forecasters in Cleveland, the bookies, had given 8 to 5 odds favoring Stokes at the beginning of the general election campaign. On the day of the City Club debate the odds were even, and at 1:00 P.M. no one was taking any bets. The old-timers at the City Club felt that many a politician had won or lost an election at the Friday luncheon hour. If the bookies were right and both men came into the City Club debate almost even, then the flashing of the letter was a significant rhetorical tactic.

Rhetoric alone was not responsible for all the dynamics of the campaign; however, it was through these rhetorical acts of the candidates that the issues—overt and covert—became known. It was through the rhetorical acts of the candidates in their assumed or assigned roles as champions of causes that the electorate found reasons for making a choice, reasons that could be articulated openly.

These reasons were articulated right up to, and including, election day. On election day in the candidates' headquarters, the voting places, suburban homes, Election Board headquarters, offices, stores, and restaurants the voters voiced their fears, justified their positions, and generally evaluated the campaign. At Stokes headquarters there were a group of men from Detroit, one of whom declared, "They should tear the town down; there shouldn't be no more Cleveland," if Carl Stokes did not win. When he was questioned about this he preached some facts of life: "The time for prayer is over. We don't care much about the white man. Take the Bible and throw it in the garbage can. I want mine the same way the white man's been getting his for years—by shooting someone to take it." Others at the headquarters, alarmed at the Detroit man's words, said his talk was "way out," that there would be no problem of violence whoever the victor was. But during the day many voters voiced the fear that there would be incidents if Carl Stokes did not win, and the National Guard stood by all day and was not dismissed until the final vote was counted.

At Taft headquarters a black man, who identified himself as a member of the League of Non-Partisan Voters, predicted that Taft would win by fifteen hundred votes because after Stokes "beloathed Mr. Taft" in the first televised debate people started to change their minds. Another Taft supporter said he had bet a thousand dollars that Taft would win by twenty-five thousand votes, but he was vehement in his denunciation of the "pseudo-intellectual ivy-leaguers" in the Taft organization who "know nothing and think they know something."

In all quarters people were rehashing both the events and the issues of the campaign. A public official's wife confided that before the debates started she was pro-Stokes, but on television he "presented himself as a glib generalizer" and never got down to any pertinent information unless it was to "cast a dig." One teen-age boy said he thought Taft would win because of the backlash but that Stokes was better qualified. Another youngster gave an instant analysis of the rhetorical abilities of the candidates in justifying why he had cast his ballot for Taft in the mock-election at his school:

> Mr. Stokes, I mean, well, he had a good personality and everything, but I really don't think he knew what he was doing. I think a lot of people put a lot of ideas into him and he'd get up on a platform and use them and he had a better way of presenting what he wanted. Taft may have had better ideas. I just don't think he came out with them right.

At Election Board headquarters were assembled the party brass, the press, and the curious—pundits and philosophers all. By 10:40 P.M. everybody knew it would be a close race, and rumors spread quickly and variously as to how close. At one time "an authoritative source" projected Taft the winner by five thousand votes; however, thirty seconds later a "Taft lieutenant" said the election could go either way by one thousand votes. Well-known attorney and political analyst Arthur P. Lambros noted that the east side precincts were still out and, at 11:00 P.M., predicted a Stokes victory. With the accomplished fact only a few precinct tabulations away, the assembled political analysts (both acknowledged and self-appointed) somehow seemed anxious now to discuss the very topic all had tried to avoid during the campaign—*race*.

A prominent Republican said that certain industrial leaders had determined that the community would be better served by the image of a Negro mayor in order to achieve labor peace at any price. He accused the newspaper editors in their "ivory tower sanctums" of going along with the attempt to get Stokes elected. "As a matter of fact," he added, "we have more international coverage on this election than any place else, and the only story they have is if Stokes is elected. If Stokes is not elected, it's backlash and there's no story."

A *Chicago Tribune* reporter admitted that the only reason he was there covering the race was that there was a Negro running in it. "I think there's national significance in this," he explained. "At least two aspects, certainly, from President Johnson's point of view. It's good news if Stokes wins; it's disappointing news if he loses, because I think he hopes that Stokes would help him hold Ohio in the presidential campaign and also be a benefit to restless Negro voters clear across the country."

Robert B. Krupansky, who was later appointed to a federal judgeship by the Nixon administration, remarked that the race issue never really surfaced until election day, because until that time no one really had to come squarely to terms with it. Only 50 percent of the registered Democrats on the west side had voted, indicating that many white voters had simply chosen not to choose. Krupansky believed the electorate would accept the results of the election regardless of who won; he observed: "Minority groups always add to the strength of the democratic process, and, if they don't have the opportunity to express themselves, then we are shortchanging ourselves in making ourselves a stronger nation. You see, that's the secret of our whole form of government—the flexibility of it."

"Yes, flexibility—," added former Councilman Anthony Pecyk, "peaceful kind of change." Pecyk said unreservedly that this was the best mayoral race Cleveland had ever witnessed: "I think it's an indication of stabilization. It will give a sense of direction to government generally. . . ."

However, indications of stabilization were not evident that election night. Just outside the city the National Guard held "practice drills." The commander was in constant touch with Stokes's headquarters. The anticipation of possible violence had resulted in the planning of control measures by all parties concerned. William Silverman said that in the event Seth Taft won, several steps would be taken immediately: "We would have met Wednesday morning at 10:00. Another meeting at 11:00 A.M. with all the Negro leaders in the city. They had all been lined up."

At 2:51 A.M., the tally board at Election Board headquarters showed Stokes ahead with 129,225, Taft trailing with 127,263. The Board of Elections declared Stokes the winner. Ostrow told Stokes to just tell the voters how he felt but to be sure and include something about America. Carl Stokes said: "This vindicates my faith in the people. This is the American dream." Fred Griffith of WEWS-TV, standing nearby, reported hearing Ostrow sigh and say, "God damn it; God bless America." Twenty-one-year-old Andy Bass, electronics technician at Stokes's headquarters, called Adj. Gen. Edwin Hostetler and informed him that all was well. The adjutant general then made the decision to dismiss the National Guard.

On Wednesday morning, November 8, 1967, the *Plain Dealer* carried the headline: "Stokes Apparent Winner: Victory Margin Is Less Than 2,000 Votes." Both parties were faced with the uneasy fact that a change of less than one vote per precinct would reverse the outcome. Seth Taft demanded a recount, but, according to Silverman, the count was made only to clear the air and make it easier for the mayor to conduct his job. "We knew a tremendous percentage of the city did not believe Carl Stokes won the election. They felt it had been stolen. And that's the only reason we had the recount—to clarify the fact that he did win."

Though many statisticians and analysts wrote off the campaign as merely a racial contest, in doing so they accounted for only one operative persuasive force—the predisposition of the voters towards having a black man assume the office of mayor. The participants in the campaign never for a moment took such a narrow view of human behavior. Thousands of dollars and manhours were invested in the belief that at least some of the electorate could be persuaded on grounds other than racial predisposition. Communication of this belief constituted the campaign.

Both Carl Stokes and Seth Taft recognized the ethos factor. Both hired public relations men to help them establish themselves as credible candidates. The public relations men did not merely promote their candidate's image; they determined the strategies and tactics by which the candidate would create his own image. They governed the activities of volunteers and precinct workers, whose function was to carry the candidate's image to the neighborhood level.

The methods employed by the campaign engineers contribute to the candidate's total image, for where there is ill will towards the machinery there develops ill will towards the candidate. Some intraparty strife develops over the methods used by the campaign engineers in analyzing audiences. In the 1967 campaign, the "Madison Avenue boys," as Ralph Locher called the campaign engineers, met resistance from precinct workers accustomed to working on gut-level hunches about where the vote was and what it would take to pull it out.

On the strength of their audience-analyses, the managers determine what strategies are necessary to overcome voter lethargy or resistance. After the primary, Carl Stokes studied a precinct-by-precinct breakdown of the vote. He knew how many votes he needed, what his goal had to be, and which precincts had produced the required number of votes. Bennett said Stokes used the primary to test his vote-pulling strength and that Stokes was ruthless in getting rid of workers who were not pulling in the projected amount of votes. On election day the Stokes people launched "Operation Doorknob" throughout key precincts. In areas where voters had been remiss in following through on their commitments, reminders (printed with instructions to turn the reminder over to the opposite side after the occupant had voted) were hung on doorknobs. Stokes volunteers toured the areas throughout the day, knocking on doors and literally pulling out the vote.

An intermediary force in creating the candidate's image is the public opinion maker: the newspaper reporter, the broadcaster, the influential public figure. Vail of the *Plain Dealer* said, "We had the man and the moment" in which the newspaper could invest its authority and credibility in making the endorsement of Stokes. Ralph Locher blamed his poor image on the media. While many still believe that Locher was crucified on a television antenna, the media did not so much create his image as to amplify some of its less appealing aspects. The television medium had to take, as given, the situation of a man trying to create his own image. But it did spotlight certain elements in that situation and could, therefore, selectively alter the image to suit the tastes of the newsmen. Television also added a new dimension to the candidate's image by focusing attention on the behavior of his supportive audiences. The radio phone-in shows offered the candidates an opportunity to demonstrate different facets of their ethos—the intellectual ability to field difficult questions and the emotional stability to remain calm under conditions of stress.

The opinions of leaders or the very absence of opinion by a respected leader constitute another dimension of the candidate's image. Stokes had the endorsement of Democratic leaders at the top of the party, with the noticeable exception of Senator Frank Lausche, the former Cleveland mayor and Ohio governor. Not until after the election was it revealed in a column by John P. Leacacos, Washington correspondent for the *Plain Dealer*, that Lausche had been insulted by Stokes's assertion during the primary that the onus of Cleveland's present problems had to be placed on Lausche's shoulders. "I, too, have self-respect," said Lausche. "To have participated in the campaign in behalf of Mr. Stokes would have given confirmation to the unjust and wrongful arguments he made against me."[13]

But politicians tend to place more importance on the endorsements of people in high places than do voters. It was probably more significant to the Cleveland voters that Stokes wrung endorsements from County Democratic Chairman Albert Porter and other local Democratic party brass than from Lyndon Johnson, Hubert Humphrey, or Frank Lausche.

Rhetoric is an affective force in any campaign in influencing the candidate's image and in influencing the candidate's strategies and tactics. It is the rhetoric of the candidates which links the candidate's goals and the audience's values. It is through speaking that the candidate conveys the qualities of mind, character, and concern which he hopes will impress the audience. The choice of language and the manner of presentation are not just matters of elegant detail. They are indicators of whether the speaker has a clear understanding of his audience, their needs and expectations. They are indicators of the speaker's habits of thought and action, his acuteness, energy, and self-awareness. The content of the speaker's message cannot be separated from the man himself. Even the uncritical acceptance of a ghostwritten manuscript reveals the man's character.

The campaign managers determined the issues and the rhetorical strategies for the candidates, but when the strategists erred, the candidate alone suffered. Sometimes disagreements among the managers or discouraging attitudes at headquarters were reflected in the candidate's projection of self. Ostrow's methods sometimes created breaches between Stokes and other members of his staff. Dr. Louis Masotti left the campaign after one such showdown over the development of issues. A deeper and still unhealed breach came when Dr. Kenneth Clement objected to Ostrow's tactic in bringing up the racial issue in the second debate. When a candidate's own campaign manager says publicly that he wishes there were a third candidate he could vote for, his image and subsequent behavior with regard to it are bound to be affected.

The public statements of the candidates, of course, were the chief means of communicating with the voters, but the machinations involved in arranging for public-speaking appearances were complex and time consuming and sometimes worked to the candidate's disadvantage. Bennett called his scheduling committee the "all-night committee," because, among other things, they would drive the route the night before Taft was to take the same route and make a tentative schedule which allowed a few minutes for Taft to greet and mingle and a specified number of minutes for the presentation of the message. The inflexibility of these arrangements often overtaxed the candidate's strength and left him with little or no opportunity to adapt to particular, unforeseen situations. To the scheduling committee, the content of the message was irrelevant, but the *context* was relevant—in length, timing, location, locale, occasion, and atmosphere. Not only were the candidates in a continual process of trying to adapt to different audiences in rapid succession, they were often faced with physical surroundings which made any kind of communication difficult at best. During one of Carl Stokes's appearances in Joseph McManamon's backyard, a jet plane flew overhead interrupting the speech. Stokes promised he would do something about that. Some months later a participant in a town hall meeting reminded Stokes of the incident and asked what he had done about the problem of jet noise. Stokes quipped that he had stopped making speeches in McManamon's backyard.

The candidate's image was also projected through the campaign literature and insignia. The Taft literature included pamphlets called "Taft Talk," "The Voter Review," and "Tomorrow." "The Voter Review" was an eight-page newspaper that outlined Taft's four programs. The Taft "Position Papers" were not sent out to the public but kept for reference by writers. An impressive "Action Kit" which contained flower seeds (forget-me-nots), pictures of Taft, and a detailed outline of his campaign was available to campaign workers. Of course, bumper stickers and straw hats were means of projecting voter commitment and identification with the candidate.

Carl Stokes had three pamphlets of about twenty pages each which told "The Truth About the Muny Light," among other things. He passed out sixty thousand bumper stickers in the primary alone and used sixty thousand doorknob notices on election day. The selection of orange and black as the campaign colors insured prominence and instant identification.

Of course, much unofficial literature was distributed by interested parties not directly associated with the campaign or, at least, not acknowledged by campaign headquarters. Most of this literature was designed to destroy the image of one of the candidates. The "Democratic Letters" were designed to raise doubts about Stokes's integrity. A newspaper called *Comment* created by Jean Capers and distributed by the League of Non-Partisan Voters pictured anti-Stokes Negroes on the front page and carried articles attacking Stokes's record. On election day a pamphlet was distributed in the Murray Hill area warning residents of what would happen if a "nigger" took over. There were undoubtedly other such forms of literature, designed to create fear and doubt, distributed in both black and white neighborhoods.

Rhetoric at all levels and in all forms is also an affective force in influencing strategies and tactics, in that the candidates respond to each other's messages, modes, and manners. The rhetoric focuses the attention of the electorate on some overt issues and gives them a rationale for making a choice. Naturally, for many, it reinforces their positions, and they listen for clues which will tell them what they most want to hear. In 1967 all these factors *plus* racial predispositions contributed to the election outcome.

The movement (which had begun with some striking events that aroused the populace) had progressed through a period of rhetorical crisis and should have been consummated with Stokes's victory. A period of relaxed equilibrium should have resulted. But it is curious to note that an air of uncertainty persisted. The victors seemed only to have won the right to advance to another level of controversy.

In effect, the rhetorical movement of the campaign was only an initial stage in the evolution of public controversy which saw agitators for change succeed in convincing society that there should be change. In the natural course of events there should have followed a second stage when speakers and writers concentrate on *ways and means* of avoiding danger and achieving some greater degree of public happiness. This "What shall we do?" stage is what Clevelanders had actually been seeking, for a campaign does not give citizens the opportunity to solve problems. Citizens merely choose the participants who, in the second level of controversy, engage in deliberation and thus decide on specific courses of action.

A third stage of controversy *may* evolve if the deliberative stage drags on and no effective solutions emerge, or if participants do not assume their responsibilities in good faith. Instead of debating the merits of plans and solutions, speakers in the third stage will insist on the *rightness* of their positions and will resort to appeals to the highest authorities or values sanctioned by society, such as "God is on my side, and to be against what I am for is to be against everything that is right and good." Then the conflict is no longer about the most expedient course of action, but about ultimate values. The speaker who arrives at this mode of argument cannot retreat. He no longer has the option of saying, "I was *mistaken* when I favored that course of action. I was not sufficiently informed of the facts or the possible consequences." At this stage, if he admits to being wrong, he must admit that he was *morally* wrong or that he couldn't discern the difference between right and wrong. When controversy reaches this "authoritarian" stage there must be a winner and a loser; the time for compromise and conciliation has passed.[14]

If there is no court of last resort to arbitrate the dispute and declare a winner, the controversy evolves into its final form wherein each side defends and justifies its position "for the record"—often just before talk is completely abandoned as a mode of social operation.

Viewed as the first level in an evolutionary hierarchy of controversy, the rhetoric which constituted the campaign becomes very important. *What* was communicated during the campaign and *how* it came to be communicated influenced the conduct of affairs during the Stokes administration more than the mere fact of Stokes's color. The mandate for change was slim, indeed, and the defenders of the status quo—never really conceding victory—hovered about waiting for the opportunity to say, "I told you so, but you wouldn't listen. Now see what's happened?"

CHAPTER 4

THE PERIOD OF ADJUSTMENT

ON NOVEMBER 13, 1967, at 10:22 A.M., less than one week after winning the election, Carl Burton Stokes placed his left hand on a Bible opened to the Twenty-third Psalm. The Bible belonged to his brother; the psalm was the favorite of his mother. The mayor's oath of office was administered by his old friend, Municipal Judge Anthony A. Rutkowski. Vowing to uphold the laws of Cleveland, the state of Ohio, and the Constitution of the United States, Stokes became Cleveland's fiftieth mayor and, according to James Naughton, "ended twenty-six years of hand-me-down rule and began a new era."[1]

In his inaugural address Stokes mentioned that the city was filled with people of diverse backgrounds and varying opinions but said that they were all basically united in their devotion to the principles of American democracy and dedicated to working together for the common good. He spoke of the problems which the city faced, problems of tangled traffic and downtown decay, race relations and job-making industrial development. He said he thought the primary duty of the mayor was to provide leadership for everyone in the community to participate in solving these problems. He concluded with the words: "Let's roll up our sleeves and get to work."

Here was an invitation to deliberation—to analyze problems and weigh alternatives. It was time to search for solutions rather than scapegoats, to deal in ways and means of achieving goals rather than merely enunciating values.

But before policy-making discussion could begin, Carl Stokes had to form a new administration. At a luncheon at Cleveland State University three years later, Mayor Stokes reminisced about the day after his inauguration. He admitted that he had been unprepared for the task. "I was no administrator," he said, laughing. "I didn't know where to begin." However, as the new mayor of Cleveland he had one week to make the decisions about important appointments to his cabinet. He was also faced with a lame-duck council. Council traditionally inaugurated its new members the first week of January, almost two months later. Although the City Charter provides time for newly elected legislators to learn the ropes before taking office, no such period is allotted the mayor. No candidate can openly plan his cabinet appointments during a campaign, nor is he in a position to solicit firm commitments from people about their availability to serve. But the candidate who does not plan at all faces a formidable task the day after election.

Within three hours after Stokes had been declared the victor, he appointed attorney Joseph F. McManamon to the post of safety director. McManamon had been a Cleveland homicide detective and instructor at the police academy from 1945 to 1951.

Stokes's second appointment was James S. Carnes as chief police prosecutor. As had been expected, Police Chief Richard R. Wagner, target of Stokes's attack during the primary, resigned. He was replaced by Michael J. Blackwell who, at sixty-seven, was a veteran policeman with forty-three years service. In announcing Blackwell's appointment, Stokes said he and the new chief had agreed on the specific steps for reassigning three hundred policemen from office jobs onto patrol beats as Stokes had promised during the campaign.[2]

After a gala inaugural charity ball, Stokes appointed six aides, including Geraldine Williams, who had been instrumental in developing Stokes's campaigns in 1965 and 1967, and William H. Stein. Campaign worker John C. Little joined the staff and was soon elevated to the important post of secretary to the mayor. Andrew Dono also joined Stokes's executive staff, apparently a concession to the Hungarian bloc whose newspaper, *Szabadsag*, had endorsed Stokes. Dono had been Locher's commissioner of printing. Richard J. Murway, a former reporter and public relations man, became Stokes's press secretary.

A significant and much applauded appointment was that of Municipal Court Judge Paul D. White, a Negro fully respected by both the black and white communities, to the post of law director. Paul White was an honor graduate of Kentucky State College, received his law degree from Western Reserve University (1950), and had served as assistant chief prosecutor in Cleveland; the *Plain Dealer* story announcing White's appointment stated that former Police Chief Wagner preferred sending his men to White over any other prosecutor, when they needed legal advice or assistance. The role of law director in Cleveland government is similar to that of a crown prince. He is appointed by the mayor and is the mayor's immediate successor. (Ralph Locher had inherited the throne when Anthony J. Celebrezze resigned.) The law director also governs the city in the mayor's absence.

Stokes next appointed Dorward C. Witzke as his finance director.

Mayor Carl Stokes, Assistant Law Directors Sara Harper
and Ruth Stromberg, and Law Director Paul White
Photograph courtesy of City of Cleveland

Witzke had been unknown in government circles until Ralph Locher appointed him to head the Little Hoover Commission. Witzke held a bachelor's degree in industrial engineering from the University of Washington and a master's in business administration from Harvard. Before heading Locher's Little Hoover Commission, Witzke had worked as a management consultant. A *Plain Dealer* editorial of November 21, 1967, praised the mayor's appointment and predicted that Witzke, as new finance director, would press for some of the reorganizations he had first recommended as executive director of the Little Hoover Commission.

Only a week after making these last two appointments, Carl Stokes met in Columbus with Governor James A. Rhodes. In an almost unprecedented flourish of good feeling, Republican Governor Rhodes had initiated the conference and dispatched a fourteen-passenger plane to Cleveland to pick up the Stokes team. Out of the meeting emerged agreements that Stokes and Rhodes would urge corporation executives to expand their businesses in Cleveland, that Cleveland would work towards a city-county or regional port authority, that the new mayor would support Rhodes's request that the Ohio legislature put a $700 million highway bond proposal on the May 7 ballot, and that the governor would continue his commitment to make Cleveland State University one of the nation's top educational institutions.

The appointment of Ben Stefanski II to the post of utilities director gave some people pause. The utilities director is charged with supervision of an annual budget exceeding $50 million and a staff of more than two thousand. Included in the Department of Public Utilities are the divisions of light and power, water works, pollution control, and sewage. Stefanski held a law degree from the University of Michigan but had never attained membership in the Ohio bar. His vita indicated that he had served as vice-president and member of the Board of Directors of the Third Federal Savings and Loan Association. Stefanski's father was president of the same firm. Speculation ran high about Stefanski's appointment. Old-time politicians shrugged it off as a concession to the Polish bloc. Others who had high hopes for an end to patronage appointments were disappointed. James Naughton pointed out: "Aside from paying his utility bills, Stefanski had no technical preparation for the job."

The Stefanski appointment followed, by one day, the revelation that Stokes's new aide, William H. Stein, had been shot in an embarrassing Christmas Eve incident. Stein was the first of the Stokes appointees to leave the administration under less than ideal circumstances. Instant detractors were beginning to say, "I told you so," but were somewhat quieted by the appointment of a well-qualified director of the city's public properties, Edward J. Baugh. Baugh had served in many municipal administrative posts and most recently had spent eighteen months with the Peace Corps. Parks, recreation, cemeteries, and shade trees seemed to be in safe hands.

High on the Stokes list of priorities for the attention of the new City Council was the creation of a county-wide port authority for Cleveland. During the campaign Stokes had been supported in his proposal for a port authority by Council President James V. Stanton. Knowing that with Stanton's help the measure would routinely be guided through council—thus fulfilling another campaign promise—the new mayor left Cleveland to spend thirteen days in the Virgin Islands.

During Stokes's absence the newly launched administration began to crack at the seams. One young political purist moaned, "The ship of state is sinking, and the captain isn't even here to go down with it." The image of their mayor sunning himself in the Caribbean was not a happy one for Clevelanders when a violent snowstorm hit the city in mid-January. Streets were clogged, and the city's snow removal efforts were more than inadequate. One particularly angry merchant reportedly threatened to sue the *Plain Dealer* if they printed one more story saying that Mayor Stokes "knows what the city's problems are." The mayor wasn't around to see what the problems were, and the merchant had just spent two thousand dollars to have a private contractor remove the snow which had piled up in front of his place of business.[3]

It has been said many times that voters will forgive a city official almost anything so long as the garbage gets collected and the streets are clean. While frustration in Cleveland mounted, Mayor Stokes interrupted his vacation to fly to Washington for a television appearance. Instead of hurrying home to straighten out the city's problems, he then promptly returned to St. Thomas for another romp in the sun.

The snowstorm which had raged outside City Hall was minor compared to the storm which had simultaneously broken loose inside. On January 15 the *Press* headlined a story, "Mayor Stokes' Secretary Is Linked to Cheat Spot." The reference was to his executive secretary, Geraldine Williams. "Cheat spot" is the local term for a club which violates state liquor laws, usually by selling to unauthorized customers or by operating after hours. The story, bearing the mysterious by-line "A *Press* Reporter," recounted its author's personal experience in being openly served liquor at the supposedly private Thirty Second

Cedar Club where only members should have had such privileges. The reporter alleged that one of the officers of the Thirty Second Cedar Club was Geraldine Williams. This was the very club in which Geraldine Williams and Jean Capers had first set upon their plan to elect a Negro mayor.

The next morning the *Plain Dealer* carried a statement of denial by Law Director Paul White in which he charged the *Press* with the "grossest kind of irresponsible journalism":

> The story relative to Miss Geraldine Williams, executive assistant to the mayor, was clearly calculated to defame and smear. . . . The administration regrets this attempted character assassination and the regression of this newspaper to "yellow journalism."

The January 16 edition of the *Press* carried two stories and an editorial about the incident. The next day the *Press* announced that Stokes had fired Geraldine Williams:

> Stokes called the *Press* from Charlotte Amalie on the island of St. Thomas in the Virgin Islands at 10:30 A.M. to announce that he had ordered Miss Williams dismissed.

Stokes also informed the *Press* at the time that John C. Little had taken over the job Geraldine Williams had handled.

The *Plain Dealer* stated that the news of the firing was released to all the media before Geraldine Williams was informed. "She cried for the next two hours until Dr. Kenneth W. Clement and Councilman George L. Forbes escorted her from City Hall."[4]

The January 18 *Press* applauded Mayor Stokes's "swift and correct" action in dismissing Geraldine Williams. Geraldine Williams put quite a different interpretation on the action. She stated that when the question first came up about her connection with the Thirty Second Cedar Club, she stated emphatically that she had resigned at the time she began working for Operation Equality, well before the 1967 Stokes campaign. She insisted that Carl Stokes was aware of her resignation because on several occasions when he was unable to reach her at the club she had told him, "You know I've given that up." When the story broke in the *Press* she reportedly took the minutes of the club to City Hall and voluntarily handed them to the safety director, saying, "Now, here. If I'm a member of the team I know you can find anything in here to justify whatever it is you want to say." Then Geraldine Williams called Charles Loeb of the *Call and Post* and said, "Look, the daily newspapers are fixing to fry me. What can you do for me?" According to Geraldine Williams, Loeb said, "Gerry, you get me a copy of that resignation [from the club], and I'll put it on the front page of the *Call and Post*." Geraldine Williams said she approached Safety Director McManamon and his assistant Frank Moss and asked for the records she had turned over to them. She reported that they refused to give them to her. "Then that's when I knew they wanted to get rid of me at City Hall. And I was just amazed!"

During those same eventful days, Law Director Paul White announced the appointment of three civil service commissioners who were later to figure in an administration scandal. They were Marvin Chernoff, vice-president and general manager of Broome Business Machines Corporation, attorney Jay B. White, and Charles L. Butts who had been a secretary to the city welfare director. Butts replaced Francis J. Hogan as secretary of the Civil Service Commission.

Also at that time, the *Press* announced that Dr. Kenneth W. Clement was to be the Stokes number-two man. Though formal appointment was not forthcoming, Dr. Clement continued to serve in an unofficial advisory capacity. It was made known through the newspaper gossip columns that Clement was displeased with the Civil Service Commission appointments.

On the day the mayor returned from his vacation in the Virgin Islands, James Naughton wrote perhaps the first really critical article about the Stokes administration. The headline read, "Open Up City Hall." In the article Naughton said that an air of depression was "swirling about the city" due in part to some of the unfortunate circumstances surrounding several of Stokes's appointees.[5] However, Naughton cited the mayor's absence as the greatest reason for the depression settling in among City Hall birdwatchers. Not only was the mayor beyond reach, but access to the mayor's news aide was difficult for newsmen. "To say that the mayor's City Hall door is open for the first time in years is to further alienate those unable to get through the door," wrote Naughton.

That newsmen did not have the free access to City Hall as they were accustomed to in past administrations was confirmed by Norman Wagy of WJW-TV, who said, "I got this phone call from Dick Murway one day saying that this new thing had happened—that the reporters have to come and talk to the secretary first and ask for whomever they wish to see. They no longer have freedom to just wander through the offices as, historically, we have been given that opportunity."

Richard Murway, Stokes's press secretary, had been a reporter on the *Cleveland Press* for some years, but in his new position he expressed no sympathy for his former colleagues. Time did nothing to mellow his new attitude. In 1969 he expressed his philosophy of government-press relations:

> I now have a clear viewpoint of the fact that no other institution in our society is subject to the scrutiny that government [gets]. Newsmen feel they have the right to know what goes on in government. Do they feel they have the right to know what goes on in General Motors? Does General Motors have reporters walking in and reading stuff that's in the secretary's typewriter? (I did the same thing.) I don't think so. These other institutions in society are just as important as government. The decisions that are made by the board of directors of any five hundred large corporations have the, a more substantial impact on the economy, the quality of life, than people who make the decisions at City Council. That's one of the little chores I've taken upon myself—to tell these guys why don't you cover the Catholic Church or Republic Steel the same way.

Two months after Murway made this revelation, Louis Seltzer, speaking to an urban media seminar, was asked what current issues he would send his top investigative reporters out to cover. "Government!" exploded Seltzer. "Government at every level. Decisions of government affect more people today than all the other institutions combined. If necessary, I would lay siege to City Hall and batter down the doors!" When asked if he thought reporters at City Hall were being denied access to news of vital interest, Mr. Seltzer said, "I *know* it."

Scandals and poor press relations were not the only problems which beset the Stokes administration in January of 1968. Even though James Stanton continued to assert council leadership in approving all of Stokes's program for the several months following, there was evidence of a developing feud. Stanton appointed a strong Stokes critic, Jack Oliver, to handle press relations for council. Stokes, in turn, appointed a Stanton enemy, former Ward Thirty Councilman John Pilch, as secretary to Director of Public Properties Baugh. A January 15 story in the *Press* headlined: "Stokes, Stanton Seek Power As City Hall Honeymoon Ends."

"Honeymoon" would indicate an emotional state in which the partners involved enjoy their relationship without worrying too deeply about each other's faults, many of which are only beginning to surface. The honeymoon in Cleveland involved not only the council and the mayor, but the businessmen and the mayor as well. According to Mayor Stokes, on the day after election, business and civic leaders came to him offering their support. According to Stanton, City Council was ready to support the mayor's wishes in order to get the city started on the road to improvement. The newspapers heralded a new era; one news editor said that they were all caught up in a tremendous feeling of brotherhood and excitement of what was to come. Newspaper criticism seemed to be coming from only one reporter—James Naughton—who openly questioned policies and activities of the new administration.

While there had been some instances of carping and complaint about actions and inactions of the new administration, as yet there had emerged no deliberative speaking because no issue had yet been opposed. Appointments were received either with praise or skepticism, but arguments for or against these decisions were not articulated in an open forum either at the executive or legislative level. James Stanton claimed that within the council committee meetings, where debate generally takes place, every effort was being made to support the mayor's programs. Most discussion and debate on ordinances occur in the City Council committees or within party caucuses, so that the legislative body usually knows how the vote will go before it convenes each Monday night. Regularly scheduled council meetings, therefore, are given over to the business of *formally* passing bills which have already been decided upon. Councilmen also take advantage of the public forum (the meetings are televised on WVIZ-TV) to take the administrative directors to task. Unfortunately, the exchanges between council and directors often degenerate into the ridiculous as both administrators and councilmen indulge in personality defamation, backbiting, and nit-picking.

Most of the Monday night rhetoric in the chamber of Cleveland's deliberative body is either ceremonial or image-building. Each councilman wants to show his constituents that he is acting in their best interests, and he uses the ploy of assigning blame to the administration for whatever may be wrong in his ward. Administrative directors counterattack by minimizing the complaint or shifting the blame elsewhere—preferably back to council. One gets the feeling that the election campaign has simply moved indoors where the politicians, having accomplished their prime objective of getting elected, can concentrate on the second objective of getting reelected.

However, a resurgence of image-building campaign rhetoric was precisely what the mayor wanted upon his return from vacationing in the Virgin Islands. His image had suffered during his absence, and he knew he could not proceed until he had restored public confidence in his ability to lead. Campaigning and self-justification were arts at which the mayor was highly skilled, so he scheduled an "Open House" at City Hall on February 15. The event served its purpose and was judged an important success. One week later, to show that his house was truly open, Mayor Stokes ordered all his directors and commissioners to list their telephone numbers publicly and become available to the citizenry.

In the rush to establish better community relations, however, the mayor chose to ignore festering internal administrative relations which were to damage the mayor's image permanently. Relations with the Cleveland Police Department were deteriorating, but the mayor refused to acknowledge this fact, stating, "All I know about the police situation is what I hear from the news media."[6] In December, 1967, 225 police had been reassigned, mainly from desk jobs to street duty. Both police morale and effectiveness suffered because, frankly, many of the men involved were no longer interested in or physically suited for beat work. But the mayor felt that satisfying his promise to put more policemen on the streets was of prime importance. Solving one problem had created another of a lasting nature. Police operations were in need of *reform*, but reassignment of personnel without notice was interpreted as a punitive measure by the policemen. Investigation had not preceded the decision, nor had appropriate methods of reform been tested for their effects on the long-range goals of the department. When Stokes made this decision he was still acting like a candidate trying to win approval rather than an administrator trying to run an effective government.

Following through on another campaign promise, Stokes requested that council create a Department of Human Resources and Economic Development. In addition, he also asked council to approve a salary of $30,000 to obtain a topnotch director for the Department of Community Development to solve the city's urban renewal problems. Several councilmen objected to establishing a salary for a cabinet member which was $5,000 higher than that of the mayor, but they went along with Stokes's request. With the announcement that the salary had been approved came the news that Richard R. Green had been appointed.

Green's credentials included a master's degree in city planning from M.I.T. and six years as "chief planner" (at a salary under $20,000) in the questionably successful Boston urban renewal program. Experts had advised Stokes to find a "promising young man bent on establishing a national reputation." The firm of Ernst and Ernst had located and recommended Green as the man who best fit that description. Green told the *Press* on February 21 that he hated long-planning processes. Green's impatience with the planning process was to serve him ill in the months to come, but, at the time of his appointment in February, 1968, all signs pointed to a relief from the past frustrations and delays caused by ineffective administration of urban renewal projects.

Stokes's new image-building attempt was strengthened by an article written by Vail of the *Plain Dealer* who openly sympathized with the mayor and blamed Cleveland's problems on a shrinking tax base, politically ambitious councilmen, low administrative salaries, and the two-year term of office for mayors. The generally popular attitude towards urban problems is that the underlying cause for them is lack of money. Seemingly, if a city could just get its hands on enough money all the problems would disappear. Early in 1968 the mayor appointed his own Little Hoover Commission to study the city's financial needs and resources. On February 26, Robert E. Walker, executive director of the commission, reported to City Council's finance committee that an .8 percent increase in the city income tax would be needed by April 1.

Council, like any other audience, needed persuasive evidence to support the commission's findings. Council President Stanton said he was confused about the fiscal position of the city. He had not seen a copy of the 1968 budget, though budget hearings were scheduled for the following week. The budget was supposed to have been submitted to council by February 1. On February 26 it was still not in council's hands. Councilman Anthony Garofoli said that the mayor was premature in coming before council and "outlining the city's needs for the next ten years, when you don't even have the experience from the first year of the [income] tax for a base." He accused the mayor of "just guessing." At a time when a thoroughly documented case should have been prepared, the administrative spokesmen came forward with only unsupported assertions.

Stokes's response to council's criticism was to fly to Washington on March 1. Three days later it was announced that the federal government had ended its freeze on funding for Cleveland's urban renewal projects and that $12 million would be forthcoming.

Council responded to this news by approving, on March 11, twelve of the thirteen bond issues in Mayor Stokes's $38.5 million program for capital improvements. The program included improvements in sewage disposal plants, streets and highways, construction of health centers, school-crossing lights, equipment for the safety and services departments. That evening Stokes's $76 million budget survived a second reading with but one comment.

At this same time, the Greater Cleveland Associated Foundation decided to help Cleveland solve its problems and gave the newly formed firm of William A. Silverman and Company a grant of $68,000 to improve the city's *image*. According to Dr. James A. Norton, director of the Greater Cleveland Associated Foundation, the foundation decided to aid the city in improving the image of Cleveland with the local and national news media and in improving the relationship between the city government and the people in the neighborhoods. The problem as seen by the foundation was strictly public relations, and the solution was simply to employ a professional persuader. The choice of William Silverman, a professional public relations man, evidenced the foundation's analysis of Cleveland's problems. (A year after Silverman's appointment, the local press questioned the legitimacy of a tax-exempt foundation contributing to a project which was designed to increase the personal prestige of an elected public official.) But Silverman did more than promote better communication from, and within, the city. He became a creator of programs for the administration and a general troubleshooter for the mayor. He also wrote or influenced every major speech given by Stokes but later admitted that the mayor had thrown away some of his efforts: "I wrote one speech that he described as the worst thing he had ever read."

The eyebrow-raising incident in March, 1968, was the replacement of Dorward Witzke as finance director. Witzke had been criticized for his somewhat highhanded treatment of council and for trying to run a political institution like a business corporation, but his replacement came as a surprise even to critics. More surprising was Mayor Stokes's announcement that Witzke's appointment had been a temporary one; no such qualification had been made in November, 1967.

The man who replaced Witzke was thirty-four-year-old Philip M. Dearborn. Dearborn had been an administrative assistant to Lakewood Mayor Frank Celeste, safety-services director of Fairview Park, and most recently, a deputy county executive for planning, budgeting, and analysis in Fairfax County, Virginia. A New Englander, Dearborn held a bachelor's degree from Yale and a master's in public administration from Western Reserve. He told the *Press* he had been interviewed for an "unidentified position" on February 24. Frank Celeste had been among those present at the interview.[7]

With money coming in from Washington, the City Council's approval of the income tax and the bond issues, and the added grant from the foundation, it appeared that the administration and Carl Stokes would experience a modicum of security in their images. The second stage of rhetorical movement was finally at hand—or so it seemed.

Unforeseen events decreed otherwise. Cleveland was plunged once again into a period of emotional rhetoric by the assassination of Martin Luther King, Jr., on April 4. On that eventful day, Mayor Stokes was speaking at Baldwin-Wallace College which is located about twenty miles from Cleveland. When he heard the news he went immediately to the three commercial stations and taped an appeal to the black community to remain calm in the memory of Dr. King. After this was done, the mayor, Richard Murway (his press secretary), Police Chief Michael Blackwell, and Safety Director Joseph McManamon met at City Hall to talk about what was going to happen next.

Members of the news media were stunned and uncertain how to handle the situation. Most of them sincerely wanted to do what was in the best interest of the community. The mayor called a meeting on April 6 to ask the cooperation of the media people. By cooperation, the mayor indicated that he wanted the media to refrain from covering anything of a violent or alarming nature in the inner city. He requested pressmen not to roam around the east side looking for incidents. Norman Wagy remembered that April Saturday when all the media people were gathered in the Tapestry Room at City Hall. "Boy, at that point we were all ready to walk through fire if it would have helped, . . . and we looked to him for leadership. . . . Some of us were honestly grieved at the assassination, and others thought, 'Holy mackerel! Is the east side going to blow up now!' "

Between April 5 and April 10, newspapers and broadcasts carried stories about Mayor Stokes walking the streets and meeting with militants and church and civic leaders in an effort to maintain peace. The stories contained touching accounts of Carl Stokes's devotion to the cause of racial peace, but they said nothing of the incidents of violence which did erupt, and they certainly did not report the threats of violence which were being voiced around the black community. When other cities were reporting scenes of violence and destruction, not even a rumor of dissent was reported in the Cleveland newspapers. The media claimed they acted as they did because the mayor requested them to do so. Norman Wagy of WJW-TV said that he refrained from sending any of his crews out to follow any lead or investigate rumors of fires and violence.

Carl Stokes did everything humanly possible to keep the city cool. He enlisted the aid of every black person in the community who might be able to influence potential troublemakers—Browns football players, preachers, business and professional people, even Geraldine Williams. Geraldine Williams contacted leaders of the Afro Unity Circle, a militant black nationalist organization. When Carl Stokes couldn't personally persuade certain elements of the community, he persuaded middlemen who could convince them.

But, by covering up the real nature of the problem and reporting only that Mayor Stokes saved the city by walking night after night through the streets appealing to people to stay calm, the media may have done a real disservice to Carl Stokes and to the city. The city, not understanding the full extent of the bitterness and hatred which permeated the Negro community, unfortunately concluded that the level of restlessness and bitterness in Cleveland was quite low. By highlighting only Stokes's heroic efforts as a pacificator, the media lulled the white community into believing that the only price of racial peace was to vote for a Negro mayor.

For the majority of the community, the crisis was passed on April 10 when the media decreed that all was well. Carl Stokes had solved the problem of riots and thus delivered another campaign promise. It put him in the not-so-enviable position of confirming the voter's assumption that all that was needed for racial peace in Cleveland was a Negro mayor. It had been a good trade.

With few exceptions, the next three months of the Stokes administration turned into an era of euphoria. Stokes's triumph in keeping the peace after the Martin Luther King, Jr., assassination was followed by a series of exciting events just as Stokes had promised during his campaign. One of William Silverman's first projects was to reestablish the Carl Stokes who had charmed even hostile audiences during his campaigns. No one knew better than Silverman the impact of a Stokes personal appearance. Out of this need were born the Stokes town hall meetings. The first was held at William Dean Howells Junior High School on the west side on the night of April 16. The mayor took with him his entire cabinet and the chief of police. Refreshments were served and baby sitters provided. The mayor was cheered that night by a grateful west side audience.

The administration was having a few minor skirmishes with council during this period and Community Development Director Richard Green told the *Press* that "Council is the whole trouble with this city," but nothing major broke the mayor's stride. Mayor Stokes was convinced that money was the answer to the problems that beset the city, and on May 1 he announced a revolutionary program called "Cleveland: NOW!" which would attack a wide range of Cleveland's problems. At a special breakfast meeting with City Council at the Sheraton Cleveland Hotel, Stokes announced to the councilmen that there would be a special program on all television and radio stations on which he was going to ask for total commitment from every segment of the community.

The three commercial television stations in town worked feverishly for three days to put together a half-hour "instant special" showing Mayor Stokes in various problem areas within the city. Four thousand feet of film were edited to tell the story and were interlaced with the mayor's presentation of his plan—complete with slides and graphics. The combined effort of all the commercial stations was in itself a demonstration of how business could cooperate to advance the interests of the city. That was, in effect, what Cleveland: NOW! hoped to do. The idea for the program had begun when Stokes asked Irving M. Kriegsfeld, then director of PATH (a citizens nonprofit housing group) to talk to the most knowledgeable Clevelanders in the areas of housing, health, and unemployment and with them develop a community program to solve these problems. According to the *Plain Dealer* chronology of events leading to the final plan, Kriegsfeld held a series of crash meetings and was able to come up with an outline of needs in four days. Stokes's cabinet members got busy investigating programs which the city could undertake. The combined findings of Kriegsfeld and the cabinet were presented to the business community on Friday, April 12. At that time Stokes asked for a commitment of $10 million and 11,000 jobs. On Thursday, April 18, George J. Grabner, president of the Weatherhead Company and chairman of the Greater Cleveland Growth Association, assured Stokes of the support of the business community. George S. Dively, board chairman of Harris-Intertype Corporation, and John Sherwin, board chairman of Pickands Mather and Company, were appointed to head the collection of money.

News media managers had assured Stokes of their cooperation and on April 25, Stokes again called the media people together and detailed the program he had worked out. All media people and many advertising and public relations firms joined together to promote the Cleveland: NOW! campaign. The morning after the television special the *Plain Dealer* devoted its entire front page, second page, and parts of pages 4, 5, and 9 to articles explaining the inception of the idea for Cleveland: NOW!, the goals of the program, and the people who had cooperated to make it possible. A chart, which appeared in that special issue of the *Plain Dealer*, summarized the goals of the program and the funding sources for carrying it out during the eighteen months following. A ten-year projection of Cleveland's needs called for an investment of $1.5 billion.

In summarizing the highlights of his first year in office, Carl Stokes said that the Cleveland: NOW! program was the high point. "Little kids sending in two cents and the Leland Schuberts with a million dollars. It was more than I could have thought."[8]

While the program was being launched, two key men left the Stokes team. Law Director Paul D. White resigned, citing ill health as his reason, and Kenneth Clement announced that he would be spending less and less time at City Hall. Local skeptics wondered why the mayor was being deserted by his most respected advisers at a time when the mayor's popularity was in the ascent. Wagy voiced this skepticism: "The fact that those two guys walked out told me something was wrong. I didn't know what, but something was wrong. I don't know of any appointment anyone has made since I've been around that got such universal acclaim as did Paul White's."

However, only those in the city who were politically astute would have taken much notice of the implications of the White-Clement withdrawals. The news media was too full of all the good things that were happening. Stokes made it possible for Cleveland to have its own liaison with the many Washington departments and agencies which would help the city move forward. The liaison man was Sidney Spector, a second Celeste man who had transferred to the Stokes camp. David G. Hill of Pittsburgh was selected to head the new Department of Human Resources and Economic Development. The city was finally beginning to roll, and Carl Stokes was providing the momentum.

Funds were pouring in for Cleveland: NOW! and the mayor continued to appear at his town hall meetings in various areas of the city. Properties Director Baugh succeeded in establishing an outdoor restaurant on the Mall (the open park area in downtown Cleveland near the Public Auditorium), and the mayor was the first to join the public in lunching there. Pollution in the Lake Erie water abutting Edgewater Beach was sufficiently controlled for the first time in years, by the placement of a plastic screen, to allow public bathing. Stokes and two cabinet members joined the happy crowd of kids for a wade-in there. The city was cool and showed signs of remaining so.

While there may have been doubters and grumblers, on the whole, the city seemed to be caught up in the charisma of its mayor—until the morning of July 21, 1968.

Over their morning coffee cups Clevelanders were shocked to see a picture of Mayor Stokes walking down the street amidst a group of young black men carrying rifles. In the background of the picture were two prominent signs. One read Stop Ahead. The other showed an arrow pointing backwards and the words One Way. The signs were prophetic.[9]

The occasion for the picture was the second annual commemoration of the deaths of four persons slain in the Hough riots of July, 1966. A parade, escorted by police, had been arranged by Lewis G. Robinson. Participants in the group sponsoring the event were the Afro Set, Hough

Mayor Stokes's "wade-in" in Lake Erie
Photograph by the Cleveland *Plain Dealer*

Mayor Stokes marching in the parade
marking the anniversary of the Hough riots
Photograph by the Cleveland *Plain Dealer*

Area Development Corporation, the League Park Center, Poor People's Partnership, the Council of Churches of Christ of Greater Cleveland, Hope, Inc., CORE, and the NAACP.

Clevelanders were taken aback. Was Mayor Stokes a black nationalist? A militant? Did he sanction the carrying of guns in the Hough area? Where did he stand?

Asked for his views on black nationalism, Carl Stokes explained that he didn't believe there was *a* black nationalist group, but that there were at least ten or twelve different groups out in the black community "each of whom has their own notion of what black nationalism is." He said he couldn't tell people what a black nationalist was thinking unless they told him which one they were talking about. For example, he said that he could tell what DeForest Brown thought, or what Harllel Jones thought, but he said, "If you ask me about what Brother Zoom or what Ahmed [Evans] thinks I may not be able to tell you about them because they happen to think about some things in this area of black nationalism that I have not been exposed to, to the same extent as I have been to Harllel and to DeForest." He said, furthermore, that he tried to explain his views to the various nationality groups he visited and to show them the similarities among the various ethnic groups, black and white. During the same interview he talked about nationalism and the Constitution of the United States saying:

> If you told any American group that the Constitution is a supremist doctrine, they'd be shocked. They don't know anything about the Constitution. They think all the Constitution is, is something that talks about everybody being equal and giving everybody their rights and serving as the basis for the "Star Spangled Banner." That Constitution really is a bad piece of paper. It wasn't written for all of us. It was written for just a few people.

But on July 21, 1968, there was no time for discussion about the history of America and the struggle by minority groups to gain equality. There was just a picture. And that picture became as popular as the one showing Carl Stokes romping in the waters of Lake Erie amidst a group of laughing children. Which one was the real Carl Stokes? Certainly that scene with the rifles damaged the image that had been painstakingly nurtured by a series of public relations men. It placed further doubts in the minds of those who were not quite ready to accept Carl Stokes as the new messiah. Stokes's image might have survived despite the picture had nothing further occurred.

Unfortunately, two days later the damage to his image was further reinforced when shooting began in Glenville.

CHAPTER 5

FALLEN IDOLS

SHOOTING BEGAN in the Glenville area of Cleveland's predominantly black east side on the evening of July 23, 1968.[1] Before the evening ended, seven people were dead and fifteen were injured. Three of the dead and eleven of the wounded were policemen. During the five days following the shooting, sixty separate business establishments were damaged or destroyed as a result of looting or arson, and property damage totalled over one million dollars.

Those are the facts stripped of inferences. But local and national newsmen described the shooting as an "incident," a "siege," an "inferno," a "disaster," and a "riot." Cleveland policemen called it a "planned ambush." It was reported "in depth" by newsmen, studied by scholars, and rehashed by local politicians in later campaigns. What happened in Glenville distracted the city from serious discussion aimed at problem-solving and plunged the citizens and their elected officials into a massive exercise of image-destroying rhetoric.

With the destruction, the images began to crumble. No one was spared; not the mayor, the police chief, the safety director, the police, the black community, the white businessmen, or the news media. Glenville was Cleveland's time of infamy—one long night which lasted from 2:30 P.M. Tuesday, July 23, until 8:30 A.M. Sunday, July 28.

The following chronology is based, for the most part, on official reports prepared by the mayor's office. On July 23, a number of intelligence reports alerted the Federal Bureau of Investigation and the Cleveland Police Department to the possibility of impending violence in Cleveland and other northern cities. The Cleveland reports concerned Fred (Ahmed) Evans and his group, the Black Nationalists of New Libya. The reports stated that Evans and his fifteen or twenty followers had assembled an arsenal of handguns and carbines at Evans's home in the Glenville area; that Evans and his followers had made trips to Pittsburgh and Detroit to collect semiautomatic weapons; that an outbreak of violence was planned for Cleveland at approximately 8:00 A.M. on July 24; that there was a possibility of assassination of five Cleveland

Negroes: Mayor Carl B. Stokes, Councilman Leo Jackson, *Call and Post* publisher William O. Walker, Baxter Hill (director of Pride, Inc. and a member of the Community Relations Board), and Patrolman James Payne (a policeman whom Evans had been accused of assaulting).

The accuracy and reliability of the reports could not be ascertained, but they were serious enough to be considered and investigated. On Tuesday morning, July 23, the Cleveland police checked some aspects of the reports and Inspector Lewis Coffey called a meeting at 2:30 that afternoon to discuss the matter. Mayor Stokes was in Washington, D.C., and newly appointed Law Director Clarence L. James, Jr., was "acting mayor." While the meeting was in progress Mayor Stokes placed a routine call from Washington to his office. When informed of the trouble, he told James to contact Baxter Hill.[2] James could not reach Baxter Hill, so he called George Forbes, councilman in the Glenville area where Evans's home was located. It was decided that George Forbes and Walter Beach, a prominent Negro leader of the Urban League, would make contact with Evans and discuss the problem.

At this same afternoon meeting, after much discussion, it was also decided to place a moving surveillance, consisting of two patrol cars and a total of five men, on Evans's home and on his 1962 Chevrolet station wagon to watch for an attempt to obtain illegal weapons.

When Walter Beach and George Forbes met with Ahmed Evans, he indicated that he was quite concerned about the police surveillance which had been placed upon him. He said he was tired of being harassed by the police. He requested that the police be removed, and he told the two men to deliver a message to Carl Stokes: "Tell Big Brother downtown that everything is going to be all right."

Councilman Forbes then decided to ask Safety Director McManamon to remove the surveillance as soon as possible.[3] McManamon, in turn, gave Forbes the mayor's private phone number and while Forbes was speaking with the mayor, discussing Evans's problem, an emergency call came through. The shooting at Glenville had begun.

After studying all the newspaper accounts, interviewing over a hundred people who claimed to have knowledge of the event, and reading a four-hundred-page report of the incident as well as the official reports, it is still unclear why and how the shooting really began.[4] Few accounts agree; many are speculative. It was variously reported that the surveillance cars were ordered out of the area, that one or both of the cars were shot at, and that at least one of them returned bullet-ridden. All accounts agree that the patrolmen in one of the surveillance cars heard a radio call for assistance. A police tow truck had been fired upon at East 123d and Beulah Avenue in Glenville.

Police tow-truck drivers in Cleveland are civilian employees of the police department. They wear uniforms almost identical to those of regular patrolmen, but they are not armed and have no law enforcement authority. Many Clevelanders assume that the tow-truck operators are full members of the department because of the overt symbol of the uniform.

Earlier that afternoon a parking ticket had been placed on an abandoned car, and the report was given to the operators of the tow truck. They arrived to pick up the abandoned Cadillac shortly after 8:00 P.M.; at 8:25 P.M. one of the truck's operators, William C. McMillan, was wounded by sniper fire. Whether the reported firing at the surveillance car and the shooting of the tow-truck driver were separate incidents or part of a planned ambush may never be determined.

The patrolmen in the surveillance car, upon hearing the call for assistance, came back into the area and parked at East 123d Street. By the time they arrived, other police cars were already coming into the area in answer to the radio call.

About 9:00 P.M., Mayor Stokes arrived at City Hall. He attempted to get information by calling those at the scene of the shooting, but accurate information was almost impossible to obtain. The city officials were listening to the police radio, but the barrage of scattered accounts was confusing. No provisions had been made to set up communication facilities in the event of racial violence. (Perhaps the "obvious" atmosphere of calm imposed after King's death had lulled the officials into believing nothing could happen in Cleveland.) Patrolmen at the scene who left their cars were completely out of touch with anyone. Supervision was impossible because of an outdated communication system designed to meet the needs of the police department in 1929. Neither the police chief nor the safety director was on hand to take command.[5]

The mayor called Governor Rhodes and requested that the Ohio National Guard be alerted. At 12:15 A.M. on July 24, Adj. Gen. Sylvester T. Del Corso and the mayor conferred with Governor Rhodes about mobilization of the Ohio National Guard, and the governor approved the decision.

At 12:30 A.M., with seven dead and fifteen injured, the shooting ended as Fred (Ahmed) Evans, thirty-seven, surrendered to the police and was taken into custody. He was considered by the police to be the leader of the group of snipers. When arrested he said he would still be shooting at policemen if the carbine he was using had not jammed.

He was charged with three offenses: possession of a machine gun without a permit, shooting with intent to kill, and possession of marijuana.[6] When questioned by homicide detectives in the presence of his attorneys, Ahmed Evans said that he had received money to support his group from Cleveland: NOW! funds. He said the money was allotted to him and other nationalists by the Hough Area Development Corporation whose director was the Reverend DeForest Brown.[7] Evans told detectives that he and other black nationalists used the money to buy a station wagon in which they travelled to Akron, Detroit, and Pittsburgh, adding: "We were meeting and talking with our brothers. We are followers of Ho Chi Minh. He's a soul brother of ours, and we believe in his philosophy." Police reported that Evans also told them that he and his group used the funds to buy guns and ammunition.

Although the Glenville shooting was over at 12:30 A.M. Wednesday, by daylight there were 26,000 National Guard troops in the city available for deployment. Sniping and looting had begun, and the mayor and Chief Blackwell issued an order to the police department that "the National Guard be notified of all snipers and they take the necessary steps and force to effect arrests. The looters and those destroying property are to be arrested by police or National Guard without the use of deadly force."[8]

At an 11:00 A.M. news conference the mayor announced, "We are constantly re-evaluating the situation and assure you that this city will not be governed by hoodlums."[9] Earlier, at 8:30 A.M., the mayor had met with over a hundred Negro leaders. Many opinions were expressed, particularly the fear that if police were allowed to remain in the area there would be further shooting. The predominant fear was that the black militants in the area would begin the shooting themselves or that, if the police were allowed to remain in the area, they would seek revenge for their three comrades who had been killed the night before. The large meeting adjourned, but about twenty of the participants reassembled across the street at the Auditorium Hotel to continue discussions. City Hall officials identified this select group as representing the more militant factions in the black community.

At about 1:00 P.M. the group of men who had retired to the Auditorium Hotel returned to City Hall and met with the mayor in the Tapestry Room. There they proposed to go back into the community and bring it under control by using their respective influence to prevent looting, burning, and additional loss of life. They wanted a specified time to accomplish this and stated that if it did not work, Stokes could then choose a different strategy. Community Relations Director Bertram

Gardner, who had been out on the streets in Glenville on Tuesday night, also suggested that Stokes take the police and National Guard out of the area and allow Gardner to send about two hundred or two hundred fifty black leaders back into the community to try to calm feelings. The same course of action was suggested by Community Development Director Richard Green, who felt that the black community ought to be given a chance to pull itself together.

At 4:14 P.M. Mayor Stokes released a detailed plan for Wednesday night. It was called "Memo for Understanding between the Safety Director, the Chief of Police, and the Adjutant General of the Ohio National Guard" and stated that within a designated square mile of Glenville, black control would be established, only black policemen would be used, and all white nonresidents, including white newsmen, were to be kept from the area.[9]

This time the mayor had not called the newsmen together; he had not offered guidelines nor persuaded them to cooperate; he had merely imposed restrictions upon them. After the death of Martin Luther King, Jr., in April, the newsmen, it seemed, voluntarily responded to these same restrictions. But the newsmen's reaction to the Glenville restrictions was one of open opposition. When the Glenville incident occurred on July 23, Cleveland newsmen, impatient since their wholehearted compliance following King's death, went after the story. Some became a part of it.

This spontaneous response by the media was disorganized, and the coverage was competitive. The age-old dilemma of whether a reporter should be an objective observer or a part of his community and a part of the story he is writing was revived.

Cleveland newsmen had imposed some guidelines upon themselves after the Hough riots of 1966, but very few newsmen adhered to them at the time of the Glenville incident. The guidelines agreed to after the 1966 riots were the result of three meetings between Director of Community Relations Bertram Gardner and the news media staffs and management. Following the code of conduct drawn up by the *Chicago Sun-Times* some fifteen years earlier, Cleveland newsmen then had agreed to use extreme care in reporting events about racial disturbances and to avoid using terms and details which would produce or increase tension. They also agreed not to broadcast information about the activities of the police or other law enforcement agencies as they were preparing to handle a disturbance and not to report the specific location of an incident until the authorities felt they had sufficient personnel in the area to control it. They agreed to avoid transmitting rumors, to avoid reporting trivial incidents, to report and not interpret what was happening, and to avoid the use of superlatives, adjectives, or other sensational techniques. Furthermore, they agreed to be as inconspicuous as possible when covering a troubled area, to confirm the source of all telephone reports to the newsroom, and to restrict themselves to responsible sources and to responsible leaders.

Some fifty newsmen were interviewed immediately after the Glenville incident. Several of them claimed they had never received *any* guidelines for reporting civil disturbances. During a television interview with Community Relations Director Bertram Gardner, Virgil Dominic, the anchor man for WKYC-TV news, asked, "Don't you think we [newsmen] should have some guidelines?" He obviously did not know that any existed. A WIXY-radio newsman claimed that most of the people who had attended the 1966 meetings to establish guidelines were upper echelon and not members of the working press.

The members of the working press, however, were the ones who converged in droves upon the scene in Glenville. Camera crews came from every television station, along with newspapermen, radio and television reporters, and representatives of national news agencies. One reporter said, "We had twenty reporters there and, besides ours, there were five from *Time Magazine*, two from the *New York Times*, three from *Newsweek*, two from the *Washington Post*, one from the *Los Angeles Times*, one from the *London Daily Press*, one from the *Toronto Globe*, and Jimmy Breslin who was free-lancing."

Several newsmen were wounded and injured, and policemen helped them into ambulances. One injured reporter was helped to safety into an alley by a patrolman. He there proceeded to interview a man who also had sought the alley for safety and who allegedly was from a militant gang. This dramatic interview was aired nationally. A photographer from WEWS-TV was attacked by a group of black youths in orange shirts who yelled, "Hey, whitey, wanna know what black power's like?" A black detective rescued him.

A black television newswoman from WKYC-TV was sent into the restricted area with two white newsmen. She said, "I was scared. It was the night only Negro reporters could go in, and it was uncomfortable. One reason was that I went in with a white crew." The white crew was from NBC.

Several local newsmen expressed disgust with these national reporters. A radio newsman said: "Those guys got out of line. I've seen those guys work. Cops say, 'Move along buddy,' and they say, 'Who the hell do you think you are? We're NBC.' They have no regard for anybody. They've got NBC and CBS pinned to them. They think it's a license to do anything they please." Literally hundreds of newsmen were in the area after the shooting began. Despite the mayor's orders, many white newsmen entered the restricted area.

WEWS-TV was the first to carry films of the violence at 9:00 P.M. They began by calling it a riot and identifying the area. A very dramatic audiotape from the scene was also aired at 2:00 A.M. by radio station WERE's news director, Bob Campbell.

The following is a short segment from WERE's newscast:

> [Gun shots.] Can you see him?
>
> No, but this ain't good, because I don't know who I'm after.
>
> Why don't you just get out? You're marked like a son of a bitch.
>
> Hey, I gotta take a leak.
>
> Go to the house over there.
>
> [Dogs barking. Confusion in background. Voices seem to be those of citizens, police, and reporters. There followed discussion about how to remove the wounded, and the policemen called for a wagon and a zone car. A reporter thought a tank with a hatch would be most appropriate.]
>
> This is Brother F—— [one of the militants, who was trying to act as a mediator]. I ain't on no side. You know how I stand. Brother, if you please, hold your fire. They'll pull their wounded off the street and we'll pull our wounded off the street at the same time. And there'll be no sneakin' and beatin' around the bush.
>
> Ask them to answer you. Tell them to fire a shot in the air if he hears you.
>
> If you hear me and believe me, fire one shot in the air and I'll come out myself, and anything you want to do to me you can do what you want to do.
>
> [When attempts failed to gain a response, the police called for a wagon.]
>
> Okay, let's go with that wagon. Can we bust those lights out?
>
> I wish they'd knock out those fuckin' lights.

Radio coverage swung from extreme caution at the beginning to more extraordinarily descriptive and dramatic accounts as the action progressed. Television viewers were able to relive the entire scene, but since at times the voices were not identified, it was difficult to determine whether the police, citizens, or reporters were responsible for the words. While gunshots echoed in the homes of Cleveland citizens who had their radios blaring, those watching television saw burning buildings and newsmen shouting over the noise and confusion. Citizens saw shattered glass raining down on a newsman from WEWS when police shot out a street light above him to provide a cover of darkness.

Newspapers selected less violent pictures for the front page, but pictures in the inside sections showed the bodies of dead snipers, looted stores, fires, and policemen holding looters at gunpoint. Feature stories about citizens who feared for their lives, lost children, policemen's wives, and a series about Ahmed Evans kept the event alive in the weeks that followed. When a city editor decided to call a halt and refused a story written by three reporters claiming to have the "real truth" about Glenville, a group of young reporters threatened to walk out.

However, by Thursday, July 25—only two days after the incident—the mayor decided that significant headway had been made towards ending the violence and lawlessness, and he made an announcement that ". . . the city of Cleveland police will be patrolling the area this evening. The citizens-group used Wednesday evening has been disbanded."[10] He said that while the Negro community did "admirably well" in controlling itself, "some of the things that happened" had to be stopped. He was referring to the looting that had taken place. The greatest problem on Wednesday night, according to the mayor, concerned young people between the ages of fourteen and seventeen. He asked the Negro community to keep the young off the streets.

On Saturday at 11:00 A.M. the mayor announced that 1,200 National Guardsmen had been withdrawn from the Glenville area. "I believe the crisis is past," he told the news media.[11] On Sunday the police returned to normal eight-hour shifts, and the National Guard pulled out the remaining units that had been left in the city on a standby basis.

The official casualty list from the mayor's office numbered the following: seven dead, fifteen wounded, one believed dead. Property losses were estimated at $1,087,000.

What really happened in Glenville is still hotly debated among Clevelanders. How Mayor Stokes handled the situation after the shooting began was a principal issue, especially his decision to cordon-off a square mile of Glenville where white policemen and white newsmen were forbidden to enter. Although Police Chief Blackwell had supported the action, many white policemen felt police authority had been undermined. News media representatives felt that the decision was correct regarding the police but wrong regarding newsmen. Dr. Kenneth Clement, Stokes's former adviser, contended that the wrong element (militants) in the Negro community felt they had won a kind of victory and were "emboldened." City Council was nearly unanimous in its criticism of the report the mayor made to council at an early morning meeting on August 9.[12] Council President Stanton called a news conference and said he could not agree with the decision of the mayor to pull the duly constituted law enforcement authority out of the riot area during the period of Wednesday, July 24. He added, "If our society is to endure, it must endure under the law, and no mayor's committee or vigilante group can be substituted on any moral basis in lieu of the duly constituted law enforcement authority."[13] A private poll conducted by a special survey showed that citizen reaction to the mayor's decisions was mixed but that, nonetheless, most supported him. The most damaging blow, however, was the disclosure by Fred (Ahmed) Evans, alleged leader of the sniper unit, that he had received money to support his group from Cleveland: NOW! funds. The mayor, noting that contributions had dropped off after July 24, appealed to the citizens to continue to work for Cleveland: NOW! He appeared on television and asked the citizens not to let the vendetta of a "handful of misguided men" poison the city and destroy all the good that had begun with the Cleveland: NOW! project.

In the months that followed Glenville a highly factionalized community was not at all satisfied with the information it had received from the news media and the mayor. The people wanted more facts and, upon hearing that a "scientific study" of what happened in Glenville was underway, anxiously awaited the results, assuming the rhetoric would be objective. It was not.

Dr. Louis Masotti, a professor in the Department of Political Science at Case Western Reserve University, was asked to research the incident. He was a member of a group of scholars in his department who had established a Civil Violence Research Center at the university. Prior to June, 1968, the Lemberg Center at Brandeis University had contracted with the National Institute of Mental Health for a ten-cities project to investigate the dynamics of urban violence and its relation to urban structures. Even before the Glenville incident, Dr. Masotti was asked to direct the Cleveland phase of this study, and Lemberg and the Greater Cleveland Associated Foundation granted financial support for the study. Dr. Masotti decided that an analysis of the Glenville disorder also should be undertaken. Since it would be somewhat similar in scope and intent to the original ten-cities project, he proposed that the two efforts be combined.[14] There is some question whether that combination was ever acceptable to the Lemberg Center, but in any event the center made further funds available for study of the Glenville disturbance. Dr. Ralph Lewis of the Lemberg Center at Brandeis University said that a total of $21,000 was given to the study. Dr. James A. Norton said the Greater Cleveland Associated Foundation financed the Cleveland portion of the ten-cities project with an additional $30,000.

What eventually came to be known as the Masotti Report was from its inception an attitudinal survey. Interviewers were requested to follow a set of guidelines concentrating on the personal attitudes of the individual being questioned. Examples of some of the questions listed on the guidelines were:

> How does the individual view the disturbance? Was it a riot, a rebellion, a criminal act? Was the activity of the riot national or not? Was the disturbance supported by the majority of the black community? Was the initial shooting a plot or perhaps a part of a nation-wide conspiracy?

There was also a set of guidelines regarding Mayor Stokes's role in the disturbance, questions pertaining to his decisions:

> Was the decision of Mayor Stokes to remove police and National Guard from the riot area on Wednesday night (July 24) a wise decision or not? Why?
>
> Was Stokes too secretive about his decision-making and unwilling to listen to those who wished to offer advice?
>
> Did Stokes tell the public all he knew or was his disclosure of information to the public done on a carefully screened basis?

The interviewers also were requested to obtain opinions regarding the administration's job in the city before the disturbance and regarding the future prospects of programs like the Summer Youth Program and Cleveland: NOW! Interviewers were asked to determine the role of the interviewee in the disturbance by seeking information about the activities of the individual questioned. "The intent," stated the guidelines, "is to have the interviewee reflect upon Cleveland and the various impacts the disturbance has had upon situations in Cleveland. As much as possible, the individual's own personal opinions are what we desire in the second part of the questioning."

The public, however, came to believe that this was an investigation into the facts of the event rather than opinions about the causes and results.

The study was well underway when Dr. Masotti attended a meeting in Washington where the National Commission on the Causes and Prevention of Violence, popularly known as the Eisenhower Commission, was recruiting social scientists in all fields to study the violence which occurred in Chicago, Miami, and Cleveland.

A contract was signed between Masotti and that commission for a report of the Glenville disturbance. This contract reportedly stated that the commission could not release its edited version of the Masotti Report without Masotti's permission and that the report would revert to Masotti's control when it was publicly released by the commission or on June 10, 1969, whichever occurred first. At that time Dr. Masotti could make whatever use he wished of the report. The Eisenhower Commission's financial support amounted to $12,500. (The commission's contribution was in addition to the $51,000 already granted for the Glenville study.)

Thus, the methods used in the investigation of the disturbance limited the study to a survey of attitudes, opinions, and interpretations of events. The raw data consisted primarily of interviews which were not sworn depositions. The people interviewed, in some instances, had been guaranteed anonymity. Furthermore, none of the interviewers had been on the scene of the Glenville incident, and too much time had elapsed between the incident and the interviews to prevent the inevitable contamination of the interviewee's opinions by such outside influences as news media reports. By the time the injured policemen were interviewed, Ahmed Evans and his followers had been indicted for murder; the fear of prejudicing the trial limited the information these policemen could grant.

In April, 1969, rumors about the contents of what had come to be known as the Masotti Report began to surface in the city. The trial of Ahmed Evans, the alleged principal in the Glenville attack on police, had begun. Angry voices throughout the city were beginning to demand that the government release the Masotti Report to the jurors in the Evans trial. The Eisenhower Commission postponed releasing the report until after the trial to avoid any possible interference in the case. The rumors persisted that the report contained evidence that would clear Ahmed Evans. Flyers were distributed in many sections of Cleveland by Evans's supporters which read: "Judge 'Rush him to the chair' McMonagle and white racist jury order the murder of Ahmed in the name of the people of Ohio. The Government ordered the Masotti report suppressed in order to pave the way for this murder. We must stop this lynching. Let's fight back."[15]

Dr. Masotti called a press conference but, when reporters assembled, would make no comment. Julian Krawcheck of the *Press* asked why Dr. Masotti had called a press conference if he had nothing to say. When Masotti responded that he couldn't take time to talk to every reporter in town on the phone, Krawcheck retorted, "Well, you took the time to call us all to come over here, didn't you?" Masotti refused to respond and walked away.

Masotti's mysterious silence added to the rhetoric of protest. A student demonstration was staged on the campus of Case Western Reserve University during which the university administration was accused of acting in collusion with the government to suppress evidence which could clear Evans. This accusation was denied by university spokesmen.

The original Masotti Report of approximately 400 manuscript pages was given to Anthony Neville by the Eisenhower Commission for final editing and polishing. It was eventually published commercially as a 126-page, ninety-five-cent paperback entitled *Shoot-Out in Cleveland.* This version, by the way, is the only evidence of the research paid for by the Eisenhower Commission in the Library of Congress.

The *Shoot-Out in Cleveland* criticized a series of articles in the *Plain Dealer*, titled "The Cleveland Police: What's on Their Mind," that appeared some months after the disturbance; it discredited the authors of the articles, claiming that they were three police reporters rather than the seven newsmen named by the newspaper. The *Shoot-Out* stated:

> Nearly all the work, however, was done by the three police reporters. It has been noted in sociological studies that policemen often develop a conspiratorial outlook on the world and a persecution complex about themselves as a group. ("We're alone, we're a football," a patrolman told one of the reporters.) While police reporters do not necessarily develop the police attitude toward the community, they tend to reflect that attitude as an unconscious or unstated condition of their continuing rapport with the police. "The Cleveland Police: What's on Their Mind" gave free rein to expressions of cynicism, conspiracy, and group paranoia.[16]

These instances of unwarranted, undocumented claims couched in emotionally loaded terms reflect as much the attitudes of the researchers as the attitudes of their subjects. Needless to say, such wholesale class indictments of both the police and the media were not received with enthusiasm. Instead of contributing to community understanding, the report caused those affected to become more firmly entrenched in their positions, and the justificatory rhetoric became bitter and more intense.

In the months following the Glenville incident dissension and distrust broke out everywhere. The police were accused of brutality by the Negro community. The Negro community was accused of promoting an attitude of lawlessness. Council castigated the mayor. The mayor would not break silence when vocal elements in the community accused him of succumbing to the militant element in Cleveland. The news media, by prolonged editorializing, incurred more distrust by the angry black community. Generally, the west side residents sided with the police and the east siders with Ahmed Evans, a separation much wider than the Cuyahoga River. But while the entire community suffered from a polarization which was continually stimulated, it was really Carl Stokes who was caught in the middle. On one side were citizens criticizing the mayor because their faith in Cleveland: NOW! had been betrayed. On the other side were angry policemen criticizing the mayor because they felt he had betrayed them. During the Stoke's years, the communication barrier created by the Glenville incident was never to be completely erased.

CHAPTER 6

FROM POLICY TO CRISIS

THE TARNISH of Glenville had to be removed. Mayor Stokes stated: "Now we've got to go all the way back to November, 1967, and start all over again."[1] Obviously stellar cabinet appointments, a larger tax base, and a spectacular fund drive were not enough to solve the real problems which plagued the city: equitable law enforcement, housing, and race relations. These were the problem areas which had been identified in the campaign, and, as the Stokes administration began its second year, it was painfully obvious that the problems had not been ameliorated. Image-enhancement had to come through active and relevant programs. Again . . . the time for deliberation was at hand.

LAW AND ORDER

Mayor Stokes's first move to regain the confidence of the people was directed towards the problem of law and order. The issue, however, was defined quite differently at the City Hall level and at the neighborhood level. At City Hall it meant the necessity of curbing Cleveland's escalating crime rate while at the same time transferring considerable police power to civilian hands. At the neighborhood level insufficient police protection was the prime issue. There were complaints that calls for help were being ignored or delayed, that police were unwilling to extend equal protection to black neighborhoods, and simply that there were not enough police. Citizens expressed justified fears of even walking from their homes to the nearest Rapid Transit or bus stop. Car insurance rates in the city soared because of the increase in auto thefts and vandalism.

After Glenville, a serious police morale problem also existed. Police morale had been deteriorating since the December, 1967, mass transfers, but the Glenville incident brought the problem into the open. At the same time that the administration was asking for stronger gun control measures, more and more citizens were purchasing guns to protect themselves from the growing criminal menace despite the first city ordinance—still in effect—which prohibited the discharge of firearms in the city. Interestingly enough the very first arrest in early Cleveland was made for violation of that ordinance. Reminiscent of a later period, the 1870s, when Cleveland merchants doubled their vigilance by employing "merchant police,"[2] merchants in the 1970s are being forced to do the same thing; the "rent-a-cop" business is booming. The private policeman has become a common sight in department stores, restaurants, grocery stores, and shopping centers.

Soon after Glenville, Mayor Stokes replaced Police Chief Blackwell with Patrick L. Gerity and announced that to end the charges of City Hall interference in police affairs, Gerity would be given absolute authority in running the department. Gerity understood the problems of the urban society and how they related to the policeman's role; he was genuinely eager to improve the department and to get the best possible recruits. He acknowledged that in previous years a policeman's shooting ability influenced his chances for promotion. "We had some great shots," he recalled, "but not that great in the brain department." One of Gerity's first acts upon becoming chief was to bring in an expert from the International Association of Chiefs of Police to evaluate the police academy and make recommendations for improvements.

Safety Director McManamon thought quite differently about the police force. Much was revealed in the language employed by the two men, especially the choice of pronouns. Chief Gerity referred to the police and the entire force, including his own role, with the pronoun "we" ("We had great shots. . . . We decided . . . etc.). Safety Director McManamon, on the other hand, constantly referred to the safety forces as "they," and regarded himself as a member of "we, the administration." When asked about the importance of police attitude, McManamon replied, "In 1968 I didn't feel that it was that important because we saw in '68 a decrease in crime in most areas and a minimal increase in other areas. 1969 was a different year. We got a tremendous increase in crime and we've got a terrible attitude *out there* [in the police department]." Furthermore, McManamon felt that the problems in the police force were related in two very basic issues:

> One, civilian control. We're now attempting, very strongly attempting, to impose this control. Been doing it from the very first day. We're saying we've looked at this. We know the people need this. *You* police are going to respond. The second thing, this is the racial thing. We now have a Negro mayor and their bigotry to the

> Negro with whom they're involved in their everyday work extends to everyone who is associated with them.

On the matter of recruiting and promotion, McManamon said he did not feel that the police chief should have authority over the nature of the exams. The Civil Service Commission is vested by the City Charter with the sole authority for classifying positions and determining eligibility rules for appointment, promotion, and disciplining of workers. The safety director selects personnel from the eligible list supplied him by the Civil Service Commission.

The City Charter provides that the chief of police "shall have exclusive control of the stationing and transfer of patrolmen and other officers and employees constituting the police force, under such rules and regulations as may be established by the mayor or by the director of the department to whom the said chief of police may be immediately responsible."[3] On the matter of transferring policemen, McManamon said he believed in "more civilian control, not less." Chief Gerity said that to take away from the chief the power of assigning and reassigning his men was to strip him of any authority whatsoever, resulting in inefficient use of available personnel and inability to fit the best man to the job.

The attitudes and opinions expressed by the two men are important in view of the debate which later ensued between them over the appointment of new recruits to the police department.

In the fall of 1968, the responsibility for recruiting five hundred high-caliber candidates for the police force was placed in the hands of the Civil Service Commission—more specifically in the hands of three Stokes appointees: Marvin Chernoff, Jay B. White, and Charles L. Butts. Although the Civil Service Commission in October of 1968 was composed of two holdover appointees, Clayborne George (who had been a member of the Civil Service Commission for approximately thirty-five years) and Thomas Ryan (a member for five years), these two men were excluded by the other three members of the Civil Service Commission who had been appointed by Mayor Carl Stokes.[4]

A bulletin was issued giving the date for the civil service examination as October 19, 1968. One week prior to the examination, a meeting was held in the home of Jay B. White to decide the nature of the exam. Chernoff and Butts were involved, but George and Ryan were excluded. Also present at the meeting were certain psychologists. A few days prior to this meeting the NAACP had conducted a campaign to recruit black police candidates. The NAACP contracted with the Cleveland Small Business and Economic Development Corporation to conduct a school to aid persons who were police candidates. Interestingly, some of the psychologists who were at the home of Jay B. White to discuss the testing were also on the staff of the NAACP-sponsored school.[5]

On Wednesday, October 16, three days prior to the scheduled police examination, the NAACP-sponsored school gave to its students an identical test that would be given officially by the Civil Service Commission on October 19.[6]

On October 19, the written tests for new recruits were officially administered. On December 10, 1968, the Civil Service Commission sponsored a dinner at the Holiday Inn, Thirty-sixth Street and Euclid, for the prospective interviewers of candidates for police training—the second phase of the police examination. Included among the guests were psychiatrists, psychologists, and communication specialists. Presiding at the dinner were Commissioners White, Chernoff, and Butts.

The interviewers were told that evening that all applicants had completed the preliminary pen-and-pencil tests and that only those who had scored proficiently on the mental ability test would be advanced to the interview (or final) phase. In addition to the Army General Classification Test (AGCT), the candidates in October had been given the Minnesota Multiphasic Inventory (MMPI) and the California Test of Personality, but the results of the last two tests were not a factor in the elimination of candidates. These last two tests were to be used only as "guides" by the interviewers. Since not all the interviewers were familiar with the criteria for interpreting all three tests, they were assured that keys to interpretation would be provided prior to the first interview. Dr. Mary Jean Thomas, of Case Western Reserve University, was one of the communication specialists invited to help with the interviewing. She asked if the group shouldn't be given some indications of police job expectations. A psychologist who had scored the personality inventories and Commissioner Jay B. White replied that the interviewers should not concern themselves with such things as job criteria. The commission, according to White, was more interested in selecting a group of "nice guys."[7]

The interviewing began on Monday morning, December 16, and continued through Friday, December 20. The interviewing for police recruitment had to be completed by December 20, because the police promotional exam was to be administered on Saturday, December 21.

Past promotional exams had measured knowledge of fine points about rules and regulations, yet, according to Chief Gerity, even under usual testing circumstances, policemen always suffer a certain amount of stress and anxiety—such anxiety that heart attacks are not an uncommon occurrence.[8] Sometimes men closeted themselves in hotel rooms for several days for intensive study sessions. The purpose of the *new* promotional exam was to test the men on their concepts of the policeman's role in the life and welfare of the community—a much wider area of inquiry than the usual rules and regulations. About six weeks before the exam the candidates for sergeant, lieutenant, captain, and deputy inspector were handed the following formidable list of readings for which they were to be held responsible on the exam:

1. Allport, Gordon, *The Nature of Prejudice*
2. Brown, William, *Police and Community Conflict*
3. Clark, Kenneth B., *Dark Ghetto*
4. Donegan, Robert, *Evidence Handbook*
5. Edwards, George, *Police on the Urban Frontier*
6. Ellison, Ralph, *The Invisible Man*
7. Erikson, Erik H., *Youth: Change and Challenge*
8. Fleisher, L. A., *Police-Community Relations*
9. Friedenberg, Edgar, *The Vanishing Adolescent*
10. Germann, *Police Personnel Management*
11. Gocke and Stallings, *Police Sergeant's Manual*
12. International City Managers Association, *Municipal Police Administration*
13. O'Hara, Charles, *Fundamentals of Criminal Investigation*
14. Paulsen, Conrad, *"Children's Court," Columbia University Forum*
15. Pettigrew, Thomas, *A Profile of the American Negro*
16. Silberman, Charles, *Crisis in Black and White*
17. Skelnick, Jerome A., *Justice without Trial: Law Enforcement in a Democratic Society*
18. Schur, Edwin M., *Crimes without Violence: Deviant Behavior and Public Policy*
19. Sutherland and Cressey, *Principles of Criminology*
20. Towler, Juby, *The Police Role and Racial Conflict*
21. *Traffic Accident Investigator's Manual for Police*
22. *The Challenge of Crime in a Free Society: A Report by the President's Commission on Law Enforcement and Administration of Justice*, Chapters 1 and 4
23. *National Advisory Commission on Civil Disorders* (identified as the Kerner Commission Report)
24. Wilson, James Q., *Varieties of Police Behavior*
25. Wilson, O. W., *Police Administration*

26. Wolfgang, Marvin E., *Crime and Race: Conceptions and Misconceptions*

These policemen were not full-time students. They were unsophisticated in methods of study and writing exams. They were full-time policemen; a great majority of them had only a high school education completed some years before and were inadequately prepared to evaluate the material.

This promotional exam of December 21, 1968, was invalidated and nullified when Chief Gerity charged that proper security measures were not maintained during the exam. A second exam was given on January 23, 1969. Common Pleas Judge Thomas W. Mitchell of Jackson County nullified the *second* exam on the grounds that the questions were "unreasonable, not practical, and unrelated to the positions sought."[9]

Judge Thomas Mitchell ordered the grand jury (which met late in March) to determine whether or not there had been violations of the law, by anyone, in connection with the January 23 police promotional examination given by the Civil Service Commission.[10] Because of the facts that developed in this investigation, it became necessary to investigate the fairness and security of the December 21 police promotional examination and also the October 19 police entrance examination (given to applicants for the police department).

The grand jury report revealed that a potential group of recruits had been given access to the mental ability test prior to the October civil service exam. Two hundred thirty-nine were approved by the full Civil Service Commission for the eligible list of March 24, 1969, yet a week later 250 names appeared on the official list in the City Record. A policeman also admitted before the jury that he was given a copy of the January 23 promotional exam in advance. There was a wide discrepancy between the number of promotional exams presented to the grand jury, the number Chernoff said were printed, and the number the Western Hill Printing Company said it had printed.

The grand jury report was also highly critical of the Stokes administration, particularly of the three Stokes appointees to the Civil Service Commission:

> It was not a well kept secret that the last three mentioned members of the Civil Service Commission, recent appointees, decided that they would run the Civil Service Commission their own way and would disregard Clayborne George and Thomas Ryan, even though they had much experience in the field of civil service. . . .

> The fact is that there are no new officers on the streets—not because of the Grand Jury inquiries or investigation—but because of negligence and mistakes made by the Civil Service Commission and local government. . . .
>
> The Grand Jury finds that the overwhelming majority of the Cleveland Civil Service Commission employees feel, and have stated, that the office is not the same as it was in prior years; that it has been very disrupted and very disorganized and that morale has been at an all time low.[11]

The three-man majority was cited for keeping their meetings secret from the other two members, hiring motel rooms to prepare police examinations ($391.68 for three days at city expense), handling exam papers carelessly, bending commission rules on applications, and allowing security leaks. Jay B. White and Charles Butts were indicted for perjury and destruction of public records.

On October 3, 1969, Commissioner Marvin Chernoff told the City Club forum that "our mistake was in attempting to make changes in an area in which those affected relate change to subversion, see progress as a threat to self-interest, and view civilian direction as outside interference."[12] He denied the grand jury charges of misconduct by the commission and said the grand jury report reflected the bias of the "police establishment." Despite Chernoff's attempts to justify the administration and cast the blame elsewhere, a typical rhetorical ploy, some very hard facts remained to haunt the mayor throughout the 1969 campaign. This initial attempt to solve the problem of inadequate police protection or to improve the morale of the police awakened a distrust of the administration's ability. Chernoff's rhetoric could do nothing to reestablish credibility, but it did serve to polarize attitudes in the community.

Mayor Stokes was never in any way implicated in the exam scandals; yet he occupied the key position. He had appointed the commissioners who had conducted the testing, and he had not kept his promise to put more policemen on the street. It was not the first time, nor the only time, that Stokes would be embarrassed by men whom he had appointed. The second year of his administration was so marked by incidents in which the people whose help he needed most fell short of expectations that Election Board Democratic member Dan Duffy was prompted to remark, "Everyday is amateur day at City Hall." Before the year was out, when Stokes's supporters were accusing anybody and everybody of doing things to embarrass the mayor politically, one political observer said, "Why would anybody deliberately go to the trouble of embarrassing the mayor? That's what his cabinet is there for."

When Seth Taft was interviewed about the office he had been unsuccessful in winning, he said: "I think Stokes has been guilty of not being tough enough and insisting that things be done correctly. I think the one thing that our American system has that is unique is that we abide by a group of rules of behavior and activity." Seth Taft also felt that Butts, White, and Chernoff acted in accordance with what they thought were the mayor's wishes. "I'm sure Stokes said to Butts and White and Chernoff, 'I want more black policemen. You guys figure out how to do it.' And I'm pretty sure he did not tell them to break the rules in doing it, but they bent them pretty far and, in a few instances, pretty clearly broke them. And Stokes said, 'I didn't tell them to break the rules. I told them I wanted black policemen, but I expected them to abide by the rules.' Well, I think the fact is that they didn't, and I think he should have realized they wouldn't."

With black citizens comprising almost 40 percent of Cleveland's population, it was both desirable and necessary that there be more black policemen. Both the Hough and Glenville incidents indicated a need for better police involvement with the community which they served. More inner-city policemen were needed, men who worked and lived in the community. Chief Gerity had felt that better testing procedures would result in the hiring of higher caliber black and white policemen. However, the idea that anybody *had* to bend or break the rules to obtain more black policemen was an insult to both the black and white men who applied.

THE SECOND ATTEMPT

Despite all the charges and countercharges, the problem was unsolved. On June 16, 1969, Mayor Stokes asked council to pass an emergency bill which would enable the city to train potential policemen during the time appointments were delayed by the grand jury probe. The bill passed, and 113 trainees were appointed on July 7, 1969. The men selected for this training had been among those certified as eligible by the commission in March.

These trainees were required to take the qualifying examinations again on August 2 after the Civil Service Commission declared the October 19, 1968, exam null and void. After the resignation of Charles Butts and Jay B. White, Stokes's new appointee to the Civil Service Commission, David I. Sindell, moved quickly to make arrangements for another examination. Preparation of the exams this time was under the direction of the senior examiner, Francis J. Hogan, and, on August 2, 785 men and 138 women appeared at the Cleveland Convention Center to take the tests. A strict security guard was placed at the door, and proctors walked up and down the aisles as a further check.

On August 8 it was revealed that 87.5 percent of the men taking the exam had passed, as had 81.5 percent of the women. It will be recalled that only 47 percent had passed the October, 1968, exam. Commissioner Sindell offered one explanation for the high percentage of passing grades. He said that many who took the August test were the same candidates who had taken the questionable October exam.

Another explanation might be found in the very nature of the mental ability test. The AGCT used in the first exam was an implicit test of verbal ability. But objections had been voiced that intelligence tests which require middle-class verbal skills for comprehension are discriminatory against members of disadvantaged cultural groups. In response to this criticism the Civil Service Commission chose a different intelligence test, the Cattell Culture Fair Intelligence Test, for the next examination. Certainly it is important to use culture-fair intelligence tests if the only purpose of testing is to measure intelligence, but if the test is also used to predict success in a job which requires a variety of linguistic skills, the use of such a test which disregards verbal ability is questionable. The police training program requires reading of a wide variety of materials from operations manuals to municipal and state law codes. Policemen on the job have to write detailed and accurate reports. They are often called upon to testify in court. Obviously language facility is an important aspect of the policeman's basic qualifications. Change in the type of test offered certainly affected the percentage of passing grades in the August exam.

The interviewing phase of the exam for the August group of recruits was handled by Professors William Arnold and Philip Emmert of the Department of Speech Communication at Case Western Reserve University. Safety Director McManamon chose them because "they seemed to be most interested in the area, most knowledgeable, and they were recommended highly."

The second round of interviewing took place at the Auditorium Hotel. Again, about one-half hour was devoted to each interview. The interviewers were six psychologists and seven speech communication specialists. Only after three days of testing were the interviewers told that a psychiatrist was available, should a questionable applicant need further screening.

It is important to establish the circumstances and goals of the interviewing portion of the candidate screening, because a controversy arose over the criteria for selection. There ensued a public contest between the relative credibility of polygraph tests as opposed to the opinions of the "psychologists."

On the first day the interviewers were given, in addition to the rating form, a guideline which listed certain desirable and undesirable characteristics of policemen. These characteristics had been derived by Professors Arnold and Emmert from their interview with Chief Gerity. The following is the list "prepared" for the professional interviewers:

CHARACTERISTICS OF GOOD POLICEMEN

Unaffected by ethnic background
Wants to do something for people
Will treat people fairly
Community relations oriented
Has a sense of dedication
Has a desire to improve himself
Is someone who approaches the job as a career—wants to advance —wants the challenge of the job
Has learned discipline through military service
Has self-discipline
Must be sensitive to people—be able to "read" motivations of people
Should be of above average intelligence—this is a very complex job
Needs communication skills
Should have some specialized skill(s) (i.e., photography, architecture, public relations, urban planning, electronics, law, etc.)
Should be willing to learn—continue formal education
(Policemen ten years from now will probably need more college education)

UNDESIRABLE CHARACTERISTICS FOR A POLICEMAN

Personal "hang-ups"—over concern with himself
Over concern with security and with a "soft, clean" job
"Bully"—abuses people who shouldn't be abused—extrapunitive
"Lacks guts"
Shouldn't be suspicious of everyone he meets
Shouldn't be prejudiced to the point where the prejudice would affect the way he treats citizens while on the job—should treat everyone equally and fairly

Most of the time, the results of the Cattell Culture Fair Intelligence Test and the Personal History Index formulated by the Industrial Relations Institute of the University of Chicago were available to the interviewers. A rejected candidate was reinterviewed, sometimes as many as three times. Interviewers' evaluations of the candidates were, of necessity, subjective and derived almost solely from revelations made during the brief interview.

Prior to releasing the eligible list, Safety Director McManamon allowed members of the *Plain Dealer* staff to examine the records of more than one hundred fifty applicants. When the list was released, Chief Gerity balked at accepting about sixty of the candidates and refused to appear at the swearing-in ceremonies. The *Plain Dealer* story which followed Gerity's refusal to be a party to the acceptance of the total list of candidates reported that staff members had studied fifty-three disputed cases and more than one hundred others in addition. On the basis of their study, the *Plain Dealer* reporters concluded that nearly all the differences of opinion between Chief Gerity and Director McManamon rested on the differences between the lie detector tests and the "psychological" tests. It appeared that Chief Gerity had depended primarily on the background investigations and the reports from his polygraph experts; McManamon relied more strongly on the summations by "psychologists" (the interviewers). It was reported that McManamon had submitted the conflicting reports to a psychiatrist for review and interpretation. The *Plain Dealer* also concluded that "both sides lacked information sufficient to make solid judgments." Chief Gerity claimed that he did not have access to the "psychologists' " reports before making his judgments. The interviewers themselves certainly had no access to the police reports before making judgments.

When asked about the controversy, McManamon said:

> The main thing is that possibly we've got to educate the police evaluators. They have got to be told that if a man has had oral sodomy performed on him by a prostitute or by someone while he was in service in Viet Nam or before he reached the age of sixteen once or twice, that he's not a homosexual.

McManamon had overruled Chief Gerity on the appointment of men who had not been acceptable to members of the police force because of reported or admitted homosexual acts, thefts, police records, and use of drugs. Director McManamon questioned the very evaluations the police felt were most important and said that when looking over the trainees from an August, 1968, group he detected that the police had employed no firm guidelines in evaluating the men *they* recommended. Turnabout, it seemed, was fair play.

Thomas Guthrie, associate publisher of the *Plain Dealer*, confirmed the fact that McManamon had come to the newspaper prior to announcing the eligible list—an action which indicated to Guthrie that the director was anticipating some kind of disagreement with the police chief. The newspaper contributed to the development of the controversy by publicizing it and by presuming to act as judge. Neither newspaper, however, was careful to check all the facts, for they repeatedly referred to the interviews as "psychological tests." One *Press* reporter interviewed Dr. Philip Emmert at his office in the Department of Speech Communication at Case Western Reserve University but referred to him in print as a "psychologist"!

The time was right for a careful examination to determine the necessary guidelines for selection of policemen and to determine methods to evaluate applicants for police training. But council did not act. The administration again resorted to justification. The news media passed judgment but never asked the essential questions. Public opinion was divided between pro-police and anti-police factions instead of focusing on police recruiting methods.

RACE RELATIONS

Another major issue in Cleveland that needed the immediate attention of the administration, council, and the citizens was that of deteriorating race relations. Glenville had succeeded in further polarizing the city. The color line was even further emphasized when Mayor Stokes barred white police and newsmen from an area inhabited mainly by the black community. The act was inferred by many, both black and white, to be an act of separatism.

The *Brown* v. *Topeka Board of Education* case in 1954 was viewed by most Negroes as signaling a new era. The old Supreme Court doctrine of "separate but equal" was seen as a dead issue. Civil rights activists had as their goal the total integration of the black and white races in every facet of American life. But the dream did not come true. Eleven years passed after the *Brown* case before Congress passed the first major civil rights legislation. By that time young blacks were more impatient and more militant in their demands.

To the world outside of Cleveland it may have appeared that the election of a black mayor in a city that was over 60 percent white was the final phase of the dream coming true. Negroes in Cleveland saw another possibility. For the first time they had presented a united front and realized that in unity they could effect political change favorable to them. As Bronis Klementowicz said, "They finally caught up with the Cosmos." Black unity began to be interpreted by some as black separatism.

Many of the black political and community leaders who joined forces with Carl Stokes were, and still are, confirmed integrationists, but another large segment of the young, the alienated, and the disenchanted reverted to a doctrine of separatism. Somehow this latter group envisioned that equality could only be realized where blacks could control their own environment and destiny. Movers of separatism began to demand separate schools, separate police and fire departments, and complete elimination of all-white profit from black communities.

Cleveland developed as a city of woodframe houses—even in the inner city. After World War II, when building materials became available, the inclination of Clevelanders who occupied old worn-out frame dwellings was not to tear down and build anew on the same spot, but to move out of the city to the newer and more spacious suburban areas. At the same time the great in-migration of Negroes from the South occurred. The new blacks moved into the older, declining neighborhoods which many whites were not reluctant to leave. As the blacks continued to pour into the city, those older black residents, who had filled up the vacant spaces left by whites in the core of the city, were financially ready to move into better neighborhoods, but the new neighborhoods into which they moved were really only a few blocks removed from the old. The out-migration of the more affluent blacks from the central area into the residential areas at the outer edges of the city's east side did not result in a dispersion of the Negroes but, in fact, created an almost solid black belt right through the center of the east side.

The effects of this pattern by the late 1960s were isolated pockets of whites on the east side of town and just the reverse on the west side. Friction between the two races occurred in the border areas where daily intercourse was most apt to occur on the streets and in the schools. Those white citizens feeling most threatened were the older residents who became afraid to remain in their neighborhoods as crime and friction increased but who had neither the means nor the desire to move to the suburbs.

Most of the white pockets on the east side were strong ethnic neighborhoods. As the unity of the black community began to manifest itself, so did the white ethnic neighborhoods pull themselves into tighter knots. This attitude worked its way down to the school-age level and resulted in a number of teen-age racial confrontations. Apart from the Glenville incident, open outbreaks of racial hostility were confined to confrontations at Collinwood High School and Margaret Spellacy Junior High on the east side where black students claimed discrimination and abuse. A brief flare-up occurred at predominately white John Marshall High School on the west side, but the complaint there was that the black minority was receiving favored treatment from the teachers and the white majority was being discriminated against.

Strangely enough, the greatest disruption in race relations in Cleveland occurred in an area where few whites lived, worked, or did business. Only three white franchise-holders on the east side were directly affected by the disruption, but the reverberations created a new kind of racial tension and, perhaps more important, divided the black community. At issue was the nationalistic cause of black economic determinism.

The conflict began when one group in the black community decided that any white firm doing business in the black community had two choices—leave, or share its profits with the community as a whole. Actually no choice was presented. White businessmen were expected to do both—leave, and contribute a portion of their selling price to a black community fund. It was no great problem to force the small white businessman to get out or pay protection money, but the first attack on white big business came in March, 1969, when "Rabbi" David Hill's House of Israel group went after three McDonald's Hamburger Systems (carry-out restaurant) franchises on the east side. "Rabbi" Hill was able to expand his movement when other organized groups joined with him and created Operation Black Unity (OBU). The first demand from OBU was $10,000 in donations and payment of 2 percent of the McDonald's outlets' gross income.

The leader of Operation Black Unity, self-styled "Rabbi" David Hill, claimed to have been born in Arkansas, to have served in the Navy, and to have been ordained a pastor of the Church of Christ. He dubbed himself Rabbi after he abandoned orthodox Christian religion in 1961. Hill had a record of more than thirty arrests and had served a one-year term for forgery, four years for transportation of stolen securities, a term in the Illinois Security Hospital for larceny by trick, and a term in the Lima (Ohio) State Hospital for the criminally insane. Hill claimed that his radio broadcasts were carried in twenty-three cities and that his House of Israel religious group numbered fifteen hundred members living in Buffalo, Louisville, and Pittsburgh.

Hill's House of Israel instigated the boycott and picketing of the

McDonald's outlets. He was later supported in his efforts by groups which made up Operation Black Unity: Cleveland Urban League, Cleveland Branch of NAACP, CORE, Southern Christian Leadership Conference, United Pastors Association, Cleveland Small Business and Economic Development Corporation, Pride, Inc., Afro Set, Council of Churches of Greater Cleveland, Welfare Rights Organization, Ohio Black Concern Committee, Federation of Black Nationalists, Welfare Grievance Committee, and the July Twenty-third Defense Committee (supporters of Ahmed Evans).

Many in the city—both black and white—were outraged at the implications of Operation Black Unity's membership, goals, tactics, and especially its choice of leadership. At least *five* of the organizations in the unity group were created and/or subsidized by tax funds, United Appeal, or Cleveland: NOW! The demands made by Operation Black Unity were described by Negro leaders Dr. Kenneth Clement and Councilman Leo Jackson as "extortion." The *Cleveland Press* agreed editorially with Clement and Jackson.

However, "Rabbi" David Hill declared that he would go on with the boycott until Christmas or until there "is no more McDonald's."[13] Charles Cook, Midwest director of CORE, told the *Cleveland Press* that whites could no longer choose which blacks they preferred to negotiate with nor dictate terms "based on racist attitudes."[14] On August 27, the Reverend Emanuel S. Branch, Jr., president of the Cleveland Urban League, said, "The time has come to do what has to be done to redeem the black man, regardless of the casualties which result."[15]

Such was the rhetoric of the times! It was not designed to persuade, but to justify and to threaten. Not only had it succeeded in further dividing a black and white community, but rumblings of dissent within the black community became more vocal. On September 3, 1969, the Urban League openly criticized the OBU's demands, and two days later there was a move to oust "Rabbi" Hill as head of OBU's negotiating committee. On September 9, Hill was ousted from his post by a vote of 22 to 0 and replaced by attorney Stanley Tolliver. That same day WEWS-TV aired a program on its Inner Circle series entitled "Black on Black." The producers of the show taped comments by Dr. Kenneth Clement and Councilman Leo Jackson, then fused them with remarks by Baxter Hill, head of Pride, Inc., and "Rabbi" David Hill of the House of Israel. The four black leaders refused to appear on the same platform together.

"Rabbi" David Hill stated that the leadership of Leo Jackson and Kenneth Clement was no longer the leadership of the black community.

Baxter Hill said that all black people "realize we are all black nationalists. Integration is dying out—separation is the big thing now." Leo Jackson declared that he had worked long and hard for black unity, but he refused to accept the methods and techniques which he believed were lawless and not worthy of the organizations that composed Operation Black Unity. On the same program Dr. Kenneth Clement revived the Glenville issue by asserting that the decision to deputize a "lawless" element for even one night was an error. He said, "I think this has been one of the most oversold ideas that has ever caught fire in the community, namely, to deputize the lawless element even for one night or a season and have them keep peace, on their terms, mind you, and when it's all over you go back and say, 'Well, I gave you a tin badge for a night. I'd like my badge back.' No lawless element so deputized ever gave a badge back to any community that so deputized them."

Press columnist Julian Krawcheck severely criticized the city administration for its do-nothing attitude in the controversy, saying that "the Black Nationalist thugs hold the Negro community in a reign of terror." He wrote, "At the time when the black community cries out for City Hall leadership and police protection to resist the thugs and the destroyers who operate under the false banner of equal opportunity, the mayor is too involved with politics to take a hand."[16]

Such words from a white man would have been labeled racist propaganda, but when Jackson and Clement were seen and heard making the same charges, there were reactions from all sides. The Cuyahoga County Grand Jury was ordered to begin a probe into the tactics of Operation Black Unity on September 13. Negro *Press* columnist George Moore that day wrote that no one man speaks for the blacks. "Right now the black leadership is like the jabberwock animal in Alice in Wonderland. It is made up of many parts."[17]

A number of Operation Black Unity leaders became disturbed that the boycott of McDonald's was not helping the climate for reelection of Mayor Stokes. However, they voted unanimously upon the motion of William O. Walker (publisher of the *Call and Post*) to restore "Rabbi" David Hill to the position of leader and head negotiator in the McDonald's boycott.

The mayor was jarred into action by this reaffirmation of faith in "Rabbi" Hill. On September 25 Stokes asserted himself and called for a meeting in his office to try to resolve the dispute which he said was causing "serious divisions" in the city.[18] On September 29 the mayor announced that Operation Black Unity had responded to his urging to call off the boycott and resume negotiations with McDonald's.

The fact that the mayor did not enter into the dispute (which had continued since March) until late in September was interpreted by the news media as a campaign tactic. Stokes was demonstrating, a few days before the primary election, that he could exercise his influence upon the city. In the white community the fact that during the dispute he did not move *against* those who marched with raised fists was interpreted as a stand *for* them. This was to become an issue during the general election campaign, and the basis for the argument was a moral one—who was right and who was wrong.

Fortunately, OBU leaders backed off from their strong positions long enough to allow Carl Stokes to engage in his campaign for reelection without the stigma of a racial confrontation. The issue which had not been pressed during the last weeks of the campaign was finally settled rather quietly in January, 1970, when franchises were awarded to Charles Johnson and Ghetto East (a spin-off from the Hough Area Development Corporation—the agency for black economic development funded by the federal government).[19]

The problem of harmonious race relations, like the problem of improved police protection, by election time, 1969, was magnified in the public mind.

HOUSING AND URBAN RENEWAL

The problem of housing and community development did not fare much better. Urban renewal and slum clearance are not really new concepts or phenomena. For example, in 1867, the city purchased its first park property in a district which had become unsightly and cluttered with squatters' hovels. There is no evidence, however, that the city made any attempt to relocate the residents of what then became Lake View Park (north of the present Lakeside Avenue). The first organized attempt at urban renewal was the Group Plan, which was first projected in 1900. The Group Plan Commission was created in 1902, and its first report in 1903 recommended the clearance of a blighted area in the heart of the city and the erection of public buildings on what is now the Mall. But, as in 1867, the concept of planning and renewal did not extend to the creation of new or better housing. Blighted and slum areas were simply cleared away and the land reused for projects other than housing.

It was not until 1927 that the city government began to show some concern about the effects of commercial developments on residential areas. Plans for the Union Terminal called for the demolition of a large number of dwellings in an area populated by low-income families. City Manager William R. Hopkins and expert advisers began to study methods for securing better living quarters and lower rental for wage earners.

In 1933 the state of Ohio passed legislation enabling the creation of metropolitan housing authorities empowered to build and maintain public housing projects. The law provided that a metropolitan housing authority have within its scope an area larger than the largest city in a given county, but smaller than the county itself. The Cleveland Metropolitan Housing Authority's right of purchase and development extends to all of Cuyahoga County except Chagrin Falls. The authority consists of a board of five members—two appointed by the mayor of the largest city, one appointed by the Probate Court, one appointed by the County Commissioners, and the fifth member appointed by the Court of Common Pleas.

One of the first acts by the Cleveland Metropolitan Housing Authority was to call for a study of a slum area situated between Central and Woodland avenues from East Twenty-second to East Fifty-fifth Street. One of the purposes of the study was to discover whether slum areas were actually an economic liability for a city. The classic study which resulted was directed by the Reverend Robert Bernard Navin, dean of Sisters College, Catholic Diocese of Cleveland, with the help and counsel of Howard Whipple Green, director of the Real Property Inventory of Metropolitan Cleveland.[20]

The authors of the study defined a blighted area as "an area that economically is not self-supporting." A slum area, in addition to being a blighted area, has deteriorated to the point of being an "actual social and moral menace to the community." The study concluded: "Without any doubt, if administration expenses and each and every minor expense were taken into account, the cost of maintaining the small section of crime, vice and delinquency would have increased to $2,000,000 or possibly $2,500,000 for the year 1932. . . . Slum areas are a luxury, a very expensive luxury for any county to maintain."[21]

The first real effort to correct slum conditions began in 1935 when construction was started on three PWA housing projects. As a result of these first projects, 1,849 low-income families were moved into improved dwellings within their own neighborhood. In the late 1930s and early 1940s the Cleveland Metropolitan Housing Authority launched several federally supported housing projects and, in a period of nine years, constructed approximately 8,500 low-cost dwelling units accommodating at least 25,000 persons.[22] But with all this accomplishment, it must be recognized that other home building had been severely curtailed by both the depression and World War II. According to the 1940 housing census, of the approximately thirty million non-farm dwelling units, the typical unit was already twenty-five years old. In urban communities 40 percent of the housing was found to be seriously defective in some respect. While the supply of decent housing had decreased, the demand for such housing was going up. In his State of the Union address in 1949, President Harry S. Truman stated that "five million families were still living in slums and fire traps, [and] three million families shared their homes with others."

The Federal Housing Act of 1949 was not really a housing act at all. Primarily, the act enabled cities to purchase land at market value and sell it to private redevelopers at a lower than market value because the federal government paid two-thirds of the cost of acquisition. In other words, a city could buy a parcel of land for $3 million, sell it for anything over $1 million, and still make money. This, of course, held many advantages for private entrepreneurs, especially in downtown areas where they could hope to realize a neat profit from a venture which had already been heavily subsidized by the federal government. Land acquired under Title I of the Federal Housing Act of 1949 could be used for many purposes—luxury housing, low-rent housing, commercial and industrial use, public parks, etc. There was apparent in the law a concern for private enterprise rather than the real housing needs of society. Because of the already critical housing shortage, slum clearance projects under this act actually amounted to little more than the transfer of families from one slum area to another.

Cleveland's experience with urban renewal in the 1950s and 1960s did little to improve overall conditions in housing. The only projects which can, even now, be regarded as successful were those which provided for the redevelopment of the downtown commercial district and the institutional development of the area lying between Central and Woodland avenues from East Twenty-second to East Fifty-fifth—exactly the same area which came under the first slum study in 1934. The "Little Hoover Commission Report of 1966" showed how urban renewal complicated rather than alleviated the problems which already existed and completely obliterated housing in a large area. The report stated that while the Saint Vincent Project, 118.1 acres, was originally planned for predominantly residential use, in 1963 the Urban Renewal Department took action and changed the reuse of the land from part residential and institutional to completely institutional reuse. Meanwhile, a premature exodus of families created a problem in another area as approximately 1,200 persons relocated in the Hough area.

An estimated 4,487 families were affected by the six Cleveland urban renewal projects. As of 1966, 1,319 of those families were still living in the project areas; 1,377 had been relocated by the Urban Renewal Department or by their own initiative; only 114 were absorbed in public housing projects; and the whereabouts of 1,696 relocated families were unknown.

As early as 1963, James Q. Wilson, in an article published in the *Journal of the American Institute of Planners*, observed that after the initial burst of enthusiasm which greeted urban renewal in almost every city died down, voters who did not like being called slum-dwellers or being forced out of their neighborhoods began to complain. A growing resistance to urban renewal and clearance manifested itself as people learned from the experience of others. Mr. Wilson said that "in cities which have been engaged in renewal for several years, the planners often find prospective renewal areas ready and waiting for them, organized to the teeth."[23]

This kind of resistance was strongly in evidence in 1969 when Carl Stokes and the Cleveland Metropolitan Housing Authority attempted to impose a public housing project on the middle-class Negro neighborhood of Lee-Seville. It recurred again on the west side after Councilman Michael Zone of Ward Three put his stamp of approval on a Neighborhood Development Program involving 1,300 acres. There also developed an association of residents in the downtown area whose two-fold purpose was to put a halt to the city's redevelopment whims and to demand renewal projects which suited neighborhood needs and desires.

The Lee-Seville housing project issue in Cleveland in 1969 was, in many respects, a copy of an earlier struggle in Chicago involving the mayor, the Chicago Housing Authority, and a Councilman Duffy who resisted a housing project on behalf of his ward. Perhaps if Mayor Stokes and the CMHA had heeded the Chicago experience they could have developed a strategy which would have made the Lee-Seville project acceptable to all concerned. Instead they imitated their Chicago counterpart in the somewhat perilous strategy of engaging in a do-or-die struggle. A struggle is a mutual endeavor to apply power, whereas negotiations through discussion often result in fuller and better communication and satisfaction with the results.

The announcement of the Lee-Seville project came in May, 1966, when CMHA revealed its plans for a $4.5 million public housing project of 277 four- and five-bedroom units on fifty-one acres at Lee and Seville roads in southeast Cleveland. It was to be the first project in the nation to provide single-family homes for purchase by low-income families. The struggle began when Mayor Stokes endorsed the project and called upon City Council to authorize $4 million in community improvements —streets and sewers—which were requisite to CMHA's proceeding with its plans. Ward Thirty Negro Councilman Clarence R. Thompson balked on the grounds that his constituents were opposed to the project, had not been consulted, that the Lee-Seville area was already suffering from inadequate city services, and that the improvements called for by the mayor would not provide sufficient services if additional residents were to begin pouring into the area. Thompson was supported in his resistance by neighboring Ward Thirteen Negro Councilman Albert A. Pottinger. Council President James V. Stanton felt obliged to support the two councilmen whose wards would be directly affected, so all the mechanisms for pigeonholing the legislation were employed.

On May 19, 1969, the issue was debated in council, with Mayor Stokes joining in to defend the project and challenge its foes. When it became obvious that Stokes did not have the votes necessary to bring the legislation out of committee, he decided to take his case to the public. More than twenty thousand invitations went out urging people to attend a June 9 rally on the Mall just prior to the meeting of City Council. Organizers of the rally, calling themselves the Task Force to Save Public Housing, provided free bus transportation to and from the rally. Only about two hundred showed up to hear Stokes indict James Stanton thus:

> We must resolve whether we believe in the democratic process or in one-man rule. . . . The dereliction of responsibility lies with four council committees and their chairmen, who won't call for public hearings on the legislation. All are appointed by Stanton.

This indictment carried weight only among those who were ignorant of normal governmental procedures. Of course, committee chairmen are appointed by the president of City Council, and the legislative leader can exert pressure on chairmen to consider certain pieces of legislation. But the mayor was trying to make it seem that the council president was deliberately blocking the legislation for his own selfish ends. Earlier in the day Community Development Director Richard Green had also jumped on Stanton, saying, "In 1966, when the city under the Locher administration bought sixty-seven acres of land in the Lee-Seville area, Stanton said the land was good for housing." The implication of that charge was that Stanton would have done it for Locher, but because of personal animosity would not deliver for Stokes.

Stanton, who stood aloof during the entire struggle except to exercise his parliamentary authority, replied to Green's statement:

> On the question of the project itself, I've taken no position. Housing, in my judgment, would be the best utilization of the land. This does not endorse in any way any project which does not provide for the supportive services, problems which Councilmen Thompson and Pottinger have raised.

The exchange was publicized by the media, but the thrust of the issue was either ignored or minimized. The original objection to the project was based on insufficient city services to support a given area in its *present* condition. Addition of new units designed to accommodate large families would worsen conditions in the neighborhood unless adequate services were guaranteed for both the present and projected density and use of the area.

When the Mall rally proved to be somewhat less than successful, Carl Stokes tried another tactic. He scheduled a town hall meeting on June 12, 1969, in the Clara Tagg Brewer Junior High School which stands adjacent to the parcel designated for the project. Councilman Thompson mailed letters to his constituents urging them to attend. Walter A. Burks, City Hall personnel director, mailed letters to city workers urging them to attend the meeting. On the day of the rally Mayor Stokes held a ground-breaking ceremony on the site. CMHA had decided to go ahead and build seven houses and townhouses on East 153d Street, the western edge of the tract, to demonstrate the various types of units which would be offered for sale and rent.

There were some ugly and bitter exchanges at the town hall meeting that night. Councilman Clarence Thompson did not participate in the debate but stood silently at the rear of the room watching. Although perhaps three-fourths of the four hundred people gathered indicated that they would like council to conduct public hearings on the matter, opponents of the housing project dominated the meeting. A member of the committee, Mr. Henry Simon, said that the community was tired of waiting for improved recreation facilities for the young and for other promised services and deplored the fact that the housing authority had not consulted with residents before planning the project. The mayor in turn goaded him about having lived in the area for thirty years and asked why it was that he had taken such a late interest in the neighborhood youth.[24] He replied simply:

> Because I have a criminal record. . . . I was a hoodlum, and I'm ashamed of it. That's why I'm so concerned about the young people. I don't want them to have to resort to the kind of life I led. Now will you tell us your criminal record, Mr. Stokes?[25]

The mayor asked Simon to sit down, but he refused, saying, "You put me on display. I want everyone to see me. I never thought we'd have a mayor who would stoop so low."

Others at the meeting took objection to the mayor's accusations that the Lee-Seville residents were against poor people, and they accused the mayor of dividing the Negro community over the Lee-Seville issue. "You called us black bigots. That was a very divisive thing. It was also the turning point of this matter."[26] Any chance for negotiation and compromise had been lost, and the only alternative was a power struggle to determine the victor. All involved had to establish a hierarchy of values and line up with the man who for them represented the highest values.

Immediately following the ground-breaking ceremony, Jean Murrell Capers, who had become attorney for the Lee-Seville Homeowners Improvement Association, asked for a temporary restraining order to block construction of the housing development. The suit she filed also charged that an ordinance authorizing $890,000 in sewer and street improvements was contrary to the City Charter. Common Pleas Judge Francis J. Talty granted the temporary restraining order on June 25, 1969, instructing the city to revoke and withdraw all building permits for construction of the housing. Said Judge Talty:

> The court has heard unrefuted evidence that for the past twenty years homeowners in the area have been plagued by raw sewage from sewers. Basements and homes have been flooded. There has been clear proof that the health, safety, and lives of these citizens are now in grave peril. Any act threatening to expand this condition would be unlawful and improper.

Councilman Thompson was aided in the struggle by divine intervention on Sunday, July 20, when a heavy rain fell and the inadequate sewers in the Lee-Seville area backed up, flooding about one hundred fifty basements. Among the angry homeowners who appeared at City Hall were some who had opposed Thompson's stand on the housing project. "But," said Thompson, "when the problem of inadequate sewers finally affected them they could see why we have been fighting the project. . . . For months I have asked that the sewers in the area be cleaned out and have had no response from the service department. Legislation for improvements in the sewers is tied to the Lee-Seville project which the people do not want."

Council adjourned for the summer without resolving the Lee-Seville issue, preferring to wait until the voters in Wards Thirty and Thirteen could voice their desires by either returning Thompson and Pottinger or defeating them in favor of Stokes-endorsed candidates. Both candidates faced a run-off after the 1969 primary. Thompson was pitted against John E. Barnes, Pottinger against Robert C. McCall. Both Barnes and McCall were known to be favored, if not openly endorsed, by Mayor Stokes. The campaigns in both wards were dirty and divisive.

A Pottinger meeting in the basement of his ward headquarters on October 5 turned out to be a genuine experience in grassroots oratory. Each of the twenty people assembled spoke without hesitation and with surprising mastery. When asked about the technique of calling small group meetings by special invitation instead of larger rallies, Councilman Pottinger explained, "They express themselves better. . . . They speak much easier. When you get a hundred or two hundred people, certain ones shy away. A small group tends to dominate a meeting."

At the meeting a piece of campaign literature depicting Councilmen Pottinger and Thompson as puppets being manipulated by Council President Stanton was in evidence. The cartoon was captioned with some ugly allegations about the ethics of both men. Councilman Pottinger said:

> The mailing of a letter which wasn't exactly smut, but—. The way they do that is accuse the councilman of not doing various things, but they are things you can't do. Not getting more schools out here—this is not the councilman's job; a lack of police protection —this is done by the administration. We can bird dog the administration, but we neither can hire nor fire policemen. We pass legislation giving the administration the authority to do this.

Since the two councilmen had been accused of opposing the mayor, Pottinger was asked if he saw as his major challenge convincing the voters that, while he disagreed with the mayor on one issue, he was with him in general. Pottinger said that he had endorsed the mayor, had, in fact, cast but one vote in council against the mayor, and yet the press had picked him up as "that man who opposes the mayor." When asked why such a stir had been raised about their stand against the housing issue when very little was made of other councilmen bucking the mayor, Pottinger explained:

> Well, I think it's the fact that we are black councilmen—Thompson and myself. White councilmen are perhaps expected to be more critical of the mayor than black councilmen. For some reason—the feeling of black unity where what one black man says right down the line each other black man must say yes. They can still back a black man and disagree with him.

On the issue itself, when Pottinger was asked if CMHA could have built the housing project against the wishes of the residents had the sewer and street improvements been adequate, he replied in the affirmative. "They own the land and that's the only way they can be stopped. Just like any individual owning the land. And once the sewers are put in they can go right ahead as long as the buildings conform to the zoning."

During the same meeting another line of argument was advanced. The remarks of one woman seemed to typify the fears being expressed by the residents about the deterioration of their neighborhood:

> When we bought our house out here we didn't know how to be homeowners. We didn't know about garbage pickup, and keeping the lawn, and making repairs, and all. But we had good neighbors and they helped us learn how to be homeowners. Now a lot of these people will move here and they don't know anything about being homeowners or even good renters—and your habits travel with you. And who's going to teach them? If it's just one family on a block like we were, O.K. But you're going to put two hundred families together who don't know anything, and they'll just copy each other's bad habits. My house is worth $16,000 now, and I want it to be worth something ten years from now. If they want to help poor people get homes, why don't they have something like a GI loan with no down payment and low interest. That way they can buy a home anywhere they want to buy instead of putting them all in fifty acres and sticking us with a slum. That's hard talk, I know, but I'm just telling it like it is. And that's why I'm for this man here [Pottinger]. He knows what it's all about out here. That don't mean I'm against the mayor. I'm against my home and my neighborhood going down hill. I think the mayor's been sold a bill of goods.

When, in a controversy, arguments aimed at settling upon an acceptable solution for both parties fail, there is a tendency for an appeal to ultimate values or authorities. If you can't identify your own cause with what is right and holy you must try to identify your opponent with the devil and all things evil. When this type of argument begins to prevail, whatever opportunity there has been for discussion and resolution of doubts is ended, and the power struggle has begun. This stage of the controversy which leads to the power struggle was reached when Irving M. Kriegsfeld, CMHA director, resigned his post after a 3 to 0 vote by the CMHA board prohibiting employees from promoting the Lee-Seville proposal during the election campaign. Kriegsfeld had altered the bounds of debate from arguments about the merits of a particular case to a debate about the merits of public housing in general. In effect, he was saying that anyone against Lee-Seville was an enemy of public housing. A similar argument was that anyone against Lee-Seville was against Carl Stokes. Thompson and Pottinger, for the most part, continued to use practical arguments, although Thompson did claim that he had been approached with both bribes and threats by persons intent on "persuading" him to abandon the issue. It was evident that one side had to win or that an arbiter had to be called in to settle the dispute.

On the west side of Cleveland many residents became exercised about a new urban renewal program known as NDP (Neighborhood Development Program). NDP is a provision of the Federal Housing Act of 1968 which allows a city to apply for small-scale, short-term renewal projects. The procedures and requirements for eligibility, however, remain much the same as for the original urban renewal program. Areas eligible for aid must be identified officially as blighted areas, and this designation alone may cause the deterioration of a neighborhood.

Until October, 1969, when the Ohio legislature offered some relief, homeowners in urban renewal areas often found themselves cancelled out by insurance companies—a practice known as "red-lining." Through 1969 approximately 52 percent of Cleveland homes were in areas "red-lined" by insurance companies. Homeowners in renewal areas were often caught in other binds. Many were reluctant to invest in home repairs when they were uncertain about relocation, while at the same time they were apt to be overrun by city housing inspectors insisting that these properties be brought up to code standards. Residents learned fast enough from the experience of others to be suspicious of anything smacking of urban renewal. NDP might be a more equitable method of attacking blight, but when 1,300 acres are declared blighted in order to obtain funding for "small-bite" projects, the equity of it all lacks some credibility. Such was the situation on Cleveland's near west side.

Ward Three Councilman Michael Zone was seriously challenged in the 1969 primary and general campaigns by a candidate, Charles Augustine, whose sole issue was that NDP would destroy rather than renew the ward. Augustine invited two of the most vocal opponents of urban renewal to address an audience in his ward: Alfred Grisanti and Milt Schulman, both attorneys. Grisanti told the audience, "Urban renewal became a dirty word, so they had to change it, and they called it 'Neighborhood Development Program.'" Schulman argued that private money would not come into an area that was not stable and that from his own experience, when an area was designated for urban renewal, nobody knew what was going to happen or when, so the policy of most businessmen was just to stay away from the area. Schulman warned the residents that the city administration had come up with no specific plans for the area and that all they planned to do was establish scattered-site housing: "Scattered-site housing means they will buy a house here and a house there and put in what we call an undesirable element—welfare people, ADC women who are on welfare." He also warned that the titles of all properties in the designated area would carry the notation that they were in the renewal area.

These were alarmist tactics designed to play on the fears and prejudices of the audience, but there was an element of truth here. There is something psychologically defeating to both resident and potential investor when his area is designated by City Council as having "conditions of blight and deterioration which are detrimental to and a menace to the safety, health and welfare of the people who reside and work in the area and pass through the area in their daily lives, and which are detrimental to the general health, safety and welfare of the entire city of Cleveland and which substantially prevent, impair or arrest the sound growth of the area and surrounding areas and constitute an economic and social liability in the present conditions and use." That all property owners in the area would have their titles so identified was somewhat of an exaggeration, since only those properties to be acquired would be registered in the Cuyahoga County Recorder's office. However, none of the citizens on the near west side knew which properties were to be acquired.

Later, in an interview, Schulman said that he didn't think the city administration really had the money for NDP. "Furthermore," he said, "I'm sure that this administration [Nixon] is coming through with a whole new program, and it won't be NDP. I think what they'll do is massive housing—building of housing. I think it'll be out of the cities, built on vacant land outside the cities."

It was later revealed that the federal government had made no commitment of $10 million in NDP funds to Cleveland, as the administration at City Hall had claimed, and that all funds for the Midwest region had run out on June 30, 1969. Community Development Director Richard Green had not presented any proposals to council until May 29, which was much too late, since the City Charter not only requires public hearings on such matters, but ten days advance notice of the hearings. Director Green's department had originally applied for $60 million for NDP but was told by the regional director for the U.S. Department of Housing and Urban Development that the proposal was too large and unwieldy.

Green contended that Cleveland's urban renewal program in the past was very small, minute, poorly run, badly done, and that although Milt Schulman was one of the main individual opponents of the plan, the real problem was City Council.

> The one thing in Cleveland that nobody really described because it is indescribable is City Council. That is the key, in my judgment, to the problems of the city in many respects, and the key ultimately to the solutions of the problems. It's a problem in the city because you have thirty-three councilmen in a ward system, and their interests don't necessarily provide a city-wide view. They tend to be segmented.

The original problem of housing and community improvement seemed lost in the rhetoric of praise and blame, accusation and defense. Milt Schulman was arousing opposition to urban renewal on the west side, Mayor Stokes and Irving Kriegsfeld were identifying opponents to Lee-Seville with the devil, Richard Green was castigating council for failure to act on his programs, and council was lashing back at Green's management of the NDP issue.

Meanwhile a group of residents in downtown Cleveland embarked on their own self-renewal program with little or no help from City Hall. Residents from Wards Twenty-three and Thirty-one formed the Near-Town Association. In the first issue of the *Near-Town News*, the editor, Frank Friedel, traced the history of the association's struggle in his article "Near-Town Association—Who? What? Why?" He stated that after a booklet prepared by the Cleveland Planning Commission in 1956 literally wrote the downtown neighborhood off the books, saying that it would be completely industrialized by 1970, the entire community sat back and waited. Friedel said:

> Houses deteriorated, small businesses were forced to leave because the insurance was not available, or became too expensive to carry. Banks refused mortgage loans for the area and the City sold our recreation playfield to industry.
>
> Too many of us felt that Near-Town living was an asset. We are close to our jobs, our schools, and our hospitals.
>
> Some of our neighbors sat back and waited apathetically, did nothing. These could almost see the bulldozers standing at their back door. Many did not give up. They continued to "keep up" their properties.
>
> Then one day, the City Inspectors showed up at the front door, demanding that our homes be brought up to City code, *immediately*. Bulldozers standing at the back door and City Inspectors at the front door!"[27]

So the Near-Town Association was formed to get answers to the questions: "Were we being asked by our City to fix up so that we could stay, or were we to become another urban renewal blunder?"

The Near-Town Association residents chose not to give up their homes and instead brought their properties up to code standards; many even went a step further—new siding, new roofing, new sidewalks, and fencing. They developed their own recreation programs for boys and girls, including softball in the summer, movies, bowling, and hockey in the winter. When, after nearly twenty years of abuse and neglect by the city the residents asked for a recreation center for their children, they were publicly chastized by the *Cleveland Press*[28] for putting their selfish interests above those of the city which needed the $400,000 to plant shrubbery along Superior Avenue and East Twelfth Street! Council and the administration eventually went through the motions of approving the recreation center, but the reality took longer. The irony of the situation bears looking into by the city planners—that so much energy is expended in trying to impose "improvements" on neighborhoods who strongly resist "help" while another's cries for assistance go unheeded.

However insignificant, the fact was that in 1969 the administration did *attempt* to solve problems in the areas of law and order, housing, and race relations. Certainly hiring better and more policemen was a step in the right direction; building more housing and staking out areas for improvements was a step towards solving that problem; working with blacks and other disadvantaged to offer better opportunities for economic development was progress. Unfortunately the type of rhetoric employed in the process inhibited rather than advanced good intentions. And what should have been a normal controversy over alternative plans for meeting the city's needs developed into a conflict over whose values were the "rightest," and these conflicts developed into crises.

Once the controversialist has invoked his plan's most virtuous and honorable sanctions he can no longer advance his cause. With an unconvinced society, at this point, the debate has reached its end. The conflict must be settled by some other means. When possible, an arbiter is usually called in. In Cleveland the arbiter was the voter. Election time rolled around again, and the arbiters were faced with permitting Carl Stokes to have another try at solving their problems or choosing someone else to assume the mantle of leadership.

CHAPTER 7

TIME OUT FOR ARBITRATION

WHILE NO ONE was winning the debate in Cleveland on the various issues, the participants involved in the struggle agreed to carry their arguments to a "higher court," but not for the purpose of allowing the court to settle the dispute. Their purpose was to ask the judges whether the contest should be continued with the same or new players. In most cases when an arbitrator is called in, he is given the power to render final decisions when the processes of popular persuasion will no longer serve. Of course, the arbitrator must command obedience to his decision.

Such an arbitrator is the voter. He is respected by all those who seek out his decision, even though it sometimes means that some highly competent contributors to the political process are shut out by the announcement of the verdict. In the winner-takes-all game of politics, the electorate gives no quarter to the also-ran on the day after election, even at the cost of losing wise counsel and great leadership. In some ways, though, the contest for the mayor's office in a large city recalls the circumstances of Shirley Jackson's short story "The Lottery." Throughout the story the reader is kept in suspense as details of the village's preparation for the great day of the lottery begin to unfold. After all the suspense about the event and the prize to be won, it is revealed that the holder of the "lucky" number wins the right to be stoned to death by his friends and neighbors.

Nonetheless it was election time again, and the time to review the facts in the dispute was at hand. Stokes obviously would have to come before the people and say why he deserved the opportunity to continue with the decision-making process he had already begun, that he had not had sufficient time to bring his dreams to fruition. Perhaps he would also say that though he had made mistakes, he had learned a lot and would ask for an extension to prove his worth. His opponent would have to convince the voters that Stokes was not capable of continuing in the task they had assigned to him.

THE 1969 PRIMARY

Again what the voter had to decide was not how to solve the various problems which beset the city, but who was capable of solving them: the incumbents or the challengers. The early excitement about the primary race that had occurred in 1967 was not evident in 1969. There was no urgency to file petitions, to begin a campaign. The city was engaged in a period of decision-making resulting from change and not beginning a movement for change. The people were curious but not terribly excited. Talk centered upon Ralph Perk, county auditor and the prospective Republican candidate in the general election. Was he ill? Well enough to campaign? He had been in and out of the hospital all summer. However, Perk did file, although the Democratic primary was not his race. He filed and simply waited for the general election.

Plain Dealer political writer James Naughton speculated whether Carl Stokes would file as an Independent. Finally Robert J. Kelly, former services director under Ralph Locher, decided to run on the Democratic ticket. Sydney Stapleton of the Socialist Workers party was the first candidate to file his petitions. Louis F. Molnar, the American Independent party candidate, filed but was ruled ineligible. Stokes filed (also as a Democrat), and it appeared that there might be a primary contest after all.

On July 6, 1969, Naughton wrote: "Whatever happened to justice? Here it is the first week of the campaign for mayor of Cleveland and the key contenders are prattling about law and order." According to Naughton, everyone in Cleveland was jumping on the law-and-order bandwagon:

> Mayor Carl B. Stokes is promising to do his all. His Democratic primary opponent, Robert J. Kelly, is pledging to do better than the mayor had in 19 months, which is not so hot. Ralph J. Perk is vowing to save tax money and use it to provide more policemen on the streets. Louis F. Molnar of Cleveland's right wing is intent upon arresting every criminal in sight. . . .

That Robert Kelly chose to challenge Carl Stokes on the issue of law and order was not unusual, for Cleveland was reflecting national as well as local concerns, and law and order was Carl Stokes's most vulnerable point. However, phrases like "law and order," "equal law enforcement," and "safety on the streets" were being tossed about by all candidates—liberal as well as conservative. In Cleveland's primary, it soon became obvious that Robert Kelly meant to question Mayor Stokes's ability to cope with the problems of law enforcement; while other problems would be spotlighted, they would be of secondary importance.

What Robert Kelly did not realize was that he had to, in turn, present an alternative. He had to convince the people that he could handle the task more efficiently and fairly. Since few people in town really knew who Robert Kelly was, his assignment was difficult. The people surrounding Robert Kelly were a colorful lot, and the news media missed a good story in not researching that organization. But the campaign to win votes never got off the ground. The Kelly forces started with sixty thousand votes and ended with sixty thousand votes, but it was a grand celebration anyway.

Among Kelly's workers was State Representative Patrick A. Sweeney, a bright, young, red-haired bachelor who felt he could learn something from this campaign experience. Sweeney's attitude revealed no hope of victory. He was alternately frustrated and cynical. "I'll never back a *non-politician* again," he'd say. At the end of the primary he was asked, "What now?" and he grinned and remarked like a Kennedy, "I intend to reassess my position."

Another worker was William Nagy, a bailiff and close friend of Sweeney's. Nagy was well read, given to philosophical statements and poetic interjections. He was also very candid. "Go easy on that academic stuff," he remarked during an interview, "or they'll [the Kelly people] never talk to you."

John P. Butler, a well-known defense attorney and an eloquent speaker himself, contributed to the speech writing efforts of the organization. When he sometimes appeared on the platform with Kelly he almost stole the show.

Al Thomas, Kelly's advance man, was constantly excited about something "big" that was going to happen (and never did). He was a fascinating study in indecision. Immediately after the primary he planned to meet with attorney Milt Schulman and discuss the possibility of supporting Ralph Perk. But the weekend prior to Kelly's announcement of support for Ralph Perk, Thomas decided to make public his intention to support Carl Stokes—the same man whose reelection Thomas had been sure, only a few days previously, would spell doom for the city.

Another man supporting the Kelly candidacy was Milt Schulman. Schulman wanted Robert Kelly to take the hard law-and-order line. Although a staunch Stokes supporter in 1967, Schulman now campaigned vigorously against Stokes, especially his urban redevelopment programs, at the ward level. Schulman believed in Robert Kelly, at the beginning anyway, but soon became irritated that Kelly wasn't taking his advice.

Many people wrote speeches for Kelly and prepared pieces of campaign literature for him. A small campaign newspaper which Doris O'Donnell, former *Plain Dealer* reporter, helped design reproduced newspaper headlines highlighting all the problems in the Stokes administration. One headline read: "[Cleveland:] NOW! Funds Buy Guns." The misuse of Cleveland: NOW! funds, the civil service fiasco, the foundation grant to William Silverman, and other similar matters were featured. The makeup of the paper was dramatic and the intended impact unmistakable; however, the paper was designed only to attack the Stokes administration, and very little of the Kelly image came through. Kelly is a tall, blue-eyed Irishman who should photograph well, but of all his campaign pictures, only a small family picture was flattering to him. A pamphlet entitled "Our Cities, Cleveland as Archetype" was distributed by the Kelly people and later, during the general election, by the Perk people (who charged twenty-five cents for it). "Our Cities" rehashed the same material brought out in the 1967 "Democratic Letters," attacked Stokes's decisions and actions on Glenville, and generally traced Stokes's career and personal life in unflattering terms. It further claimed that Stokes had purchased a half million dollars' worth of property at Queen's Cove, near Freeport, on Grand Bahama Island. Another item stated that "red Killer [Ahmed] Evans [was] financed by a Stokes project." The author also cited one little publicized incident concerning Jean Capers, the original Stokes supporter and more recently the attorney who had filed suit on behalf of the Lee-Seville Home Owners Improvement Association to prevent construction of the public housing project in that neighborhood. According to the article, "On March 17, 1969, the *Plain Dealer* reported that Mrs. Capers' office had been destroyed by fire. Firemen reported smelling gasoline. Again Stokes' opponents seemed to be the victims of Voodoo." While the pamphlet committed to print all the ugly rumors used in the whispering campaign of 1967 and summarized events of 1968, it served only to bind the radical right to Robert Kelly and to alienate the moderates and liberals.

Even after viewing all the literature about Kelly and speaking to all his supporters, Kelly somehow lacked an identity. The question in the minds of many Clevelanders remained: "Who's Kelly?" Norman Wagy,

WJW-TV, shed some interesting light on the man's background:

> I recall back in the days I was covering City Hall and was in his office every day that he was indeed the one bright ray of hope. We had many arguments about his decisions [as services director]. I had tremendous respect for him. In the days I covered City Hall it was kind of a pleasure to talk to Bob because he was not the drone, not the timeserver.

The man Wagy had known never came into focus during the campaign. The political picture of Robert Kelly that did emerge was most clearly defined by television newsman and commentator Hugh Danaceau, who made these comments midway during the campaign:

> Robert Kelly's major mistake, if one can call it a mistake, because in order to make a mistake you usually have to have a choice of one or more things. What he did was this. When he filed he immediately had the extreme right wing, and the extreme right wing—Kelly could wave a Communist party card with his name on it and the right wing would still vote for him. And yet, through the whole campaign, instead of appealing to the middle and the liberal, he has continued through the campaign to appeal to this narrow right wing, which may be the way he feels personally. I, personally, feel this is not the way he feels, but *somebody* has talked him into this. And he has directed everything towards the extreme right, and they all applaud him in their small numbers, and they turn out in their small numbers, as they have tonight, and they will all vote for him, but nobody else will. So, from a political point of view—and we've heard him outline all the promises Carl Stokes made to get elected and never kept—the fact is Carl Stokes got elected by doing certain things and Bob Kelly is not going to get elected because he has not done certain things, and that is trying to appeal to as many voters as he can. He has kept his appeal to these people whom he knows are for him, and it's all very comfortable and there may be a psychological—maybe he should go to a psychologist about that—but it's all very comfortable for him to appeal to these people because they applaud him and his message is the same to these people. He knows all the code words—law and order and all that.
>
> He's neglected the middle and liberals, and he should have gone after them and he never would have lost the right wing. He's a

> white man and Carl's a black man. The name of the game is "get elected." And if you're going to play this game with Stokes, there's nothing wrong with playing a racial game for votes because Carl does and did. That's how he got elected.
>
> Let me give you a few little figures. Ken McGee, who is not with Carl anymore but who helped Carl get elected in 1967, in 1965—these are McGee figures, they may be off a little bit—in 1965, 35 percent of the qualified electorate—this doesn't necessarily mean they're registered—but the qualified electorate in Negro wards went to the polls. If in 1969, this year, we have 70 percent going to the polls, that would be a pretty good turnout in any area. And if 70 percent went to the polls, Stokes would lose, because in 1967 he got 85 percent, so if it drops just that much—

And in the Stokes camp they were worried that it might drop just that much. Carl Stokes and his workers began Operation Voter Registration. On July 10, 1969, Stokes began a push to register 50,000 new voters by August 20. The push was financed by the $100-a-plate dinner honoring the mayor in April. A registration rally was arranged by the Reverend Arthur LeMon, a Stokes aide then on leave from his City Hall post. In spite of all the accompanying hoopla, the first registration effort was unproductive. According to the *Plain Dealer* of August 16, "The special county-wide neighborhood registration conducted in August was poor. Just 6,862 Clevelanders, mostly white, registered to vote. About 15,000 fewer persons were registered than in 1967."

A special drive to register voters in predominately Negro wards was then undertaken. Employees of the city of Cleveland received letters asking them to volunteer for the drive. City administrators were made responsible for registration in Wards Thirteen, Thirty, Twenty-four, Twenty-seven, Nineteen, Twenty, Seventeen, and Sixteen. Despite all the effort, however, there was still a decrease of 10,000 voters, with most of the drop occurring in the Negro wards. The two wards with the largest reduction in the number of registered voters were Ward Seventeen (in the Central Avenue SE area) and Ward Eighteen (in the Cedar Avenue SE area near University Circle).

From all these voter registration activities in the Stokes camp, Kelly derived what he believed was his first real campaign issue. He charged irregularities in the voter registration and demanded an investigation by the Board of Elections. The charge centered around the report that some young Stokes workers had set up a table outside a school and asked prospective voters to sign a registration sheet. At least nine of these

Fun Day on the Mall
Photograph courtesy of City of Cleveland

persons were misled into thinking they had registered to vote.[1] While Election Board Democratic officers John J. Carney and Dan Duffy contended no serious harm was done, Robert Kelly said, "Someone has attempted to make a farce out of a very sacred thing."

Kelly hit this issue over and over again in his early speeches but derived very little publicity from his efforts, with the exception that he scored a moral victory when he forced City Hall to write letters to all city employees informing them of the civil service laws and urging them not to participate in campaign activities. Kelly claimed city officials had coerced employees into campaign work. John P. Butler and Milt Schulman filed a petition with the Court of Common Pleas charging coercion of city employees to work on behalf of the mayor's election. Kelly's lawyers contended that "coerced" city workers had been used to stuff envelopes with campaign literature, to register voters in pro-Stokes wards, and to prevent registration in predominantly white wards. An agreement was reached in the chambers of Common Pleas Judge Bernard Friedman, and city department directors were given three days to get letters to their workers advising them of civil service laws prohibiting political activity by civil service employees.[2]

Robert Kelly's victory in the registration matter received little notice throughout the city by the local press, however. Despite the moral overtones of the issue, its appeal was "trivial" to most newsmen and to most of the public.

In early August open dissent appeared within the Cuyahoga County Democratic party leadership. County Chairman Albert S. Porter resigned. There had been a confrontation between Porter and James Stanton when Stanton refused to second the Stokes nomination. At a meeting of the Cuyahoga County Democratic Executive Committee on July 31, Stokes received the nomination. In an effort to help Kelly, John P. Butler, however, moved that the Stokes nomination be tabled and that the Democrats have an open primary where no candidate would have the party endorsement. Butler asked that the vote on his motion be made by secret ballot. Porter ruled the motion out of order. The motion to table the Stokes nomination was tabled.

Theoretically, political parties in this country are designed on a pyramidal model in which the total party membership of a county elects representatives by precinct to a county committee. This body of elected representatives from the precincts elects from its members the officers and executives of the county committee. Again, theoretically, primary elections are held so that the party members at the bottom of the pyramid can indicate which candidates should be the party standard-bearers in the various election races. Unfortunately, this model of democratic participation in the political process rarely operates that way. The county committee is usually too large and unwieldy to operate efficiently as a policy-making group, and a great deal of control and power is placed in the hands of the committee officers and executive committee. The model, under such circumstances, is overturned, and the power descends from the small group at the top to the individual voter at the bottom. Instead of heeding the wishes of the general party membership, the party brass tries to impose its wishes on the party electors. The purpose of a party primary is completely negated when the party brass steps in to endorse candidates. In recent years the general party membership has been independent enough to disregard such "bossist" interference during the nomination of standard-bearers in the primary elections. However, the party brass still tries to invoke sanctions against candidates whom it disfavors. Such was the case in Cuyahoga County when on August 22 Dr. Samuel R. Gerber, who became acting chairman of the Democratic party, *ordered* party leaders not to allow unendorsed candidates to speak at party functions. Such orders have the effect of cutting off a candidate from the very audience he must reach. Possibly because of pressure from councilmen who objected to the ruling, Gerber wrote to Kelly on August 26 giving Kelly permission to speak at ward meetings *so long as no one else spoke for him, so long as he didn't criticize the endorsed candidates, and so long as he did not personally pass out campaign literature!*[3] Not one of the news media thought this callous flouting of the democratic process significant enough for comment.

On August 9 Kelly officially opened his campaign by calling Cleveland a "jungle." This was the real thrust and key to his whole campaign—the return of law and order. According to the *Plain Dealer*, Kelly stated that if necessary he would ask assistance of the Ohio National Guard in restoring order to the city. The point Kelly actually made about the Ohio National Guard was unfortunately distorted. Kelly and his advisers had met with Ohio National Guard Adj. Gen. Sylvester T. Del Corso and were told that until Cleveland's police force was brought up to its authorized strength, arrangements could be made to use Ohio National Guard personnel by means of temporary assignments to the force. Both voter and mass media response to this issue was insignificant. A month later, on September 9, the *Cleveland Press* ran a cartoon on its editorial page showing Stokes and Kelly in a fight ring. It was captioned, "Pretty Dull, So Far." Because of the general atmosphere of the campaign, as defined by the *Press* cartoon, reporters just couldn't get excited about Robert Kelly.

Kelly's organization was anything but solid and efficient. Al Thomas voiced disapproval of the entire structure. Patrick Sweeney was frustrated by the candidate. Kelly workers would not stay in the downtown headquarters after 5:00 P.M. because they claimed the streets were not safe. Scheduling was mishandled with alarming consistency as Kelly's campaign appearances often failed to coincide with his announced schedule.

The newspaper accounts revealed an inept organization to the public, which naturally reflected on the abilities of the candidate, and the Kelly people became irritated with the media—with some justification. On September 30, 1969, the *Plain Dealer* stated:

> Kelly thought he was invited to speak to the Democratic Women's Club of Cuyahoga County, meeting in the Hotel Statler Hilton. He was met by the president, Grace Giblin, who told him, "We didn't expect you. We've got business to conduct. You'll have to wait." So Kelly stood around for a half hour. Every once in a while, a member would pop her head out the door to say, "Five more minutes." Finally Kelly told Mrs. Giblin he had to go to another meeting. She pleaded for him to wait five more minutes, but he stuck his head through the door and yelled at the 75 or so women, "Hello, I'm Bob Kelly. Don't forget to vote on Sept. 30." Five minutes after Kelly left, Mayor Carl B. Stokes showed up, was introduced, made a speech and went his way.

The newsmen were standing in the corridor *outside* the meeting, so that their story was made up of inferences, not facts. Grace Giblin told the members she was not going to introduce Robert Kelly before the mayor showed up. Most of the members interviewed about the incident were displeased that Grace Giblin had not allowed Kelly to speak. The fact was that Robert Kelly had shown up on schedule and the mayor was late. Grace Giblin dragged the meeting on, much to the chagrin of several restless members. She introduced Clerk of Municipal Courts Helen J. Lyons who came to the podium and spoke briefly. It was apparently Grace Giblin's logic that, out of courtesy, the mayor should be allowed to speak first and that Kelly should wait, no matter how fidgety the assembled members became.

What really happened was that Robert Kelly opened the door to the meeting room, stepped halfway in and, over Grace Giblin's protests, said that he was Robert Kelly and "Please remember to vote." Grace Giblin rushed to the door, as if to bar the intruder, and said confusedly, "Oh dear."

Grace Giblin nervously continued the "business" of the meeting for another five minutes before Carl Stokes appeared with a flock of "Stokes Folks" and made a few remarks. His speeches were typical of the incumbent candidate. Recognizing the nature of the rhetorical task, he reviewed his record and asked the voters to retain him so that he could complete the job.

Stokes began by introducing Helen Lyons and talked about the pleasant day he had had: "I bowled tonight for the first time in almost ten years, just bowled two balls, but after ten years, what do you want? Then played a little basketball, and of all people to beat me, a newsman beat me at playing. Now you know he's got to tell everyone about it." He spoke glowingly of a new dining place on Harvard Avenue and then launched into the main topic—defense of his administration:

> Let me tell you briefly what being mayor has been to me. I've enjoyed the last two years. They've been, very often, we'd incur frustrations. We'd encounter some problems over which we had never had any experience to work with, but it meant we had to use our imagination and inventiveness to get the advice and help of other people and in some kind of way we worked through every problem and come out with the city better for it and ourselves better for it. There's one thing you cannot buy and that's experience, and the mistakes we made, I think you know we've acknowledged our mistakes and what we've tried to do is learn from those mistakes so that, in fact, they teach you how to do things better, so in this way I've been given the opportunity to grow and learn things and be able to respond to problems better. I would want to feel that in carrying the banner of the Democratic party that I've acquitted myself in office in a way to make you proud.

Stokes talked about developing civic pride, saying that Cleveland: NOW! had brought people together. "We've tackled housing, transportation. We've demonstrated that we can do the kind of job the city needed to have done." He claimed that, "We can go to any section and say that the million dollar recreation center is going up. We're able to talk about streets being surfaced, that the street cleaning has been better." He spoke about obtaining federal money, putting in mercury-vapor lights, and he finally launched into the improvements in the police department, claiming that there wasn't a police automobile over two years old, that there were seven tactical units with the finest equipment, that 213 policemen were taking college courses paid for by the department. He said, "The city of Cleveland that ranks eighth in population ranks tenth in crime. A job is being done in public safety, at least to the extent that is possible. We put 300 policemen on the streets, took them off desk jobs." There was a running theme of "everyone makes mistakes" (also used by Mayor Lindsay in New York). Stokes delivered the speech quietly, somberly, and left immediately upon its conclusion to attend a class reunion on the east side.

Later in the campaign Kelly became the subject of another instance of observation-inference confusion by the media. On September 24 at Clara Westropp School on the west side, Robert Kelly uttered something that sounded like the word "nigger."

That night Jim Cox of WJW-TV seemed to be the only newsman present who tape-recorded the disputed passage. He gathered up his crew, phoned in to the station that he had the "hottest story of the campaign," and sped back to the station where Marty Ross and Doug Adair, the anchor men who were not present at the event, decided how the film clip should be used, where to edit the film to show the essential information, and what remarks to make about it.

There is no doubt that had Kelly actually used the term there would have been a story worthy of note, but it would seem that an alert reporter would have interviewed Kelly, Stanton (who had just left the stage), and anyone else available who might have clarified the matter. Sydney Stapleton, the Socialist Workers party candidate who was on the platform, insisted he had heard the word and called Kelly a racist. Interviewed in the back of the room at the time, Kelly's friend, Arthur Pagel, said he hadn't heard anything, looked puzzled, and claimed it "must be a smear tactic." Several other people in the back of the room hadn't heard anything unusual. John Butler was stopped as he was leaving, and he claimed he had not heard the word. The people in the front rows, obviously, had heard something, because they were the first to question Kelly about his use of the word.

From the front near the stage it sounded like Kelly had said "nigger neighbors," a startling comment to make unless Kelly wished to lose the election. Jim Cox went out into the hall to replay the tape. Intent upon the utterance itself, rather than the sense of it, the tape certainly sounded, at the time, like "nigger neighbor." When Marty Ross listened to the tape he remarked:

> Well, it stuck in his mind, and it slipped out without any meaning at all. "Well," he said, "we're getting a lot of them." I think I'll pick it up earlier. He's talking about Negroes and his mind stuck

> on it and that's how he refers to them, and there's no doubt in my mind about that.

The WJW-newsmen went into the viewing room and ran the film. What Kelly had been talking about "getting a lot of" were complaints. This is the context in which the controversial word or utterance appeared:

> Well, I want to tell you a few more things. I have a few minutes left. I have to run out. I've been with you and this city working in your behalf for thirteen years as your city traffic engineer. Left some records behind me, some pretty good ones I'm proud of. Many times I've argued with *you* [nigger?] *neighbors* about traffic regulations, but it was for a good cause because we did in fact break the records on fatal accidents. I'm the guy picked up your garbage for you. Used to wait thirty days to pick up rubbish, then it was done weekly and can be improved further.

Note that the pronoun was "you" not "your." The audience was white, and there were no black neighborhoods bordering the neighborhood in which Kelly was speaking. Nothing in the subject-matter context nor the context of the locale could explain the use of the term.

Kelly had stumbled on words many times before; at times during the campaign his speech had been almost unintelligible. That night he had a rasping throat; when he was asked about the controversial word, it was obvious he did have a real problem with his voice.[4]

Later that evening, Kelly wanted to hear the tape of the speech for himself. It took several minutes to find the statement on the tape. Kelly grew impatient. He didn't believe he had said the word. His wife, Anne, called to say that she had called the station, WJW, and they had played the tape for her. Kelly's friend Arthur Pagel was with him, and he was worried. "Do you think this will lose us the colored vote?" he asked. He appeared perfectly serious. His next question was, "Do you think he should apologize?" Then Pagel went over to Kelly. "We think you should apologize."

"For what?" said Kelly. "For a cold? Never!"

The incident was aired over and over again by the television and radio stations until it was firmly implanted in the minds of the audience that Kelly had, in fact, used the word. The story went on television three times and on radio six times until Hal Morgan, WJW-radio newsman, called in orders to kill it. (At William Franklin's headquarters in Ward Ten on primary election night, an elderly gentleman not sophisticated in the ways of broadcasting, said, "He [Kelly] said that nigger word *three* times. He ought not had done that." The man had obviously heard the soundtrack three times and assumed that each was a report of a fresh occurrence.)

Speculation on Kelly's motives ran as high as whether he had, in fact, committed the unspeakable. Kelly claimed the next day that he said "nearby" neighbors. Politicians and newsmen didn't think it mattered much one way or the other. Robert Kelly had been written off early in the primary. True, he had not gathered around him an effective organization, nor, seemingly, did he have a particularly loyal organization. Kelly was apparently lacking in sufficient money to run even a meager campaign, and he certainly had no newspaper support. Even his major thrusts at the Stokes administration were not penetrating enough. Kelly tried to warm up the issues of the civil service scandals, the lack of pollution control, and Stokes's refusal to step into the McDonald's dispute. But just as the registration drive issue was deflated when Stokes's department heads sent out letters reminding city employees not to participate in the campaign, so was the McDonald's issue deflated when Stokes finally did step into the negotiations on September 26. In effect, Kelly's criticism allowed Stokes to demonstrate that he was capable of correcting his own mistakes.

Probably the most eloquent public speaking during the 1969 primary campaign came from attorney John Butler, a Kelly supporter. Always immaculately attired, Butler's penetrating knowledge of government, his easy, articulate delivery, his choice of meaningful and appropriate language held audiences entranced. Butler usually gave the "warm up" speech for Kelly. He would begin by placing their cause into a moral perspective:

> The first obligation of any government in the history of the world has been the protection of life and property. The ancient cities of Athens and Rome, from which we derived our patterns, didn't have any Muny Light Plant, . . . but they had a police department. And that is the primary function of government. Without it, nothing else is any good. We contend that there has been a complete breakdown in the protection of life and property that has shocked the nation. That's why we make that our main issue of the campaign.

In concluding, Butler would visualize for the audience what impending disasters would face the city if Kelly were to lose; then, dramatically dropping the level of his voice, he would say, "Ah—but he can't lose." The crowds loved Butler and his performance. Kelly would acknowledge in his opening remarks how hard it was to follow Butler. Unfortunately, Kelly generally had to follow Butler, and the comparison was unavoidable.

However, in the Stokes camp, no one seemed to notice. It was obvious that no one was listening to Robert Kelly or his eloquent aide. Everyone was busy trying to discover how to campaign. Information from the 1967 campaign was not available. Ostrow was out of the picture. Though William Silverman was around, at the time of the City Club debate he said that he had not been involved. The knowledgeable workers of the 1967 campaign were noticeably missing. One worker who had been around in 1967 said, "It's not the same, believe me."

In the office of Gwen Scott (Arnold Pinkney's secretary), a worker came in wanting some figures on ethnic distribution on the west side. She was advised to call Dr. Thomas Campbell of Cleveland State University. Dr. Campbell was the resource person for the campaign, filling much the same role that Dr. Louis Masotti (then of Case Western Reserve) took in 1967.

Even Arnold Pinkney, Stokes's new campaign manager, was uncertain. He asked if there were any records of how many bumper stickers were ordered in 1967—how many balloons, buttons, etc. Pinkney said he was trying to put together some sort of organization, but that they wouldn't really get started until the general election. Plans were being formulated to recruit young people as workers, to get high school and college students involved. "We want to run a grassroots campaign now," Pinkney told me. "The mayor's good with small groups." Kelly as an opponent was simply dismissed. "The mayor's strategy is to ignore him," said Pinkney.

Stokes "ignored" his Democratic opponent in interesting ways. First, he challenged Ralph J. Perk and "any other legitimate candidates" to debate the issues of the campaign. Although he made this statement on the day he filed, Stokes obviously did not consider Robert Kelly's candidacy "legitimate" because he not only would not debate Kelly, though challenged repeatedly; he would not even acknowledge the challenges. The one exception was the traditional City Club debate. Several times Stokes referred to Kelly as "that other fellow" in the race. Except that he was pressured into stepping into the McDonald's dispute at the last minute, Stokes never specifically answered Kelly's charges about the civil service mess, the increasing crime rate, etc. Instead, Stokes mournfully decried the "base tactics" used by the "other guy."

Stokes's strategy paid off. Kelly was never able to establish an image of himself, but Stokes was successful in creating an unfavorable image of Kelly as a faceless, insignificant man given to "base tactics," a racist who was playing upon the fears of the city with his law-and-order theme.

Furthermore, this early in the campaign Carl Stokes was not about to reveal his true strength. He attended meetings, but he didn't say much. He went east and he went west, but somehow he did not project the eager enthusiasm that he had in 1967. At one of Stokes's speaking engagements, in a west side hall that was not primarily a "Stokes" audience, one could sense some tension. Stokes was somber in his presentation. A listening reporter whispered, "Take a look at the women. They're not hostile." The mayor had not lost his ability to charm even though his manner was less outgoing than it had been two years before.

Carl Stokes was more relaxed among groups on whose support he knew he could count. At a Ward Three gathering he danced with the Puerto Ricans, and at a breakfast meeting on the east side he just talked, laughed, and philosophized. This particular breakfast was given for the mayor by Ward Ten council candidate William Franklin. Most of the guests were Franklin workers, but when Franklin's opponent John C. Armstrong arrived, Mrs. Franklin graciously seated him and saw to it that he had breakfast.

When Carl Stokes arrived he was hugged by all the women. He sat down next to Naomi Wilcox, a ward leader who had first started Stokes on his political career as state representative. She obviously was a respected person in the Mount Pleasant community. Another woman from Ward Ten said that Naomi Wilcox called Carl Stokes to her home and told him that she knew he couldn't come out and support William Franklin, but he'd better not say anything against him. Carl Stokes listened. He treated Naomi Wilcox with considerable deference that morning.

Harllel Jones came in to say hello and to remind the mayor that he had "black power." "Well, you're going to see some white power," answered the mayor. At the table a discussion about the election began and the mayor remarked that people just didn't understand what was going on. Mrs. Thomas Whelan objected:

> Mayor Stokes, we here understand better than you think we do, and we're not colored—our minds are not colored by what we read. We read in between the lines nowadays and I think the majority of the people are both black and white and I think we do understand that there are a few things behind the scenes that we

> never hear of. We understand much more, and this is an intelligent public out here.

The mayor listened graciously and responded:

> I believe that, too. But you know what's going to happen on Tuesday and on Tuesday, November 4? We're gonna win. And in the story—even as our own people are concerned—we won, but the whole process of what happened—some of the things that were done, all this really ought to be recorded.
>
> There's a book that I rely upon heavily called *Who Governs* by Robert Dahl [New Haven, Connecticut: Yale University Press, 1961]. Tells the story of the ethnic and minority groups and takes you just about through the time of Fiorello La Guardia. Now what he does, he basically records certain topics and he has the capacity of some insight. He deals with the interplay of what happened in that European and ethnic group—its recorded events. I'm a little more interested in recorded events behind the scenes. We're watching some things going on—this Corrigan—that's the kind of low—but Corrigan got Thompson out of it. Got him out from underneath that thing when we were gonna burn him. [Referring here to Clarence Thompson's charge that he had been threatened and offered bribes to keep quiet on the Lee-Seville issue. County Prosecutor [John T.] Corrigan called Thompson in to hear his story but did not investigate.] When a guy [Civil Services Commissioner Marvin Chernoff] criticizes, criticizes a grand jury indictment, right away the prosecutor says, "Well, if you have something you know, we'll call you in before the grand jury." You know what that's saying to the people? It's not saying anything. This is the way the police states are formed.

At this point the mayor was reminded that everything was being tape-recorded. "Well," he replied, "you're the only one I know who is. You know, someone ought to keep a diary of everything that goes on at City Hall." Then, laughing, he added, "And if I ever catch anyone doing that, I'll fire him."

The mayor was in good spirits that day. After the breakfast meeting he went to the opening of the Steel Workers Credit Union. His brother, Congressman Louis Stokes, was there, as were Congressman Michael A. Feighan and County Auditor Ralph J. Perk. Stokes kidded Ralph Perk about his Florida tan and said he'd have to be careful or Perk would take

Mayor Carl Stokes and Congressman Louis Stokes
Photograph courtesy of the City of Cleveland

away "his" votes. It was a dreary, rainy day and they stood under a canopy at the new building which had just been dedicated. Campaign fare that day was ham and eggs in the morning, hot dogs and beer for lunch.

Throughout the campaign Carl Stokes continued to ignore Robert Kelly; however, the Democratic voters did have one opportunity to view their candidates together when Kelly and Stokes debated at the traditional City Club meeting.

The most significant aspect of this debate was that for the first time Robert Kelly emerged as a personable and aggressive contender for the office of mayor. Kelly spoke energetically about the failures of the administration; cited the civil service scandals; reminded the audiences (in the room and at home) that the voters had authorized $100 million in bonds for the elimination of water pollution and that the mayor had failed to take appropriate action to issue the bonds and activate remedial programs. Kelly presented proposals with regard to finance and recreation and insisted that the protection of life and property was still the first and foremost obligation of government. The mayor, in his opening remarks, spoke with pride about his administration and through the use of elaborate graphs and charts stressed that Cleveland's crime rate was not as bad as it had been painted by the opposition.

The prime issue raised in the question-and-answer period was Stokes's handling of the Glenville issue. Kelly said, "My actions before the Glenville massacre would have been different. I would not have sent agents out to make a contract with the snipers." He was referring to George Forbes's conversation with Ahmed Evans prior to the outbreak of shooting. The mayor answered very solemnly:

> Nothing in the two years I have been in office was as crushing to me as what took place in Glenville. I took an action, after eight agonized hours of deliberation, calculated to save the lives of policemen as well as civilians. I valued human life over property. This did result in the cessation of those hostilities. I feel I did the right thing. If the circumstances were exactly the same, and God forbid they would be, I would act the same.

The audience was heavily salted with Stokes supporters, and the mayor was rewarded with applause several times. Kelly was hissed once after he referred to Stokes's crime charts and said, "I wish I had taxpayers' money so I could make pretty charts."

The only election promise made by Carl Stokes was the establishment of a program of "bloc grants" to the various wards in the city for the accomplishment of specific projects particularly desired by the people in the ward. Stokes said the money for the projects, amounting to between $40 million and $60 million, would come from the rental of Cleveland-owned property in the suburbs. Presumably the mayor was referring to the city-owned land in Warrensville Township where Seth Taft (and later Stokes himself) proposed building a new housing development.

One can only speculate what might have happened if Robert Kelly had had other opportunities to appear on platforms or in front of television cameras with Carl Stokes. However, it is doubtful that he could have overcome the lack of organization, of financial and numerical support, or of endorsements from newspapers and organizations. Though Carl Stokes also had obstacles to overcome, most of them arising out of his first two years in office, he was politically astute enough never to give a forum to his opponent. One Stokes worker declared, and rightly, "Carl Stokes wins his own campaigns." The favorable showing Robert Kelly made at the City Club was not enough to make an impression on the uncommitted electorate, for by that time he was already too strongly identified with a right-wing law-and-order platform.

The primary election results were in early the evening of September 30, 1969. At 7:25 P.M. Tom Kelly of WGAR news phoned in this report:

> Most of the mayor's campaign workers are drinking coffee, smiling confidently, but are not overconfident this early. Hugh Corrigan, campaign director, is not here; neither is Arnold Pinkney. With the voter turnout light in most sections of Cleveland, most observers give Robert Kelly almost no chance. One campaign worker said they expect first reports here at Stokes headquarters in minutes. If the mayor wins there will be a victory celebration at the Pick Carter Hotel later this evening.

Kelly's next report indicated some frustration on the part of reporters who were supposed to be keeping the public informed about the latest returns:

> All the veteran political reporters on hand at Stokes headquarters agree that there has never been a setup like the one we are experiencing tonight. The tabulation room is off limits to reporters. There has been no indication as to what figures, if any, might have come in. Add to that the fact that there is no blackboard anywhere. All early returns have been kept a complete se-

> cret. A three-piece band plays in the background. Arnold Pinkney is expected with that magic key to open up the lock on those returns. All of this with smiles and a relaxed atmosphere.

At Stokes headquarters reporters were getting very edgy about having no results to phone in. The front rooms were crammed with people, but the hallway leading back to the tabulating room was carefully guarded. Bob Crumpler of WEWS-TV grumbled, "We're supposed to be telling people what's going on, and we're the only ones in town who don't know anything."

Richard Murway, Joseph McManamon, and television reporter Jim Cox chatted casually about the campaign, but nobody had any predictions to make. There was a general feeling that victory was assured, but the newsmen were left with nothing to do but stand around and wait.

Outside Stokes headquarters at Nineteenth Street and Euclid Avenue there were busloads of teen-agers filling the air with political adaptations of football cheers and fight songs. Even though the night had grown quite chilly, they seemed content to wait for the appearance of their hero.

Kelly headquarters was grim, but a large tally board was in plain view. The newsmen there were only waiting for the moment when Kelly would arrive to make his concession speech. The Kelly lead, which had come from the early returns on the west side, diminished three times within the space of five minutes. A Kelly worker at the front desk was close to tears. The press looked bored. In the back room an NBC engineer was monitoring the station to pick up a stand-by cue from master control for the cut to Kelly headquarters for his concession. As it happened, NBC chose to telecast Stokes's victory speech first. The mayor thanked all those "nearby neighbors" for his victory. The one question all the reporters wanted to ask Kelly was whether he now intended to support Stokes in the general election. Kelly dodged the question but left the unmistakable impression that he would not.

Before midnight the final tally showed Stokes the winner by a margin of 92,219 to Kelly's 60,899. Why Kelly? Kelly's campaign was not the campaign of a man determined to win. The primary didn't really identify the strength of the anti-Stokes vote, because barely half the registered Democrats bothered to vote. The Republicans couldn't really even gauge how well a law-and-order platform would sell. It is impossible to say who benefited from Robert Kelly's candidacy, but it wasn't Robert Kelly. He returned to the obscurity from which he had come, carrying with him the hazy, uncertain image of the man who ran against Carl Stokes.

THE GENERAL ELECTION CAMPAIGN

Unlike Kelly, Ralph Perk, the Republican contender in the general election campaign, did have an organization behind him. In fact, Perk's campaign was organized highly but, strangely enough, ineffectively.

During the primary several Stokes supporters worried that Ralph Perk would "hit hard" at Stokes. Their fears were never realized. Perk had been known to wage vigorous campaigns in the past. His campaign to unseat County Auditor John Carney had been anything but low key. Perk was the only Republican official in the predominately Democratic county, and that kind of victory doesn't result from diffidence. Perk began the campaign with many factors operating in his favor. He had won in the past over Democratic opponents. He had strong ties with, and a great deal of sympathy from, the various nationality groups in the city. Perk had strong financial backing and the blessings of the Republican party—local, state, and national. But his campaign never met the exigencies of the moment. Perk did not recognize his rhetorical challenge, and he did not seek out the audiences he needed to persuade. In that respect his campaign resembled that of two other losers—Ralph Locher and Robert Kelly.

At no time did Ralph Perk reach out to the city as a whole. Often it seemed that Ralph Perk's campaign managers were protecting him. They protected him from Carl Stokes, from black east side audiences, from television debates. One wonders if they really explored and analyzed Perk's good points as a man and as a speaker. Ralph Perk, in question-and-answer formats when he had no script, relied on his memory and experience and presented a picture of a well-informed, forthright candidate. But these occurrences were rare. Perk's schedule was too tight for questions at most personal appearances. His schedule was strictly adhered to, and it was set up well in advance. The decision not to debate Carl Stokes was made early in the campaign and remained irreversible though the atmosphere was conducive to reassessment and reversal.

The men surrounding Ralph Perk were dedicated to their statistics and precise schedules. Robert Bennett, campaign manager, again worked on voter projections. It will be recalled that Bennett had campaigned for Perk in 1962 and shortly thereafter joined Perk in the county auditor's office. He ran Perk's 1965 mayoral campaign and then ran the campaign office of Seth Taft in 1967. Besides Bennett there were other young men of the new breed at Perk headquarters. Robert Hart, thirty-four, was campaign coordinator. William Petro, a young lawyer, had charge of the rigid scheduling and carefully planned advance arrangements. At downtown Perk headquarters one day, the following dialogue took place between Petro and an elderly gentleman who had just walked in. The gentleman was inquiring if Mr. Perk could come to a card party given by Our Lady of Good Counsel Church. The dialogue illustrates one kind of communication barrier—missing the meaning—and may help to explain why the "gut" politician is still distrustful of the "Madison Avenue" approach to politics.

GENTLEMAN: Can Mr. Perk come and take a bow at this card party?

PETRO: I doubt it.

GENTLEMAN: Why not?

PETRO: What time is it on Friday?

GENTLEMAN: Seven-thirty.

PETRO: Nope.

GENTLEMAN: Course it'll keep on going until ten.

PETRO: His schedule is finalized through Friday and there's no way, because you see all his time is blocked out—so much travelling time, so much appearance time, right down the line.

GENTLEMAN: If we have a dance on the twenty-fourth, could he appear there?

PETRO: Possibly. That's all I can say. Send in a letter, an invitation of some kind. We'll put it in the schedule and see if we can block it in. Okay?

GENTLEMAN: Well, you see the reason I say this is because there's a lot of votes.

PETRO: I know that's the biggest ward in the city, so send us a letter and we'll block it in, but you see because we have to send our schedule to the news media, we're blocked in three, four days in advance, and we can't deviate. Tomorrow he starts at nine o'clock in the morning.

GENTLEMAN: His sister goes to our church, you see.

PETRO: Well, just send us an invitation and we'll try and get it in his schedule.

GENTLEMAN: I'll try and get through his sister.

PETRO: You mean the invitation?

GENTLEMAN: No. Perk's sister is married and she belongs to our church. I've met her. I want to see Perk in there.

After the elderly gentleman left, Petro said: "A candidate really helps;

he helps by not being an obstruction, doing what you want him to do. One thing I told Perk was go where I tell you, do what I tell you. The issues—that's yours and the people working with you, but when I say make an appearance, when I say two minutes on that platform and get off—that's it."

A large campaign organization requires a division of labor among workers who are assigned specific tasks and areas of responsibility. It is not enough that each of these specialists manages his tasks at top efficiency. The several efforts of the specialists have to be coordinated and integrated in a total effort to assist the candidate in the primary task of projecting himself as the best person who can be fully entrusted with the public welfare. The campaign engineers and technicians reflect upon the candidate their own actions, and they need to understand how they individually and severally add to, or detract from, the candidate's interests. It may be more convenient for the campaign engineers if the candidate submits to their attempts to mold him in their own images of what he should be, to perform like a puppet on a string, but does the candidate really benefit from this manipulation?

If the campaign managers happen to misjudge the candidate's strengths and weaknesses or the totality of the challenge facing him, they are apt to propel him into actions which are detrimental to the establishment of his ethos. The *manipulated* candidate manifests an ethos manufactured by someone else, but in the final analysis, it is he alone who must bear the responsibility for the image which emerges. Whatever is said or done in behalf of the candidate becomes a part of his total public self, but he alone must suffer the consequences of a distorted image.

Whether by accident or design, Perk's campaign plan served more to amplify his weaknesses than to capitalize on his strengths. After seventeen years of boldly asserting and characteristically risking himself in the political arena, Ralph Perk changed his tactics and this time maintained a nonaggressive style. Perk never moved in for the kill, the moment of truth never arrived, and the crowd had little reason to cheer.

Ralph Perk, the man, was smothered in tactical details. At the opening of a headquarters on St. Clair Avenue, all the advance preparations were in evidence. Spotlights outside the building attracted passersby. A small, brightly uniformed troupe of musicians played foot-tapping music and summoned one and all to a celebration. Inside, the press corps had taken their positions in front of a cleared area in the small room, leaving almost no room for the assembled crowd to enter the headquarters and meet the candidate. A caravan of cars covered with Perk signs pulled up to the curb, the candidate emerged amid cheers, waved, smiled, and was whisked inside by his lieutenants. He took his place behind the microphones, hidden from almost everyone who managed to squeeze into the room except the reporters and cameramen, and delivered a short speech. Immediately after speaking his prepared message, Perk was hustled through the crowd, out the door, and into a car already waiting with the motor running. All this took place in less than ten minutes. A group of young boys with Perk signs who had been watching for him outside were still innocently waiting for the excitement to begin as the candidate drove away. No time had been blocked in for chatting and handshaking, for reinforcing the enthusiasm and loyalty of the faithful. The scene was replayed down to the last detail a few days later at the Perk headquarters on West Twenty-fifth Street.

Similar scenes were enacted when Perk made brief appearances at the 98-cent Republican Dinners. These gatherings were supposed to emphasize Perk's financial responsibility and were initiated to counter the $100-a-plate dinner for Stokes. Perk never *joined* the diners on these occasions. His entrance was timed to coincide with dessert and coffee. Warm-up speeches and introductions of ward leaders and other Republican notables were disposed of before Perk's entrance. On signal from the advance crew, the band would begin to play, Perk would walk in smiling and waving, step to the microphone, read his speech, and leave amidst another fanfare.

On two occasions Perk abandoned these ritualistic performances and got down to the business of expressing himself. On neither of these occasions could Perk be sure of the inclinations of his audiences because the events were nonpartisan. On both occasions he sought understanding from his hearers, and his methods revealed a different candidate from the packaged commodity set out on display by his managers. The first occasion was at Cleveland State University where Perk effectively related to an audience of young people by speaking extemporaneously and responding thoughtfully and completely to questions asked by the audience. There was a striking difference in his whole manner, and he was quietly impressive in the informal, unstructured situation. When reading from a manuscript Perk sounded artificial, stilted, and cold. His voice was pitched higher than normal, his phrasing was not always meaningful, and faint traces of the definite accent of his Bohemian heritage came through his reading. These nervous characteristics were not apparent when he spoke at Cleveland State.

On another occasion, at the Chesterfield Apartments, Perk spoke casually, without notes, carefully answered all questions, looked and sounded knowledgeable, relaxed, and warm. This was one of the few

Ralph Perk
Photograph by Odyssey Associates

occasions when Perk attempted to capitalize on his personal qualifications and political background. Of himself, Perk said:

> In 1953 I was elected as a member of the Cleveland City Council, in a ward that was about 4 to 1 Democratic, by a majority of 2 to 1. In 1955 I was elected by a majority of 4 to 1. In 1957 they had no opposition against me. In 1959 I was reelected and by a majority of 6 to 1 in a ward that is still 4 to 1 Democratic. In 1961 I was reelected and received four times as many votes as all three of my opponents combined. In 1962 with the assistance of the people of this city and the county I was elected county auditor and the first Republican elected to county office in nearly thirty years. I was able to reduce the administrative budget of the auditor's office by 19.9 percent the first year. The second year I reduced it even further and the third year again even further. . . . When I ran for reelection as county auditor in 1966, I had the endorsement of the Citizens League, the *Press*, the *Plain Dealer*, and every labor organization in this city.

To emphasize his record of service as well as his vote-getting ability, Perk went on to tell his audience how he had dissolved the notorious 2 percent "flower fund" which had flourished in the auditor's office and still operates in some county offices today.[5]

> For years the employees were required to pay back to the county auditor's flower fund 2 percent of their salary. This had to be paid back in cash in an envelope every payday. This meant that the County Auditor was getting between $30,000 and $50,000 a year in a flower fund, and you know you can buy a lot of flowers for $50,000.

Prefacing an attack on the Stokes administration's extravagance in increasing the costs of government by excesses in hiring, Perk told the audience that he had not only abolished the kickback operation in his office but got rid of the woman whose chief job was administering the "flower fund" and the man whose job it was to write news releases on "what a great guy the former auditor [John Carney] was." He indicated he would rid City Hall of all such excess baggage.

Those who had seen Perk's performances at several of the Republican 98-cent dinners were astonished by the impression of the experienced and knowledgeable public servant that emerged that night at the Chesterfield. William Petro, the Perk advance man, was asked, "Why don't you let him campaign in his own style?" Petro just rolled his eyes in dismay—a symbolic vote of "no-confidence" in the candidate's oratorical qualifications. But Perk's ability to field questions about the function, scope, and limitations of the mayor's office that evening was impressive. Since most of Perk's speeches were attacks on Stokes's performance in office, there never really emerged the possibility that Perk carried within him the political know-how to step into the office without a wasteful on-the-job training period. At some point in a campaign, attack for the sake of attack has to give way to attack for the sake of establishing oneself as a person qualified to remedy the ills.

One of the few intriguing moments of the campaign came with the public exposure of the "Blueprint for Victory" memorandum. This document, written by public relations man William Levy and addressed to Mayor Carl B. Stokes and his aides, John C. Little, Sidney Spector, and Arnold Pinkney, was headed "personal and confidential" and the subject was noted as "PR Strategy for General Election." Somehow Republicans obtained a copy of the document. Stokes accused County Republican Cochairmen Saul Stillman and Robert E. Hughes of outright theft—breaking and entering his office and the locked files therein.[6] The Republicans reproduced hundeds of copies of the document and made it available to all who attended Perk rallies. Perk referred to it repeatedly in his speeches. Part of the document is included here as an excellent example of a public relations strategy that parallels on the local level what Joe McGinniss's *The Selling of the President, 1968* (New York: Trident Press, 1969) illustrates on a presidential level. The portions quoted here suffice to demonstrate why the Republicans prized the document so highly:

> We are again faced with the prospect of running a segmented campaign—one directed at the black power base and the other directed at the "soft" white community, where we must make a significant showing if Mayor Stokes is to be re-elected.
>
> Fear is the one weapon that will effectively increase the turnout of black voters. Though the job is primarily one of organization, we must instill in the black voters the thought that unless they turn out better than in the primary, Mayor Stokes will lose the election. . . .
>
> According to the Sorenson survey, the key to gaining any significant numbers of voters in the General Election is reaching the white-Catholic voter on the West Side. . . .
>
> Mayor Stokes must run a vigorous campaign. He must be exposed to as many white voters on a man-to-man basis as is humanly pos-

sible during the next four weeks. There are two reasons for this: because of his health, Ralph Perk's activities probably will be limited and a busy Mayor will tend to show this up; the Mayor is a "great" personal salesman who can win voters by his charm and sincerity in person. . . . The Mayor should do some symbolic doorbell ringing in selected West Side wards. We must show that he is interested in winning the support of the people in this section of town. . . . Wherever possible, the Mayor should make speeches to groups of Catholic religious leaders. Father Murphy has indicated he can set up a speaking engagement at St. Joseph's Mother Home, where some 200 nuns can be assembled. These nuns are not only voters, but they can have some influence in swaying other voters. We must pull out all stops to arrange teas and coffee sessions, where the Mayor can make brief appearances. The Lubell survey points out that women are leaning toward giving the Mayor another two years, and we must exploit this. We should strive for one massive West Side rally in late October and bring to Cleveland a leading Catholic who will speak in support of the Mayor. It has been suggested that Ethel Kennedy be approached for this. We should immediately approach Mrs. Kennedy to determine if she would be willing to do this for Mayor Stokes. Otherwise, we will have to seek an alternate. Similarly, we should attempt to get Mrs. Coretta King here for a huge black rally on the East Side.

One of the key points brought out in the Sorenson survey is the feeling among West Siders that Mayor Stokes has directed a majority of his effort toward the East Side. We must dispel this feeling. If we rely only on radio, television and newspaper advertisements to tell the West Side story, it will not be properly told. . . .

Every day must be a news day at City Hall. This is a way in which Mayor Stokes can dominate the news, without Ralph Perk being able to call for equal time. . . .

Ralph Perk has a record, too. And it should be scrutinized for flaws which can be pointed to in speeches and in statements issued by the Campaign Headquarters. Unfortunately, there is little in his public record that can be criticized. Both newspapers generally agree that he has been a good County Auditor, who put an end to the wheeling and dealing of the previous administration. . . . Perk's health must be a silent issue. He says he will work seven days a week, 52 weeks a year and has criticized the Mayor for being away from the city. We must point out that he has been in Florida twice

> this year, the Bahamas once and Arizona once. He has also been hospitalized for eight weeks. . . . Let's lace Perk quickly again on the statement he is starting his campaign with $500. We'll point out that he already has 64 billboards posted at a cost of $5,000. An overriding theme as far as Perk is concerned should be the relationship to Saul Stillman and Bob Hughes. Let's plant the idea that Cleveland will have a "three-headed" mayor if Perk is elected and two of the heads will live in the suburbs. . . . Though there is a risk of alienating a segment of the Nixon Administration, we must tie Ralph Perk to Washington and to the administration which: is leading the country down the road to the worst inflation the country has ever known; has played ball with the bankers so that today the little man can't get a mortgage for his house unless he pays an eight percent mortgage—if he can get the money. . . . We must indoctrinate people who will be speaking for the Mayor at campaign rallies and ward meetings with this philosophy, so they can spread the word about bossism and Perk's ties to the National administration.

The strategy revealed here is, in itself, neither new nor unique. This sort of planning has been going on behind closed doors and in smoke-filled rooms for generations. The shock came from seeing everything spelled out so graphically in print.

Perk, of course, tried to use the document to his advantage. At the Chesterfield Apartments he said: "The public relations director for the Stokes campaign has outlined a campaign which Mr. Stokes is following, because if you look at the document you will find that he is following each and every recommendation. The recommendation is that he run a segmented campaign." Perk, too, was running a segmented campaign, but unlike Stokes, Perk wasn't addressing an appeal of any kind to the black community or to the "soft" white community.

The "Blueprint for Victory" should have been Perk's "golden kazoo" —that irresistible, universally appealing gimmick every pitchman dreams of finding. But he could not make it so by continuing to limit his campaign to those audiences already committed to him. And, except for the *Cleveland Press*, the news media did not award coverage to the issue. When asked whether there was any hesitation in publishing parts of the memorandum, Boardman of the *Press* remarked:

> No, this was an interesting document which was available to us through perfectly legitimate sources, and it's news, and we're in the business to print news. I frankly was quite surprised that it be-

> came such a large issue. To me it was just an interesting look into the background of the campaign. I didn't think about it; as a matter of fact I don't think too many people did.

Perhaps if either newspaper had published the memorandum in its entirety many more people would have "thought about it." Except for Richard Maher's one article excerpting a few paragraphs from it, the public at large was rather carefully shielded from its contents. WJW-TV mentioned the "Blueprint" only twice, as opposed to twenty-three mentions of the question "Will Stokes and Perk debate?"

In answer to the repeated question about his refusal to debate the mayor, Perk generally came up with the answer that he was already drawing crowds and he wasn't going to draw them for Stokes, that he wasn't going to spend one more hour listening to Stokes's false promises and lies. Perk said that in 1965 he had appeared on the platform with Stokes thirty-nine different times and Stokes stole his ideas and used them.

During any campaign the image of a man unwilling, or unable, to engage in a personal dialogue with his opponent is a devastating one. The man who ducks confrontation arouses suspicions as to his ability to handle himself in a critical situation. A most damaging film clip appeared on television late in the campaign when Stokes cornered Perk outside a meeting place and challenged him on the spot to exchange a few words. Perk excused himself weakly, saying that he was late for another meeting. In this contest Stokes's role was that of defender of his administration, and Perk should have been the aggressor. Instead Stokes took on the aggressor's role and put Perk on the defensive about his refusal to debate.

An astute campaign manager would have recognized that Stokes was highly vulnerable and that Perk had nothing to fear from a confrontation. Even if he could not approach Stokes's oratorical heights, Perk could have scored a lot of points with only two strategies: (1) pressing hard and (2) staying cool. Stokes in 1969 was not projecting himself as the same warm, delightful, often ingratiating entertainer he had been in 1967. He was operating impatiently and had on several occasions displayed his irritability at sharp questions from newsmen and audiences.

One night the mayor's appearances on both the east and west sides of town were taped in order to compare his performances before partisan and potentially hostile audiences. On the east side Stokes danced, laughed with the children, introduced his supporters, and in general pre-

European Night in Cleveland for Mayor Carl Stokes
Photograph courtesy of the City of Cleveland

Campaigning at West Side Community House
Photograph courtesy of the City of Cleveland

sented a lively picture of a beloved mayor glowing in the warmth of his people's adoration. On the west side he was sometimes defensive, dignified, reserved, and even a bit testy. He made little attempt to mingle with the audience. It was easy to talk to the mayor on the east side after his speeches, but on the west side his aides closed in about him, and he left the halls immediately. After one west side meeting the mayor misinterpreted an attempt to question him. He must have thought it was a request to ride with him to his next meeting, for he barked, "I've got six in that car now!"

At another west side meeting, the audience did not honor the mayor by standing either when he entered or left, but even the hostility, which was sometimes present, was never unanimous. Of course, Stokes people were always scattered through every audience, and the mayor often called upon them to perform some service. At Saint Ignatius Hall a lady complained about repeated requests for a street light on a certain corner, and the mayor immediately called one of his aides seated in the middle of the audience to take the lady's name and make a point to check into the situation. At the same meeting another lady rose and asked the mayor whether he was planning to replace the police chief. The lady cited an article in a Lake County newspaper which the mayor immediately identified as written by "a woman reporter." There was no doubt in anyone's mind that he knew about the article and the identity of its author, Doris O'Donnell. The mayor's response was to keep insisting that the lady from the audience had not read the story in a Cleveland newspaper, as if that somehow answered the question about whether he was going to replace the chief. Stokes did offer some words of praise for Chief Gerity but dodged the question of his replacement. The lady who asked the question showed signs of dissatisfaction which had a contagious effect on others in the audience.

Because of his official position, Carl Stokes was more defensive in 1969 than in 1967. He became very agitated during a television interview on WJW-TV on October 25. The subject in question concerned funds raised for Stokes in Philadelphia and Washington. The exchange between the mayor and the *Press* reporter Alan Horton went like this:

> HORTON: You raised roughly, according to estimates given by our Washington reporters, forty thousand dollars in Washington and Philadelphia.
>
> STOKES: You're not telling the truth! You're not telling the truth! Your Washington correspondents—
>
> HORTON: Then what are the facts?

STOKES: No! You're not asking that. Your Washington correspondent has not told you that. Which one of your Washington correspondents told you that?

HORTON: Will you answer my question?

STOKES: I'm not going to answer an untruth. If you think I will sit here and let you on public television tell an untruth then you're certainly wrong and no one in Washington told you that.

HORTON: They have.

STOKES: Who? Who, Mr. Horton? Who? Tell us their names.

HORTON: We have two. Bob Crater and John Russell are our two Washington correspondents.

STOKES: I don't believe you. Because, first, they weren't at the affair and, secondly, they haven't told you that and I think you ought to be ashamed of yourself for having said that.

This small exchange between Stokes and a reporter should have been a signal to the Perk people that the mayor could be goaded into an ugly display of temper with the slightest provocation, and that a public confrontation would be to Perk's advantage. But they remained steadfast in their refusal to let him debate.

The *Press* wrote an editorial supporting Horton, albeit tempering the criticism by suggesting that "Cordi's tears triggered the mayor's temper." (Cordi, the mayor's daughter, had reportedly created a scene at the breakfast table because her daddy was never home anymore. On many occasions when the mayor was under public attack he brought a member of his family along to support his image.) An interesting series of events followed the Stokes-Horton encounter. First the mayor personally hand-carried a note of apology to Alan Horton. Thomas Boardman, commenting on the note, said, "The mayor can still turn on the charm when he wants to." Soon after the election there was a shake-up in staff assignments. City Hall reporter Norman Mlachak, who impartially took bites out of everybody's hide, was reassigned, and Alan Horton replaced him at City Hall. In his new position Horton tended to criticize City Council and to justify the administration. Stokes, indeed, was still winning his own campaigns.

For all the lessening of the mayor's outgoing approach to audiences in 1969, he was at least willing to expose himself to more and different audiences than was his opponent Ralph Perk. Hugh Corrigan overruled several top men in the Stokes camp and convinced the mayor that he must campaign all over the city. The mayor appeared all over the east and west sides of town and on television. However, he shied away from the radio programs that involved lengthy question-and-answer sessions. On the other hand, Perk confined his appearances primarily to friendly white audiences. This schedule of appearances during the most crucial campaign time (October 16 through November 2) evidences the highly selective nature of Perk's appearances:

Sachsenheim Hall, 7001 Denison
*Hofbrau Haus, St. Clair and East 55th Street
*Roman Gardens, 12207 Mayfield Road
Trent Civic Association, Saint Procop's Hall, West 41st and Trent
Our Lady of Mount Carmel Hall, 6928 Detroit
*Nottingham United Methodist Church, 185th and St. Clair
*Cleveland State University
Polish Women's Hall, 7526 Broadway
Ampol Hall, 4737 Pearl Road
Brooklyn YMCA
Saint Mary's Romanian Orthodox Church Hall, 3256 Warren Road
Carpatina Hall, 1303 West 58th Street
*Bohemian National Hall, 4939 Broadway
*ICA Hall, 15901 St. Clair
*Chesterfield Apartments
Anton Blazen VFW Post 2079 Hall, 5949 Engel
Saint Rocco's Church Hall, 3205 Fulton Road

None of the east side appearances (asterisks) were in black neighborhoods. Almost half the gatherings were the 98-cent fried chicken dinners which were, in fact, a real bargain whether one liked Perk or not. Most of the scheduled appearances provided for only a very brief speech to an already convinced audience.

After a month of lackluster campaigning the candidates and electors cast their votes on November 4, 1969. Mayor Carl Stokes and his wife, both stylishly attired, voted in the garage of an apartment building just off Shaker Square. Mr. and Mrs. Ralph Perk, conventionally attired, cast their ballots at 7:35 A.M. at Barkwell Elementary School. A total of 238,843 Cleveland voters went to the polls, and Carl Stokes was re-elected mayor by 3,753 votes—twice his margin in 1967.

The arbitrators had decided to let Carl Stokes try again, but they put a few stumbling blocks in his way by electing several councilmen who could be counted on to keep the mayor in check—among them Clarence

Thompson, the Ward Thirty councilman who had blocked Stokes on the Lee-Seville housing issue. Groups all over the city learned the lesson of checking power from the Lee-Seville residents. One group attempted to check the mayor on election day. By midday on November 4 rumors abounded about voting irregularities and the presence of two hundred off-duty policemen manning east side polling places as witnesses and challengers in behalf of the County Government Reform Issue. Arnold Pinkney, Stokes's campaign manager, claimed that the off-duty police officers had been intimidating black voters. Clarence James, the law director, claimed their actions violated the provisions of the City Charter.[7]

Attorney Paul W. Walter forecast another breakdown in already strained relations between the mayor and the police department when he said:

> The Chief of Police realizes the rights that the police have as citizens and he knows what the law is insofar as witnesses and challengers are concerned, and if they are legally appointed they have a right in the booths regardless of whether they are policemen, firemen, or whosoever they may be as long as they are an elector and properly there.[8]

However, by evening the city settled down to await the results of the arbitration. Election-night headquarters for both candidates were set up on the same floor of the Sheraton Cleveland Hotel. Stokes supporters jammed the Grand Ballroom while Perk supporters gathered in a smaller assembly room.

Ralph Perk made an early appearance at his headquarters and told the crowd, "You are wonderful! You really turn me on!" Later when it became obvious that the vote was going in Stokes's direction, Perk again addressed his supporters, thanked them for the good fight, then made his way to the Grand Ballroom to congratulate the winner. The Perk people had gathered without hope of a victory celebration. Even the music sounded spiritless.

On the other side of the hotel the "Stokes Folks" seemed more confident of victory. The Reverend Jesse L. Jackson, a member of the Southern Christian Leadership Conference, and the Operation Breadbasket band were on hand to add to the excitement. Stokes people confidently crossed the barrier and wandered into the Perk party, flaunting the Stokes ribbons and buttons. When word got around that Stokes was on his way to the ballroom to claim victory, a crowd of over six thousand

Election Night 1969:
Mayor Carl Stokes and Councilman George Forbes
Photograph courtesy of the City of Cleveland

pressed into the ballroom. They linked arms, swayed to the music, and when the mayor finally arrived they cheered loudly, then burst into "We Shall Overcome." The crowd was so keyed up that the mayor had difficulty making himself heard over the general hubbub. He kissed his wife and thanked his campaign workers. When Ralph Perk arrived to offer his congratulations, Stokes tried to get the crowd to applaud the gesture, but there was more booing than applause.

Bob Crumpler of WEWS-TV offered the most colorful and descriptive commentary on the events at Stokes headquarters. He transmitted a part of the mood to the viewers at home when he said, "It's jubilant. It's overflowing. It's bountiful. Stokes is happy."

After it was all over and the shouting had died down, Richard Maher, *Press* political writer, presented his sage analysis for the City Club:

> Now Stokes won by 3,753 votes on Tuesday.... I think Perk lost because his people failed to get out the vote. Just think, only 5,000 more votes would have wiped out the Stokes margin and put him in—provided, of course, they were Perk votes. There's no substitute for shoe leather in getting out the vote. A corps of several hundred of the young, personable folks gathered about Perk for this campaign could have been thrown into the precincts where he was most likely to get votes. They could have gone door to door even in the rain and induced lazy, timid, or indifferent voters to go to the poll—even if they had to transport them.

While it is true that the Stokes workers did go door to door and got out the vote, that busloads of college students from Oberlin and Wilberforce came in to ring doorbells and transport Stokes voters to the polls, it is too simple to say that a similar effort by the Perk people would have turned the tide. The alternatives to Stokes were not strong enough to move the electorate. The risks in returning the city to its pre-1967 condition were greater than the perceivable rewards. Or maybe, like the the villagers in "The Lottery," the people were piling up stones to throw at the winner, for it wasn't long before Carl Stokes got caught in another crossfire.

CHAPTER 8

ENDGAME

ON MONDAY, January 5, 1970, Mayor Stokes, his cabinet, a packed gallery, and thousands of television viewers looked on as thirty-three newly elected representatives of the people of the city were sworn in. A new decade had begun and with it a new resolve to make the instruments of government serve the needs of the people.

Despite disenchantment and weariness, the administration and council announced they would renew their attempts at problem-solving. However, no indication that council or the administration would refrain from engaging in personality debates was forthcoming. In fact, a major confrontation in 1970 involved a personality conflict between the mayor and a new safety director.

It began when Joseph McManamon resigned his post as safety director and the search for a replacement was under way. The law-and-order issue was never so pressing. At the end of 1969 the overall crime rate in the city was up 54 percent from 1968—almost three times as high as the national average for cities of comparable size. Added to this alarming figure was the fact that the two top men in the law enforcement area had been publicly feuding. When McManamon resigned, speculation about Chief Gerity's tenure as police chief followed.

Actually Stokes had been looking for a replacement for Gerity since the November elections when the police department had been involved in the challenging scandal at the polls. He felt that he must develop leadership in the police department responsive in *fact*, rather than theory, to some form of civilian control. He was advised to seek aid through the White House and was referred to the Justice Department Law Enforcement Assistance Administration. There George W. O'Connor, Chief of the Police Programs Division of the Law Enforcement Assistance Administration (LEAA), and another Washington contact put together several possible courses of action for the mayor. They stated that because he already had a police chief and a safety director, the first possibility would be to keep both of them, and the advantages and disadvantages of that action were spelled out. Another possibility was to replace the police chief and keep the safety director. A third possibility might be to keep the police chief and replace the safety director, and the fourth was to replace both of them. O'Connor advised the mayor to first find a safety director and then let this director, given time, look around in the department. He said "Find somebody, if possible, from the inside and, if not, go outside—but make it clear that the safety director was doing the selecting."

According to O'Connor, the Stokes administration chose the worst option from the possibilities offered. Stokes searched for a safety director and a police chief, replacing both at approximately the same time. An attempt was made to get James F. Ahern, at that time the police chief in New Haven, Connecticut, as the new police chief. According to O'Connor, the Stokes administration promised Ahern tight security. Ahern didn't want his mayor knowing he was in Cleveland talking about a job. O'Connor stated, "Ahern got out of New Haven and checked into the hotel in Cleveland. He no sooner got to the door when he received a phone call. Someone welcomed him to Cleveland and said they were happy he was coming—or unhappy. He was very upset over the lack of security and left."

Still determined, Stokes made the decision to replace Gerity while the search continued for a new safety director. Lt. Gen. Benjamin O. Davis, Jr., the highest ranking Negro officer in the United States Air Force, was being wooed for that position, and it was reported that he had accepted. However, the general was still in Florida awaiting retirement when, on the morning of January 26, 1970, the mayor demoted Gerity and appointed William P. Ellenburg, former Detroit policeman and safety director of Grosse Point Park, Michigan. According to the Cleveland administration, replacing the two top men in the law-and-order department was an initial attempt to attack the problem of public safety.

Unfortunately the problem was only compounded—and for several reasons besides the ones mentioned by O'Connor. One was that Chief Gerity had been gaining stature steadily in the eyes of his men. At a banquet of the Fraternal Order of the Police just a few days prior to his ouster, Gerity had been given a standing ovation from the over three thousand guests. Another reason—unforeseen at this point—was that new Chief Ellenburg would enjoy the shortest tenure in office ever held in Cleveland.

The appointment of William P. Ellenburg was announced on January 26. Ellenburg brought with him as chief assistant Thomas R. Cochill, also a former Detroit policeman and, before coming to Cleveland, the safety director of Grosse Point Shores, Michigan. The news media's reaction to the appointment was generally favorable. The *Cleveland Plain Dealer* wrote: "William P. Ellenburg is a lean man, tall and soft-spoken. He reminds you of a man from whom you last bought insurance." However, in the same paper, Allen Wiggins wrote: "Richard R. Wagner became a campaign issue. Challenger Carl B. Stokes said he would fire Wagner if he won. Wagner quit when Stokes took office. Stokes's choice for a replacement was Blackwell, uh, Gerity, uh, Ellenburg . . ."[1]

On Wednesday, January 28, a City Hall reporter discovered that Ellenburg was under investigation by the *Detroit Free Press* for alleged acceptance of protection payoffs from a Mafia lawyer. The *Plain Dealer*'s editorial staff immediately made the decision to send a reporter to Detroit to inquire about the allegations. The reporter learned that the *Detroit Free Press* was indeed investigating Ellenburg and that the new chief allegedly had received money to protect an abortion ring. The *Cleveland Press*, by this time, also had the story, but they remained cautious. By Friday, however, the *Plain Dealer* reporter related that the *Detroit Free Press* was going to publish the story in its Sunday edition. On Sunday, the *Plain Dealer* published an eight-column, double-deck bannerline story: "Ellenburg Accepted Payoffs Detroit Mafia Lawyer Says." The story related how former Mafia lawyer Lawrence Burns of Detroit had named Ellenburg as one of the three Detroit policemen who had taken payoffs between 1959 and 1963 for protecting an abortion racket operating out of the Medota Clinic.

On Sunday night the mayor responded to the *Plain Dealer* article over a three-channel television hookup during which he defended his actions, noting that the television stations and the *Cleveland Press* refused to publish the allegations until they were substantiated, thus condemning, by implication, the *Plain Dealer*. He also stated that Ellenburg's accuser was under the influence of drugs. Stokes actually called Burns a "drug addict."

Ellenburg held a press conference on Tuesday, February 3, but this only succeeded in raising more doubts about his ability to handle the role to which he had been assigned. Not only could he not remember events of ten years back but was hazy about events of the past few days. An excerpt of his interview with the press indicates why a *Plain Dealer* reporter stated that the interview raised more questions than it answered:

> Q: Chief, may I ask a last question? A week ago when you were sworn in, I asked you at City Hall whether you contemplated

any changes, and you said no. And within a half hour, changes were made. Who dictated the changes?"

A: I asked for a list of names of people who would help me to establish a staff for a new man.

Q: How would you know these men—how did you know these particular names?

A: Well, policemen have a way of knowing about other policemen.

Q: How did you find out so quickly?

A: I didn't find out so quickly. I talked several hours about this thing, and I went over several names. One of my chief aides, who is a director of personnel, is Deputy Inspector Harry Antel, whose district function has been extremely efficient, who is a qualified attorney.

Q: How did they come hauling out so fast?

A: I was told all of these things. Some recommendations were made that I might bolster up this area or that area. I know you are referring to the transfers. They were made from a higher level; this is partially true, but only with my agreement. Suggestions were made to me: "If you want to help this area, here is the man."

Q: Who made those suggestions to you—those kinds of suggestions?

A: Well, I don't remember. I really don't know.

Q: Would it be in the mayor's office?

A: Well, naturally it would be.

City Council was particularly disturbed by the administration's failure to use a single, normal channel in its investigation of Ellenburg's background. According to Alan Horton of the *Press*, Richard McKean, assistant safety director and former FBI man, was not asked to check with his former associates about Ellenburg because Mayor Stokes feared this type of check would leak Ellenburg's name to the news media. Perhaps the experience with Ahern had made the department leery of the press. However, this reasoning was not acceptable to council, and young Councilman Dennis J. Kucinich was prepared to invoke Chapter 5, Section 46 of the City Charter and submit a resolution calling for an investigation of the selection procedure used in hiring Ellenburg. Council President James Stanton stepped down from his chair during the council meeting and made a plea for discretion and caution in pursuing the matter, a move which made Stanton appear more a statesman than a politician. In asking that council be compassionate and compromise a hard-line stand, he emerged as a more receptive leader, appearing more lenient than his usual role of adversary.

As a result, Stokes was granted a reasonable time to conduct his own investigation into the charges before council would take action. Mayor Stokes departed that night for Detroit, returned late Tuesday after a day of consultation with law enforcement agencies, and discussed his findings with his new chief.

At a 10:00 A.M. press conference on Wednesday, February 4, 1970, Ellenburg's and Cochill's resignations were accepted, and Inspector Lewis W. Coffey was sworn in as Cleveland's new chief of police. The selection of Lewis Coffey, a veteran of thirty-one years, was heralded by policemen, who respected Coffey's efficiency and effectiveness.

But the whole affair had a demoralizing effect upon both the police and the public. It also had many ramifications. It marked the beginning of a series of investigative features about the Stokes administration by both dailies which, in turn, prompted the mayor to accuse the newspapers of being responsible for many of the ills of society. Stokes stated, furthermore, that he would not accept a *Plain Dealer* endorsement for himself in the future. Actually the media did not prolong the Ellenburg discussion, and the problem was not explored further by either council or the administration. An investigation into the method of selection of police chiefs did not occur, and the entire event was dismissed after Ellenburg's resignation.

Fortunately at this point, the administration's face was saved by the timely arrival of Lt. Gen. Benjamin O. Davis. The general, recently retired, had agreed to accept the safety director's post. His acceptance was heralded as a major coup by the administration. The general's impeccable background and his quiet, but firm, demeanor added stature to the sorely bruised image of the administration.

In a private interview, the general said that when he arrived in Cleveland, the morale of the department "was about zero." He added: "It was just a terrible situation, because at the time I got there Ellenburg had just been there a few days and the day after I was appointed, Mr. Ellenburg resigned." The general felt that the first problem which faced him "was to establish personal relationships and organizational relationships within the department of public safety."

General Davis said that he and Chief Coffey understood each other from the very beginning. "Consequently, I immediately achieved something that had been missing for a long time—namely, confidence between the director of public safety in the City Hall and the chief of police."

Policemen themselves generally admitted that the morale of their department was highest during the time General Davis held the post of safety director. Not only did he earn the respect of the police, but he quickly established his image as a public leader as well. He was visibly present whenever a disturbance occurred. At Cuyahoga Community College, when students staged several disruptions, General Davis appeared, and his presence had a quieting effect upon the crowd that had gathered.

The general brought with him William Hendrickson, a retired colonel in the United States Air Force, as his aide. Colonel Hendrickson stated that the general worked steadily within the administration to establish a more efficient operation. He built a budget and made department heads responsible for their own budgets. He developed projects and assigned them to the proper departments, requiring datelines and progress reports. He reviewed merit raises for the first time in many years and, in an attempt to rehabilitate facilities, reanalyzed the maintenance department, scheduling 80 percent of the men for maintenance and 20 percent for emergencies. The general also answered all correspondence and responded to all citizens' complaints.

The general quickly observed that there still existed among policemen and firemen a lack of confidence in City Hall. He remarked, "The Glenville affair still cast its shadow. . . . July 23, 1968, was as real in February, 1970, as if it had been the day before. . . . Part of my problem in doing my job was to avoid the efforts that a whole lot of people were making to continue raking over the coals of Glenville, going backwards, instead of going forward." General Davis said he cast a cold eye on anything that had happened in the past because there were enough things happening from day to day.

However, there were many black citizens who felt that the problems that had created the Glenville disturbance were the ones that needed attention, and it is possible that they interpreted the general's refusal to look back as a refusal to solve the problems of Glenville which for them were still very real.

Nonetheless, things seemed to be going along splendidly until early in the spring when several items appeared in the *Cleveland Press* which suggested personality differences between the mayor and the general. Bob Williams of the *Press* stated that at City Council meetings "while Stokes has been under attack, the former general has been heartily ap-

Safety Director General Benjamin O. Davis at City
Council meeting; Council President James V. Stanton presiding
Photograph by Odyssey Associates

plauded by white audiences critical of the mayor." He also said that the *Call and Post* criticized Davis for allowing heavily armed police task forces into black areas, claiming he did not do the same for incidents in white areas.[2]

In the spring at a meeting at the First Methodist Church on Euclid and East Thirtieth, Harllel Jones spoke before a group of Cleveland State University students who were enrolled in a course called The Rhetoric of Black America. He said:

> The great General Davis that's been indoctrinated in the white boy's schools and Air Force academies and places like this here have went up and got this man brainwashed. This man is telling the police to make all the arrests and then suffer the consequences. You understand, and what Davis ought to understand is that one of these times they might grab the wrong black woman or the wrong black man and all kind of hell is going to break loose down in the inner city and then we'll see if General Davis can take his influence in the ghetto there and tell them "hold up and stop," because I believe sincerely that the *black revolutionaries will run him out of the community.*

On Monday, July 27, less than six months after General Benjamin O. Davis assumed the office of director of public safety, he, too, sent his resignation to the mayor. It stated:

> I find it necessary and desirable to resign as director of public safety.
>
> The reasons are simple. I am not receiving from you and your administration the support my programs require, and the enemies of law enforcement continue to receive support and comfort from you and your administration.
>
> I request your acceptance of my resignation at your earliest convenience.

Local pressmen considered this the worst political blow the mayor had yet received. The general firmly refused to identify the "enemies of law enforcement" when the mayor publicly challenged him to do so. General Davis's reply was, "I just don't have anything more to say. I'm not going to refuse [to specify the charges], but I'm not going to get into a public debate with the mayor. I don't have anything more to say."

Carl Stokes then proceeded to list the names of the "enemies of law enforcement" himself—after first conferring with the individuals and organizations he (Stokes) had designated. John Little at City Hall spoke about the mayor's decision to name specific men and groups after the general had refused to do so. Little said that the day following the general's letter of resignation, he and the mayor met with Richard Murway and Arnold Pinkney and together decided upon this particular course of action. One of the reasons, said Little, was because the national magazines were coming in: "*Look* and the others," he said, "and they were making implications about Mafia connections and all that. So we had to do something quickly."

The general would not engage in verbal battle because, as he astutely observed, "There would be no end to it," but the mayor could not afford such a stunning blow without responding. Armed with his public relations manager, William Silverman, he met with reporters in the Tapestry Room at City Hall. He had his son, Carl, Jr., with him. According to *Cleveland Press* reporter Dick Feagler, "He [Carl Stokes] had gotten into battle with Benjamin Davis, Jr., a real genuine American hero whose image he had helped to enhance. He had taken on a black Steve Canyon. It was his integrity against the integrity of the United States Air Force."[3]

At City Hall that day Carl Stokes alleged that Davis had asked him to tell the Welfare Federation to cut off funds to the Cleveland Council of Churches to silence that group's Metropolitan Affairs Commission and to ask the United Appeal to cut off money for the Friendly Inn Settlement House, an alleged meeting place for the National Committee to Combat Fascism. The mayor further alleged that the general asked him to "contain" former Community Relations Board representative Baxter Hill, Jr., who had resigned under fire. According to Stokes, the general "could live" with Harllel Jones, prime minister of the Afro Set, but wanted the Reverend W. Arthur LeMon, director of the city Community Relations Board, fired for mixing with those opposed to the general's programs. Also on the general's alleged list of "enemies of law enforcement" was the *Call and Post*.

The general refused to respond, but the news media was not averse to continuing the show.

For the WKYC-TV "Open Lines" show, the producer gathered those named as "enemies of law enforcement" by Mayor Stokes and decided to question them before the camera.

The reporter who opened the show said, "I'd like to ask the three men *who were personally named by General Davis* whether you had any personal run-in with the general and if you did, what was it like?"

LeMon said he did not recall any personal run-ins with the general. Harllel said he had met with the general a month prior to the resignation and discussed the alleged harassment of members of the Afro Set by the police. A man named "Rock" who represented the National Committee to Combat Fascism said: "We definitely consider ourselves enemies of those racists and those fascists that wear badges and carry guns. . . . What we're working for is the total liberation of the black people in the colonies and revolution in the oppressed section of America, and the way we view these policemen—we feel they should be removed from the communities, and the communities should be policed by the inhabitants of the communities. We feel we have to work on the enemy of all mankind, which is these imperialists, these capitalists-exploiters of our people. We are the oil of the well-run machinery of imperialism and colonialism."

Charles Loeb of the *Call and Post* stated simply: "We examined him [Davis] and found him not to our liking."

Once more the community became polarized. The television media had presented the mayor's point of view. Sides were drawn and Davis's supporters felt compelled to speak up. Dr. Kenneth Clement stated: "It's a tragedy that the general's charges are true."[4] Thomas R. Guthrie of the *Plain Dealer* said, "Ben Davis was another who had the courage to tell the mayor when he thought he was wrong."[5] Descriptions were attached to the two men: Carl Stokes, the orator with the flashing smile and brilliant style, born politician, astute balancer of political ramifications, etc.; Benjamin Davis, a justice-for-all-on-equal-terms man, a believer in the police as the proper instrument for impartial enforcement of all society's laws, disciplinarian, straight-shooter, etc. The news media stayed with this story long after the event.

Meanwhile, the general was called upon to be a member of the panel to investigate the Kent State disturbance in which four students were killed. Soon after that he was appointed to the Office of Transportation in Washington to head the investigations into the numerous hijacking incidents. George W. O'connor was eventually chosen by the Cleveland search committee to fill the safety director's position.

General Davis was interviewed in Washington on November 13, 1970. Since the general had made no public statement after he had released his letter of resignation, it was most important that his own words set the record straight.

The general said that though the mayor had originally promised him a free hand, "the mayor was unable to keep his promise to stay out of my business. There were decisions made counter to the efforts I was making." He further stated, rather emphatically, "It became very clear to me that the faster I got out of that job, the better for me, for sure, because I was going to be *had* one way or the other, very simply, around that time. So it was my move—or else—be *had*. Now, the reasons for that I can't support. It might have something to do with progress being made in the area of law enforcement. That's one thing. Another thing might have to do with personalities. I think I am fairly simple and direct. For example, if someone were to come to City Hall to see me, I'd just tell them my opinion. And I, undoubtedly, in doing so didn't take the position that the administration is always right and that because I am part of the administration I can't have an opinion that is counter to the administration. I was probably becoming a real thorn in the side of the administration."

When asked how he came about writing his resignation, the general replied, "I had been extremely well received in Cleveland and although, from a standpoint, it might have been desirable for me to leave in the way that some other people had left by just going into the mayor and saying, 'Mr. Mayor, for personal reasons I must leave' and he would say, 'General Davis, I thank you for all of your efforts and I'm sorry that your personal reasons require you to leave'—and the reason I couldn't do that was that I had had a lot of support from a whole lot of people in the city of Cleveland, so my reasons for leaving had to come out. They had to be spelled out. Now that is an important point that I never said to anybody. . . . In the end it was always to come back to 'Why did you go?' and the reasons I stated in that letter are the exact reasons for going—namely, that the mayor did not support my important programs, and he did support some people and organizations who were actively working against me."

In analyzing Davis's role in the showdown, it should be noted that he had attacked Stokes, and therefore the responsibility for proving it was his. According to debate procedure it was the general's job to support the allegations and Stokes's role to refute them. Stokes's response was entirely necessary and also effective. He produced citizens whose backgrounds and actions did not clearly define them as "enemies" of law and order. For example the *Call and Post* served the black community. For the black audience to accept Davis's message, they would have to reject the *Call and Post* as a credible source of information. Stokes raised doubts as to the legitimacy of Davis's claims—which in turn made it necessary for Davis to reply, since he had instigated the debate. But Davis's refusal to continue in the role he had selected as well as the media's eagerness to step into the debate without any real evidence caused the entire affair to become just another exercise in image-destroying rhetoric.

Perhaps if the citizens who had opposed the general's policies and those who had supported him had not been forced to take sides in a personality battle, the bitterness in Cleveland over this affair could have been avoided.

But the polarization continued. Defensive about the attack upon Stokes, black members of the Cuyahoga County Democratic party demanded more representation at the leadership level. When this was not forthcoming, a group of black leaders under the leadership of Louis Stokes, congressman in the Twenty-first District, formed the Twenty-first District Caucus. The caucus withdrew from the Democratic party. At the city level, black councilmen withdrew, forming a mini-caucus which weakened the positions of both the mayor and council president; although council president retained a majority vote, he was stopped on any issue which demanded a two-thirds vote. Indications of a stalemate were in evidence as withdrawal further hindered any attempt at conciliation or compromise.

However, there was one encouraging sign. After being assured of his congressional seat in Washington, Council President James Stanton stepped down from his position in the city, and Anthony J. Garofoli took command.[6] Reports were that Garofoli was setting a "softer style" in City Council. Gene I. Maeroff of the *Plain Dealer* said that "the personality conflict is ended. The logjam is broken. The checks and balances will begin checking and balancing again. No more Stanton vs. Stokes. No more cabinet members silenced at council meetings. No more attacks on the council president by the mayor." Garofoli stated that he was a different sort of person: "Jim had a flamboyance and a style all his own, and I'm not like that at all." He maintained that the Establishment was responsible for the tensions that had developed between the blacks and the white ethnic groups and said, "I would like to see blacks and whites stress their common interests and move against the power structure together."[7] Garofoli was faced with the same problems that had plagued the man he replaced. When he took over the gavel, the future of public housing in Cleveland was still dim. Although council had introduced legislation to allow CMHA to build 3,700 housing units, it was pigeonholed by council, partly because of CMHA's plans to build in Ward Four and Ward Nine. These wards, represented by former Council President James Stanton and Councilman Richard Harmody, led the opposition to CMHA and to Director Kriegsfeld. Harmody and Stanton maintained that CMHA did not plan the location of its units properly and said that Kriegsfeld should be fired. Other councilmen, worried about the reaction of the people in their own wards, objected to the fact that a single councilman under the terms of Cleveland City Charter had virtually no power to keep public housing out of his ward. Eventually the debate erupted into physical confrontation.

But the real showdown was over taxes, and the voters were used as a court of last resort. The showdown occurred because the leaders of Cleveland indulged themselves and violated still another sacred rule of politics—never play politics with money. In 1967 Stokes put the money issue into politics when he said he could reduce taxes. Instead, he increased the .5 of 1 percent to a full 1 percent. Under state law this can be done without voter approval. Since this small raise did not affect the public unduly, it was not heralded or debated. But in the year 1969 various unions in Cleveland threatened strikes, and the administration yielded to union demands which resulted in significant money adjustments across the board for all employees at City Hall, in spite of the fact that under Ohio State law one cannot authorize expenditures unless the money is in the till. There was no legal contract, of course, merely an agreement by the administration. But City Council also agreed to the raises, thereby compounding the blunder. Klementowicz, who had served the city for twelve years under three different mayors, said, "This was not a mistake. This was not a blunder. This was an act of suicide."

The mayor then put a tax package together. He proposed raising the city income tax to 1.8 percent. He also proposed lowering property taxes and putting an end to sharing city tax money with Cleveland suburbs. Council approved the ordinance but then refused to support it, or as Klementowicz described it, "took a walk." In a recent analysis of the situation, Klementowicz stated that if council "didn't like the mayor's tax program, they should have amended it. We've done that in the past. Called for more discussions on it. Come to some agreement."

Discussion did not take place. Instead, the mayor had to go out to the people and campaign alone to raise the city's income tax. He had William Silverman run a campaign to put the tax over. Councilmen, on the whole, were silent. A few east side councilmen openly endorsed it and campaigned with the mayor. Dennis Kucinich of Ward Seven staged an effective campaign against it. He had not voted for the package and obviously felt no loyalty to the councilmanic decision.

The rhetoric of the tax campaign also took on an emotional flavor. The tax became "Stokes's tax." Councilman Anthony Stringer said, "Stanton wanted to hand Stokes a defeat before he left Cleveland." Stanton was campaigning to become U.S. representative in the Twentieth Congressional District.

The mayor charged racial motives. He said, "It was not considered on its merits. The income tax failed because a majority of the council made a racial issue of it."

After the tax's failure, which Mayor Stokes blamed upon City Council, the public was informed that severe cuts in the city's budget would be made, that all plans for winter recreation programs would be halted, activities of health centers would be curtailed, and numerous other cuts in personnel would take place.

Council then asked the accounting firm of Price Waterhouse to study the city finances. That firm's report stated that Cleveland did indeed need more money but not as much as the mayor had asked for. They suggested an increase to .6 of 1 percent. Once more the issue was put on the ballot, this time with council's approval.

It was again defeated. Though eighteen east side wards voted for it, the voter turnout was slim—only 29 percent. Fifteen west side wards voted against it, and the turnout on the west side was heavier (45 percent).

The mayor blamed everyone in the city of Cleveland for its defeat. But the citizens' distrust had run too deep. They could not believe councilmen who at first told them to vote against the tax and a few months later advised them to vote for it. They also simply would not accept the role of scapegoat. Council tried to justify itself by blaming the administration for mismanagement. Newspapers began another series of exposés. Actually, at this stage in the rhetorical game, nobody admits that he is wrong, because each (mayor, council, and citizens) has to defend his own action, and personal attack is used as a substitute for debate on the alternatives.

On February 1, 1971, council and the administration indulged in a name-calling contest that was culminated in the administration's complete withdrawal from public dialogue with council. The *West Side News* reported the fracas sardonically:

> Francis Gaul said the city commission of weights and measures was acting as judge and jury in suspending a member of that division who lives in Gaul's ward.
>
> Mayor Carl B. Stokes said that Gaul (who had replaced Stanton in Ward 4) was doing the exact same thing, "acting as judge and jury" in condemning the commissioner of weights and measures.
>
> Then Council President Anthony Garofoli said that Stokes was doing the same thing, "acting as judge and jury" in condemning Gaul—who you will remember was condemning the commissioner.

According to the *West Side News*, it sounded a little like the house that Jack built.

A fault had finally severed the foundation upon which city government is built. Amidst shouting and further name-calling, during which time the council president vainly rapped on the desk with his gavel, the members of the Stokes administration left the chamber floors, accompanied by a sympathetic following from the audience. Carl Stokes asserted that personal attacks would not be tolerated. He attended no more council meetings during the rest of his term of office.

Cleveland had advanced to the final stage of justification, and the cries of "I had no choice but to act as I did" could be heard from all sides: council, black caucus, mayor, as well as the citizens.

Since no one would back down, there was nowhere to go, and the cycle had to begin again. A change was mandated. New voices outside the government started claiming ability to resolve the impasse.

Early in February, Cleveland citizens became aware that two men were actively seeking the mayor's job. One was Ralph Perk, who felt 1971 would be the ideal year to attain his lifelong dream of becoming mayor of Cleveland. The other was Patrick L. Gerity, the ex-police chief, who felt Clevelanders now were ready for a grassroots campaign and ready for an honest candidate. Despite a slapping incident involving a fellow officer, Gerity's honesty was a strong point in his favor.

Gerity discussed his decision with several prominent businessmen and politicians, all of whom encouraged him. Gerity, in weighing his own decision to run, was curious and eager to know more of the details about the Stenvig-Cohen campaign in Minneapolis (1969), for certain facts of this campaign appealed to him. While the national press had written Stenvig off as something of a "bumpkin" and the campaign as a law-and-order campaign, it had not been as simple as all that. Anyone who could beat the Republicans, the Democrats, Eugene McCarthy, the *Minneapolis Star* and the *Minneapolis Tribune*, a major department store, and the president of the Minneapolis council couldn't have been that much of a "bumpkin." Nor was it a law-and-order campaign. Stenvig had stressed *equal* law enforcement and had worked on the Human Development Commission which gave Minneapolis its first blueprint for civil rights. At the time Stenvig entered the race both the Democratic and Republican parties had split, Mayor Arthur Naftalin had decided not to run, and the Republican candidate had been stigmatized by the label "millionaire." In addition to these facts, it is important to note that Minneapolis holds a nonpartisan election: eight people ran

Empty chairs at City Council
Photograph by Odyssey Associates

in the 1969 primary. What interested Patrick Gerity was that Stenvig spent $19,000 on his campaign (both primary and general combined), while his opponent spent over $150,000. Here, in fact, a mayor of a big city had been elected with no money, no business support, and no media support. And it happened during the television years—in 1969. Patrick Gerity thought it could happen in Cleveland in 1971. He was right, but, as it developed, he was not the man to do it.

It will be recalled that after his defeat for the office of mayor in 1969, Ralph Perk had swept into a third-term victory for the office of county auditor by a 143,000 majority, the greatest feat of any GOP candidate in the county, including even presidential candidates. But his goal was still the mayor's chair, and in February he campaigned for the City Charter change that would allow a nonpartisan mayoral primary so that he could be assured of a one-to-one race against Stokes in November. While the Perk supporters succeeded in obtaining enough signatures to put the City Charter amendment change on the ballot, they did not succeed in making it applicable to the 1971 election.

After Gerity and Perk announced, several other names began appearing in the newspapers. State Representative Anthony J. Russo and Cleveland lawyer Milt Schulman announced their candidacy, John Hawkins of the Socialist Workers party and Jean Murrell Capers, Independent, also announced. Several prominent suburban Democrats began looking for a downtown address. Ray T. Miller, scion of the Democratic dynasty, gave up a Lakewood "gold coast" address to settle within the city limits. Cleveland Port Director W. Kiely Cronin moved into a Cleveland apartment. A timely, necessarily shortlived, flight back from the suburbs was beginning.

In the midst of all this activity, on April 17, Mayor Carl Stokes invited fifty guests for dinner. He walked into the middle of his living room and announced his decision not to run again. In a carefully worded speech he said:

> I have decided not to seek reelection to a third term as mayor of the city of Cleveland.
>
> I have spent the last fourteen years in local government and have aggressively sought not only to bring more citizens into the governmental process, but also to bring out into the open the real issues and problems confronting our urban society.
>
> I have been privileged to serve in high public office and during America's most trying times. But my service has, of necessity,

> been limited to a relatively small constituency. I want now to expand my efforts beyond the Cleveland area to assist others—particularly the locked-in minority groups—to better understand their role in politics and government. In this regard, I want to devote more time to stressing, throughout this country, the need for reestablishment of priorities at a human and humane level and the necessity for an honest, blunt appraisal of the root ills of our cities.
>
> As a purely personal matter I must repay an immense debt of unselfishness which my wife Shirley and our three young children have exhibited for these many years. I want to be free now to return to those I love the patience, understanding, and compassion which they have so steadfastly extended to me.
>
> Finally, from the bottom of my heart, I wish to thank the people of Cleveland who twice gave me the honor, privilege, and opportunity to serve them as their mayor.

The people of Cleveland responded to the news of Stokes's withdrawal with mixed emotions. Depression swept over the city. Treated to government by crisis for so long, the people had little energy left to respond to what might have been an explosive announcement. Depression swept over the announced candidates, too, as the realization hit them. Against whom would they be running now?

After commenting upon Stokes's withdrawal, the newspapers continued their steady probing into city government. *Cleveland Press* investigative reporter Paul Lilley wrote several articles which resulted in the investigation by the grand jury of the utilities department.

The most significant investigative reporting, however, was done by Robert G. McGruder and Allen Wiggins, the *Plain Dealer's* City Hall reporters. Armed with a city budget, a calculator, some finance department records, and a great amount of graph paper, they reported that funds were alarmingly low for *twelve* city accounts. Two important paragraphs of their article were somehow ignored by the candidates:

> If the city can cut back to its own estimated budget of $96.5 million and the income losses are as *PD* projections predict them to be, the city will be at least $9 million short, not counting the loss in real estate property taxes.
>
> But—and this is the biggest but—if the city spends as it is now and losses are as predicted *the city could come $21 million short.*[8]

Robert G. McGruder followed that investigative report with a feature story in which he cried for a good sturdy rack. "We need to set up a rack in the sub-basement of City Hall and every few hours haul a city official down for some stretching," he commented.

The citizens were aware that the city was in trouble and that neither the Stokes administration nor City Council was going about the business of trying to solve the problem nor, perhaps, had the wherewithal to do so. The rhetorical game could not be won by any of the players—the city was at a stalemate.

The final lineup of candidates included James M. Carney, Democrat and industrialist who had supported Stokes in his past two campaigns; Patrick L. Gerity, Democrat and ex-police chief; Anthony Garofoli, Democrat and council president; Arnold Pinkney, Independent, president of the school board, and Stokes's favorite; Ralph Perk, Republican and county auditor; George V. Voinovich, Republican and state representative; Joseph Pirincin, Socialist Labor candidate; and John Hawkins, Socialist Workers candidate.

Then, as though it had never stopped, the campaign rhetoric was once more heard all over the city. Even with a campaign that initially did not promise much excitement, crowds gathered to hear the candidates. Cleveland was still the campaigningest city in the United States. A young student from Penn State came to study Arnold Pinkney's campaign and, after two days of listening to speeches, dancing the polka, listening to a rock band, eating chicken, hot dogs, and drinking beer, sighed, "We don't have this where I come from."

Three candidates ran in the Democratic primary and two in the Republican primary. The primary race between Republicans Ralph Perk and George Voinovich never took form. Voinovich campaigned on a bicycle while Perk visited church groups and met small club groups and ignored his opponent. When they did meet at the City Club, they were not abrasive, and each promised to solve the city's ills. Perk offered his record of integrity, and Voinovich proposed several plans to better manage the city. The attractive, young Voinovich ran a limited and poorly organized campaign. People just never got very excited about him, so Perk managed to maintain his supporters. Of significance in the Republican primary was the fact that Robert Hughes, cochairman of the County Republican party, did not endorse either candidate, and a reported rift between Hughes and Perk widened.

The Democratic primary, however, was another story. Anthony Garofoli, James Carney, and Patrick Gerity were all Catholic and all white.

The strategies employed by these three candidates are interesting to review because of the new campaign techniques revealed in this primary.

On the mayoral level James Carney used the most modern techniques of persuasion. On July 9, the *Cleveland Press* ran an editorial urging James Carney to enter the race for mayor. The editorial claimed Carney could bring unity to the community, that "he has the respect of just about everyone." From that editorial, the strategy "Vote for Carney for Cleveland" and "Carney for Unity" was developed. The staff for Carney consisted of Patti Knox, originally from Detroit, Michigan, who had been involved in the Howard Metzenbaum senatorial race; Howard Broadbent, Carney's law partner; James A. Kaval and James Schiller, who claimed to be Gilligan's brains in Cuyahoga County during the governor's campaign; James Carney, Jr., Carney's nephew; and John Carney, Sr., the candidate's brother. Public relations were handled by Joe Manak, who had worked on Perk's campaign in 1969; William Levy, who had helped Carl Stokes in 1969; Donald H. Marcus, who had filmed the Metzenbaum commercials; and Allen Schlick, a student at Cleveland State University.

Marcus was responsible for the Carney commercials. To the people of Cleveland who previously had been inundated with the Metzenbaum commercials, only the main character had been changed. The message was the same: one black, one hard-hat, one elderly person, and a hippie all rapping with the candidate as he stood in his shirt sleeves with his coat slung over his shoulder. The theory was that if the hard-hat liked Carney, Carney must be all right for hard-hats, and if the hippie liked Carney, then he must appeal to all hippies, etc. A man for everyone.

It was a rerun and, unfortunately, the central figure was not as articulate as the original which Metzenbaum had portrayed. What the voters saw was a hesitant, often stumbling, bespectacled man. The Carney camp claimed that people didn't know Carney until television made him visible.

While it was true the people had not seen Carney, they knew the *name* Carney. He had been a shadow behind Carl Stokes in 1967 and 1969. He and his brother had been the cochairmen of the Democratic party for years and the men behind many council races. Carney was the man who had made millions from downtown investments and urban renewal and the man whose brother had been defeated by Ralph Perk in a previous county auditor's race. Carney was the man who built the Hollenden House, Cleveland's newest hotel. Most people wondered why, when he could control city and county officials, he wanted to become mayor. It was speculated that he really wanted to run for the U.S.

Senate. Nonetheless, prior to the campaign television commercials, Clevelanders' only image of James Carney was that of an aggressive businessman and political power-broker. After the commercials, the people recognized Carney, but the image was weakened.

Money poured into the Carney campaign. Television and radio spots flooded the media. A new "beeper" system was used. Allen Schlick handled it and said: "I followed Carney around as he spoke to groups and at press conferences. I would record his speeches on a portable reel-to-reel recorder for future dissemination. I called up all of the radio stations early in the campaign and made my services available to them. I would feed them an edited actuality (that is, a short statement that Carney had made somewhere) over the telephone and they would use it in the news broadcasts. Of all the candidates, only Carney had the 'beeper' system." Because Carney was not a great orator Schlick said he often took parts of two or three sentences and made one flowing statement of about thirty-five seconds. Schlick felt his service was a godsend to smaller stations whose news staffs consisted of perhaps two newsmen. Through this system the radio stations could use the actual statement on the air and appear to have covered the campaign. "Sometimes," said Schlick, "if Carney was speaking to a black group and said something pertinent to their needs, but perhaps might alienate the whites, I would feed it exclusively to the two black stations, and they would almost always use it in the news broadcasts."

Anthony Garofoli, the second man in the Democratic race, was unduly disturbed that James Carney fed one message to the east side and another to the west side. In fact, Garofoli went on television and produced literature to prove his point. The people, having been indoctrinated in the tactics of campaigning, were not surprised that politicians aimed their messages at specific audiences. The audiences were more upset (and perhaps a little amused) at the petty bickering in which these two candidates engaged. On WEWS-TV, Garofoli accused Carney of coming from outside the community, "with a telescope from Fairview Park," and pretending to be an expert on every neighborhood. Carney retorted that Garofoli had only been an active citizen for seven years while he, Carney, had lived in the area all his life. Garofoli responded, "To permit Mr. Carney to indicate I've been in Cleveland seven years is such a ridiculous statement that I'm surprised a man of his intelligence would say such a thing. Jim has known me for more than seven years. I came to Cleveland at the age of seventeen. I'm thirty-four. I've been married for thirteen years. I'm surprised Jim would tell such a known falsehood." "Well," responded Carney, "I resent that.

Now its true he's been here thirteen years, but he was a *student* part of the time. Sure, the body has been here for other purposes, but as an active citizen—seven years." Garofoli was relieved and said he was glad Carney conceded that his body had been here for thirteen years.

While these two candidates exchanged words about city and council problems, Patrick Gerity's role became one of conciliator. "Permit me to be the peacemaker," he would say. "The mayor has to set the tone in this city. He has to say we're going to live here, to work here, to get along together."

Patrick Gerity campaigned continuously. His auto caravan consisted of a Volkswagen and a Gremlin. He stood at the Terminal and greeted the early morning transit riders, he visited the ward clubs, he attended a Glenville festival with his wife and two little children. He was a shy candidate, soft-spoken and smiling, often standing aside with hands in his pockets waiting for someone to recognize him. He was always treated kindly. People came up to him, shook his hand, wished him luck. But people did not really think he could win.

The media completely ignored him. He sent a letter to the newspapers protesting, but to no avail. Television stations were not much better. Jim Cox of WJW-TV said, "Near the end of the primary we started counting things up and realized he hadn't been covered. I was sent out to do a quick one and one-half minutes." With no money, no endorsements, and no media support Gerity tried to bring his campaign to the people. He consistently promised honesty and integrity in office. But he was too shy, too uneasy in his role of politician. And the public sensed it. They liked him, but they knew he didn't have a chance. The comment heard most often about him was, "At least *he's* honest."

In both the primary and general campaigns, the men who refused to bicker, refused to attack their opponents' images were the men who lost the battle.

In the primary campaign there were two important and exciting moments. The first occurred at the Cuyahoga County Democratic Party Executive meeting. County Democratic Chairman Joseph W. Bartunek and seven elected Democratic county officials asked the party to endorse Carney. Notwithstanding, on a secret ballot the endorsement went to Garofoli. The Garofoli camp was ecstatic. Bartunek considered resigning but then decided to follow the will of the majority and support Garofoli. The party, however, was seriously divided over the election. The implications of the endorsement were far-reaching. It was felt that a coalition of Garofoli forces, Stanton, and the liberal suburbanites of the party could gain control with Garofoli as the new mayor; thus, leadership would change within the party. From then on, the general feeling was that Garofoli would be the next mayor. Even Garofoli seemed to have gained confidence. His short, stout body bounded with energy. He smiled more, spoke with authority about his abilities. Garofoli's endorsement was a severe blow to Carney. Carney had controlled the party for a long time; he had been instrumental in giving and withholding endorsements. And now that it was his turn, the party had failed him.

But he was not to be denied another endorsement—one from the mayor of Cleveland. It was the second most important move in the campaign. In a formal letter, Stokes reiterated his support of Arnold R. Pinkney but endorsed James Carney in the primary:

> I am sure you are aware that I want Arnold Pinkney to succeed me as mayor in November. However, Arnold is not in next Tuesday's Democratic party primary election, and we have the opportunity to remove from the final contest in November a man who would be extremely bad for Cleveland—Council President Anthony J. Garofoli, whose years in office have been devoted to racially dividing our city.
>
> As you know, part of the Ward (19) Garofoli represents is Murray Hill where we have had one disgusting and horrible racial incident after another.
>
> You can help make sure that Mr. Garofoli will not be around for the general election in November by casting your vote next Tuesday in the Democratic primary for a decent man, James M. Carney.
>
> Vote for James M. Carney in the Democratic primary on Tuesday, September 28, 1971.

Copies of the Stokes letter were stuffed and mailed by Carney workers. While Stokes had been active in the primary campaign, he had concentrated on the council races rather than on the mayoral race. He attended a few meetings with Arnold Pinkney, where he urged citizens to rid council of some of the east side councilmen who had actively opposed him. With a vengeance he went after Clarence Thompson and Mary E. Yates, who had replaced his arch black adversary Leo Jackson when he became a judge. As the final hours drew near in the primary, however, Stokes decided to use his political power to turn the vote out for James Carney and defeat Anthony Garofoli, whom he labeled "Stanton's man." On the weekend preceding the primary, thousands of Clevelanders picked up the telephone and heard their mayor say:

> This is your mayor speaking. I urge you to go to the polls and vote next Tuesday. I believe it to be in your best interest to vote for James M. Carney and against Anthony Garofoli.

Carney forces who footed the bill had rigged an electronic device so that even though fifty calls went out simultaneously, each person received the message immediately when he picked up the receiver. Weeks later, many east side citizens were still certain their mayor had personally talked to them.

The last personal appearance the candidates made together was, of course, at the City Club. There Carney stressed unity, Garofoli vowed he would end confrontations and unify Cleveland, and Gerity pledged to restore safety, security, and justice.

Tempers flared in the question-and-answer period when Councilman Richard M. Harmody asked Carney how he expected to end confrontation with council when he was always attacking council. Irritated, Carney insisted that Harmody had not been listening: "I haven't been blaming you. If you accept the blame that's your fault." The audience responded by booing Carney, which further infuriated him. Finally, after more bitter exchanges, Carney told Harmody, "If they can take you in the Ninth Ward, or wherever you are, let them have you." He then berated another councilman for doing a "miserable" job. It was obvious to the audience that Carney's prepared text and his extemporaneous performance were in conflict.

Gerity's performance was affectionately received by the audience. He received great applause when he stated that the city was sick and needed a doctor, not a quack.

An interesting aspect of the City Club debate was that the *Cleveland Press* covered Garofoli's and Carney's performances but claimed that Gerity's speech was "not available" at press time. Gerity did not have a written speech; his remarks were extemporaneous. However, if the newspapers *claim* to cover an *event*, not merely report the *written* speeches handed to them by candidates, then it seems incredible that such a statement of unavailability should appear in print. In this age of tape recorders and audiovisual instant playbacks, even a reporter with no memory can cover an event and meet a deadline as quickly as he can read a speech and comment upon it—unless the paper goes to press *prior* to the event. To cover a speech aimed at an immediate, persuasive effect is not to look at mere words on a piece of paper. A speech at the moment it is given is a social force. In order for the public to obtain the flavor of the moment, the reporter must re-create that moment; speech, speaker, audience, occasion—all are important. To dismiss a candidate's performance by saying "his talk was not available at press time" is to acknowledge that the reporter was not there. Accurate reporting would state what the candidates *intended* to say when they met at the City Club. Of course the practice of covering an event prior to its occurrence by printing parts of a written text is not new in the newspaper field. Knowledgeable candidates adjust their time to the media or send in the material. Those candidates who want to be quoted in the *Cleveland Press* on their City Club "talk" must type up their remarks and submit them before lunch. It would be interesting if someday a candidate handed a *Press* reporter a copy of his manuscript and then threw his own copy away when he reached the podium. On a national level this has happened many times, to the embarrassment of the newspaper.

The *Cleveland Press*, however, suffered only the embarrassment of not predicting the outcome of the primary correctly. Having endorsed Carney and having lavished space upon him, it nonetheless predicted a Garofoli win. The *Cleveland Plain Dealer*, after having endorsed Garofoli, did little but write a few editorials; it also predicted Garofoli the winner.

Seventy-two hours before the ballots were cast, Richard L. Maher, politics editor of the *Press*, also predicted that Garofoli and Perk would win in the primaries. However, he said that one factor could upset the Democratic calculations: "Will the black voters turn out? If they do, Carney will profit."

The black voters did come out—for Carney. Carney defeated Garofoli by almost fourteen thousand votes. A heavy east side vote helped him win. So Carney did profit, at least for the moment. The victory, however, was not celebrated at Carney headquarters. As far as Clevelanders were concerned, the real victory was going on at the downtown Pinkney headquarters where Carl Stokes commanded the platform. On election night, Stokes's performance was reminiscent of 1967. He was filled with joy. He had commanded his people, and they had responded. Not only had they defeated Garofoli but they had defeated several councilmen and councilwomen who had irritated their mayor. Specifically, the Twenty-first District Caucus led by Carl Stokes and his brother Louis defeated Mary E. Yates in Ward Twenty-four and Clarence Thompson in Ward Thirty. Several Stokes favorites had won. The only setback (as far as Stokes was concerned) was the success of Issue One which called for a

Mayor Carl Stokes accepting congratulations for
Carney's primary victory at Pinkney headquarters.
Arnold Pinkney is second person to right of Mayor Stokes
Photograph by Odyssey Associates

nonpartisan primary and a general election for the office of mayor. Considering the entire picture, the crowd at Pinkney headquarters was jubilant. Carl Stokes was in fine form. He was eloquent; he was witty. The audience laughed and shouted. "The Man," the people said, "was the greatest." Arnold Pinkney told the crowd that he was happy because "Carney's campaign would not be as racist as if Garofoli had won." The polite manner in which Carney and Pinkney had treated each other in the primary was reminiscent of the Taft-Stokes relationship in the 1967 primary. However, in the general election, Arnold Pinkney would be facing James Carney as an opponent, and the velvet gloves would have to be removed. Unfortunately for both men, they took too long to do so.

The day after the primary all conversation centered about Carl Stokes, "the Man," who could not only talk about power but who could deliver votes. Though a poll had predicted that Ralph Perk would be the beneficiary if Carney won, few members of the media considered the significance of that poll. Only one reporter, Robert Burdock of the *Plain Dealer*, had warned his readers that Carl Stokes was playing a dangerous game. He said:

> There are all sorts of seers in the streets who convincingly argue that Stokes is somewhat less than sincere in his efforts to see Pinkney as his successor.
>
> Should Stokes succeed in his efforts in Carney's behalf, it could doom Pinkney's chances. A $5000 poll contracted by the Democratic organization predicts:
>
> "If Carney becomes the Democratic nominee Perk would be elected mayor, with Carney running a distant third—30% for Perk, 26% for Pinkney and 19% for Carney, 25% undecided."

When Carl Stokes shouted, "We won," wresting the victory from Carney, Councilman Dennis Kucinich knew he had a campaign to run. Calling the media together he made his announcement. It was the most significant single act of the general election. He said:

> I believe it is unfortunate that a formidable voting bloc of our community has been willfully manipulated with the result that the Democratic party has as its standard-bearer a person who has little or no genuine support anywhere in the community, a person who is ill at ease in communicating or relating to the people he now wants to lead.

He went on to say that he could not support the Democratic nominee, that partisan politics was a luxury Clevelanders could not afford at the moment. He pictured Carney's nomination as "a signal of the treachery that has racially divided this city and has split the ranks of the Democratic party." He concluded by announcing the formation of a Democrats-for-Perk drive and offered to serve as its chairman.

Dennis Kucinich, age twenty-five, diminutive in size, was a little man with a big voice in Cleveland. Since taking office in 1969 he had relentlessly opposed the Stokes administration, calling the directors to task on council floor, accusing the administration of inefficiencies and mismanagement. He actively opposed the city income tax and constantly attacked the mayor. He considered himself the watchdog of the administration. For two full years since he gained office he had engaged in one campaign after another. The media called him a gadfly but found him a colorful figure and devoted more space to him than to the combined members of council, including Council President Anthony Garofoli.

In his own ward, three recall petitions were taken out against him but came to no avail. A group that supported John Bilinski, the defeated councilman, was relentless in its criticism of him. Members of the group said the community was suffering because of Kucinich's constant battles with the mayor, that Cleveland: NOW! money had been denied them because the mayor didn't like Kucinich. He survived it all, including a vicious attack upon his life. While investigating a noise outside his house, he was struck with a rake and suffered a severe concussion.

He recovered and returned to council, determined to work even harder to unseat the Stokes administration. He became even more vocal on council floor. At first, Stanton, who had helped finance Kucinich's campaign, gave him the floor at City Council, looking over him like a benevolent guardian. But when Stanton went to Congress, Garofoli tried to curb Kucinich's fiery oratory. Nonetheless, Kucinich admired and respected Garofoli, supported him, and was convinced he would make a good mayor. When Garofoli lost he said, "Let me tell you the ironic thing about this election. I know Garofoli personally. He's the kind of guy that could have done a lot about getting away from the public relations approach to handling racial relations in the city and actually getting to the community leaders on both sides. Garofoli is that kind of guy. But Stokes made him into a white devil. They could have made a freedom rider look like a white devil. This guy is not a bigot. He's for real. He has a social conscience."

If Stokes made Garofoli look like a white devil, Kucinich retaliated by making Stokes look like a black devil. Coupled with his determination to beat Stokes, Kucinich had no affection for James Carney. "It makes it easier to campaign when you really hate the guy," he told a group of college students. To Kucinich, Carney represented big business control of city government.

Immediately after the primary he put an office crew together composed mostly of students under twenty-five years of age. The day after he made his announcement, his phone rang all day. For he was a popular man. People called to give their support, to offer to help in any way.

Dennis made up a file, obtained a complete list of block workers from the Garofoli campaign, and called for their help. Over half of the block workers were apprehensive about openly campaigning, but they did agree to talk to their neighbors and friends. An eighteen-year-old student who was part of the crew explained, "We had to convince them to show the whole world that they had the guts to cross party lines in order to support the best man." Five thousand signs with black lettering on emerald green background proclaimed, "A Democrat For Perk."

Republican headquarters arranged town hall meetings on the west and northeast sides of the city. Kucinich became the "advance man" for Ralph Perk. He warmed up the audience—excited them—so that when Ralph Perk stepped up to the platform enthusiasm was at a high pitch. He went everywhere with Perk and once jokingly said, "It's the Dennis and Ralph show." Perk corrected him, "Oh no, the *Ralph* and Dennis show." The show-biz quality brought into the campaign by Kucinich was very much like the Carl Stokes appeal in that respect. Both men were excellent organizers, they knew how to use the media, they thoroughly enjoyed speaking and persuading audiences, and they both loved the rhetoric of confrontation. Kucinich was in love with words; he wrote all the new literature for Perk. "How does this *sound*?" he would often ask his associates.

Kucinich perceived the challenge to be: "Who is the best man to run the city, Ralph Perk or Carl Stokes?" His slogan was "Beat Carney, Pinkney, Stokes. Vote For Perk."

Ralph Perk needed the support Kucinich gave him. He needed to tell Democrats that it was all right to vote for a Republican. He told his audiences:

> Some older people keep calling my house and saying, "Mr. Perk, or Mrs. Perk," because she answers the phone most of the time. She's a good Italian girl, Lucy Gagliardi. And they keep saying, "Mrs. Perk, we'd like to vote for your husband, but we're Demo-

Councilman Dennis Kucinich and Ralph Perk
Photograph by Odyssey Associates

> crats, and we're told we can't do it." And all she says is, "Just take a look at Dennis Kucinich. He's the best Democrat in the city of Cleveland, and he's voting for Ralph Perk. And we need more like him."

Perk still sounded nasal and ponderous, but he faced one opponent who stammered and was easily excited and another who tried to remain composed and logical. In that kind of atmosphere, Perk held his own. Besides, he tried not to appear on the *same* platform with his opponents too often. Kucinich and Nicholas A. Bucur, a lawyer with a large Puerto Rican following, often spoke for him. Nonetheless, it was generally conceded that of the three candidates, Arnold Pinkney was the best speaker.

Arnold Pinkney's speeches when the campaign opened were beautifully organized. He told his audiences that the debate question was: Who is best qualified to lead the city forward? He suggested that all the candidates had perceived the problems of unemployment, housing, decay, crime; certainly none were *for* crime or *for* further decay. He felt the people wished to know why one candidate was better than the other and how he would tackle the problems. To this he addressed himself, hoping that the people would then perceive him as a thoughtful, intelligent man capable of decision-making and problem-solving.

He proposed a coalition of city and suburban precinct committeemen to take control of the Democratic party by means of the Twenty-first District Caucus. He proposed reorganizing City Hall and said he would reduce the directors from thirteen to eight, as recommended several years earlier by Locher's Little Hoover Commission. He stated he would seek a police chief from within the city, suggested tax incentives for housing "a coalition of private enterprise and public agencies to obtain more housing for poor." He had a plan of health care for all, and he outlined how doctors would donate free time, business would purchase medicines, and schools would donate space. He said it could work and cited other cities where it was in progress.

When he appeared with the two other candidates, he did not engage in any petty bickering or personality clashes. In fact, the polite exchanges between Pinkney and Carney were almost too kind.

No one could accuse Ralph Perk of being too kind to his opponents. He lumped them all together and said that watching Stokes, Carney, and Pinkney in action was like taking on a riverboat gambler in a game of three-card monte. "Whichever card the voter might choose, Carney or Pinkney, they wind up getting Stokes." He described Stokes as a free-wheeling big spender who regarded Cleveland taxpayers as a golden goose which would continue to lay golden eggs. When he wasn't attacking Stokes, he concentrated on Carney. He said specifically:

> Carney owns the Hollenden Hotel. He talks about being a businessman, and says, "Look what I did for the city." Every year this guy comes in and goes before the Ohio Board of Tax Appeals and wants a tax reduction. Last year two Democrats on my board, against my will, voted him a $314,000 reduction for '68 and a $278,000 reduction for '69. He's here for another reduction in 1970, and I appealed those reductions, and they're down in Columbus waiting to be heard.
>
> He did the same thing with the Investment Plaza. He paid about fifty-nine dollars a square foot for the Investment Plaza. You know what he wants to pay on taxes? He says it only has a value of thirteen dollars a square foot!
>
> The land under the Investment Plaza cost the city $3.1 million, but his dear friend Carl Stokes gave him that land for $900,000. Isn't that a beautiful Christmas present?
>
> In 1967 Jim Carney, before the City Club of Cleveland, nominated Carl Stokes as President of the United States. Before that he tried to force Locher out of the race in order to make a clear field for Carl Stokes.

And he went on and on. Inevitably, when the two faced each other Carney would scream, "That is an unequivocal falsehood. Ralph Perk has a propensity for that." Perk would not back down, and the exchange would at times embarrass the moderator who had to suggest that both men go on to the "issues."

Carney would then promise that he would reopen the police academy, establish a metropolitan "Narcotics Enforcement Agency" to fight drugs, transfer the transit system to regional authority, minimize crime by beefing up the police protection and insuring police officers adequate support and equipment. He was always confident he was the man to do the job, that he could get state and federal funds, and that he would solve these problems *immediately* upon assuming office. When he was told that the city had a $10 million deficit, he said, "I don't believe it."

Perk's platform, when he wasn't attacking Carney, included a "Support Cleveland Plan" (rather than the existing Equal Opportunities Plan), where goods and services for the area would come from companies in Cleveland who employed Cleveland residents. He proposed a "New Town in Town" from 30th to East 105th, Hough and Wade Park to Gladstone. He promised war against crime and stated he was against gun licensing and gun control and also for women in his cabinet.

Meanwhile, the media was busy running its own campaign on paper and on the television and radio. The *Cleveland Press* devoted itself to electing James Carney and, in doing so, completely lost touch with what was happening in the Perk campaign. They did not catch the crowds, the enthusiasm, the grassroots flavor of the campaign. They did not hear the crowds around Kucinich who urged him on. Phrases like "I'm proud of you," "I'm a Democrat that is going to vote Republican for the first time," "Lot of courage, good job, Dennis," "I want to shake hands with a real American, Dennis," and "Good to see you've got guts" were repeated over and over again. The newspapers conducted their own polls and concluded that it was Carney or Pinkney, and very close. Thomas Vail later admitted the *Plain Dealer* was not in touch with the people.

But supporters in the Pinkney campaign were beginning to have second thoughts. They talked to the black community and began to realize it would not be that easy to convince people to change their vote. About a week and a half before election day the Pinkney strategy belatedly took on the fervor of a campaign. On October 18 Pinkney staged a "March Over Troubled Waters" and invited the citizens of the east side and west side to join him in a historic march across the Lorain-Carnegie Bridge, one hundred feet above the symbolic Cuyahoga River. With a hard-rock band and a Puerto Rican band blaring, the people from the east side met a small band of people from the west side, and together they sang "No More Troubled Waters—We're All Together Now." The master of ceremonies said, "This is soul city. Soul city. We got soul here like you never heard before. We got white soul! We got black soul! We got Spanish soul! And we got this Pinkney you heard about, right here!"[9]

Perk called the march a Barnum and Bailey attempt to turn the campaign into a carnival. But Pinkney went right on. A week before the election Jesse Jackson and popular vocalist Aretha Franklin came into town. The realization that Perk *and* Carney had to be defeated was finally apparent.

The rhetoric changed. Carney was attacked. Carney then made the mistake of flooding the radio with spot announcements claiming he had soul. At church gatherings Jesse Jackson ridiculed Carney's use of the word soul.

Jesse Jackson and the Operation Breadbasket band visited churches,

Pinkney's "March over Troubled Waters"
Photograph by Odyssey Associates

schools, civic centers, and open air meetings. On Sunday evening before the election, his appearance in the Olivet Baptist Church was magnificent.

The program opened with a number of solos by members of the choir. Then the choir sang spirituals to involve the audience in the beauty of the sound and spirit of the message. The Operation Breadbasket band began to play and the trumpet wailed. Several young girls, overcome with emotion, were carried out of the church. During the fervor, Jesse Jackson marched in followed by Carl and Louis Stokes, Arnold Pinkney, and a number of candidates running in the council races.

On stage, the guests joined hands and swayed to music supplied by the band. Prayers were offered for the candidates who were seeking office. It was, however, Jesse Jackson's night and he alone addressed the crowd, some of whom had waited for four hours to hear him.

He began with his now famous audience-participation speech. "I am somebody," he said and the audience repeated, "I am somebody." Then he spoke of the need to keep the white man out of City Hall. He spoke of the years of trial and tribulation, the years it took to convince black people that their votes counted. He talked about the registration drives, recalled the years of the Civil War and the setbacks that had occurred after the war had been won. "It took so long," he said, "for us to come this far." Could they afford a setback? "No white man could have soul," he said, laughingly referring to the commercials produced by the Carney camp. He said Perk was on one mountain and Carney on another and Pinkney must walk through the valley below.

The audience enjoyed the entire evening. They were moved by outstanding music and the rhetoric of a compelling spiritual leader. The total effect was magnificent, but shortlived.

It was too late to help Arnold Pinkney. The black community had already been through three campaigns, through some of the most eloquent and emotional messages in the history of the city, and they had become quite knowledgeable about campaign persuasion. The entertainment and emotion of the evening had little influence upon their vote.

They looked at the candidates once more, and they listened, once more, to the promises. They realized that most of the promises made by all three candidates had little to do with the actual job of mayor of the city. The promises of all the candidates were empty offering to a bankrupt city, and while the people listened politely, they knew better. Many of them had long since begun projects in their own neighborhoods. The Glenville Development Corporation had spent three long years of negotiations with the federal government and had finally obtained funds to rehabilitate 270 structures. The Antioch Baptish Church, with funding by the federal government, had built condominiums in Glenville that received a national award for design. Years of work had brought about this now visible dream of better housing. The Near-Town Association in downtown Cleveland at long last broke ground for their new recreation center. Years of struggle were behind that very special day when they stood in the rain for one hour and a half waiting for the mayor to inaugurate the day. The sign "Thank You Mr. Mayor" soaked and dragged in the wind. He sent word he was on his way. And he was—to Washington, D.C.

Unlike 1967, the people were not looking for another "dream of the future" plan. They were looking for someone who would work hard every day, an administrator who could run an efficient government, clean the streets, and protect their property.

It is significant that none of the three candidates received their mandate. Of the people who went to the polls 38.7 percent voted for Perk, 31.7 percent voted for Pinkney, and 28.7 percent voted for Carney. The people had elected Perk mayor.

The Perk camp was jubilant. Kucinich said, "The power is with the people." He put the bosses of the political machines on notice that their days were numbered. Ralph Perk promised a coalition government and asked for the cooperation and friendship of everyone. He said, "I love you. You have done a tremendous job. This is a victory for the people."

Carl Stokes said, "Carney and Pinkney between them got 63 percent of the vote. I backed both men—Carney in the primary and Pinkney in the general election. Posters around town proclaimed that a vote for either was a vote for Carl Stokes. So I interpret the election as a referendum for Carl Stokes with 63 percent of the votes in my favor."

In the winner-take-all game of politics, the rhetorical game of one-upmanship by the candidates continued long after the final vote was counted.

Carney people claimed that the voters of Cleveland lied to the poll-takers. They were convinced that when the people who promised to vote for Carney went to the polls, all their racial prejudices rose up and confronted them and they switched to Perk. For Carney's law partner Howard Broadbent, it was an anti-black, therefore anti-Stokes, vote. Pinkney and Councilman Forbes appeared on local television (WKBF Channel 61, Sunday, November 14, 1971) and publicly blamed the 20 percent of the blacks who believed the white man's "lies" in the newspapers and voted for Carney. Charles Patterson, host of the television program, consistently referred to these voters as "niggers."

On his inauguration day, Ralph Perk faced a packed gallery. There were some people dressed in native costumes, a handful of blacks, and a barrage of cameramen who obscured the audience's view by placing cameras directly in front of all the speakers. Perk asked for divine guidance and human cooperation. The people of Cleveland listened and hoped that now the campaign was really over.

Government by crisis cannot long endure. The people get tired of it—tired of the denial of the right to be rational. A campaign is a highly charged, emotional period of time, and it must be contained. It is too exhausting to continue forever, though politicians declare that they must campaign every day. General Davis observed that in politics the campaign starts the day after election day and that he could not sanction that kind of life for himself. Several senators have made the statement that 60 percent of their time is spent campaigning. It is often true that the politician that is best known to his constituents is the one that misses more roll calls. Campaign rhetoric, of necessity, is neither deliberative nor logical. It serves a purpose. But it cannot last forever.

The problem in Cleveland was that the first phase of the rhetorical movement, the phase when the Jeremiahs who advocated change raised their voices and awakened the people to the dangers in their society, went on too long—in fact, it lasted until 1972. It never really advanced to the second stage.

It was kept alive by politicians, citizens, civic leaders, and the news media.

News inadequately reported, limited in scope and clinging to the archaic concepts of reporting only conflict and drama, has a tremendous effect upon society. While there were, and are, some notable exceptions to this type of reporting, on the whole, journalists in Cleveland have lacked both the historical perspective and the adequate preparation to evaluate the changes taking place in society.

In the early sixties while crimes of blacks against whites were reported, crimes of blacks against blacks were ignored, and the problems of the Negro were termed not "sexy" or significant. The tensions went unnoticed unless there was a "confrontation" in Sowinski Park. The conditions in the ghetto were not considered news. Journalism failed to explain the significance behind the migration from the South, the problems of the aged in the urban community, the effects of new technology upon behavior.

Take as an example the $6 million Police Communication Center. The newspapers reported the conflict between the administration and Chief Gerity about *where* it was to be located and, after it was installed, noted that an integral part of the system, the "walkie-talkie" units, constantly in for repairs. The "news story" about the wheeling and dealing that went on in awarding contracts was the main thrust of the story. The *information* about a communication system that affects the community and the police was not worthy of a news story. Communication is the heart of the command and control system in police departments. It is the key to mobility. Problems with outdated equipment are rising daily in proportion to rising crime. The solution is *supposedly* in new equipment. The news media could convey the news, too, about the vast and intricate communication system. It involves the radioman who first receives the call (who often enough is serving as punishment rather than by choice) and who sends it to a dispatcher who, in turn, contacts the zone car. The news media could illuminate the chain of people involved in sending the message. While the new system increases the number of radio and dispatcher positions, has the news media made clear that there are not enough policemen to man these positions? That a patrolman after receiving the call is often hindered by inadequate transportation (because of patrol cars that need repairs)?

And how does the patrolman react to a system he has been ordered to accept without adequate training? What about the patrolman who is given a new set of codes and told to learn them in a week, who is told that the human voice which he considered to be an indispensable mode of communications is now augmented with a digital communications link? How does the patrolman who found comfort in his relationship with a dispatcher react to rotating dispatchers, to female dispatchers? Are the walkie-talkies—considered essential for the modern well-equipped police force—controlling the behavior of the patrolman, limiting his range, expanding it? And what about the news that is both local and national in nature, the news about integrated police communication centers *between* cities, counties, states? Why not inform the public and the police about the trends in law enforcement departments across the nation? Prepare them for tomorrow?

If the newspapers realize that the news they print is old before it is delivered, they may realize that they have a new responsibility—to serve and to communicate as an *information center* for society. Of course the scoop, the deadline, the choosing-up of sides, the picking of a winner, is admittedly a simpler task. For, if the reporters happen to end up on the losing side, in Cleveland the newspaper publishers merely "retire" the offending reporters or rearrange the editorial staff in a way that will reestablish the strength of the press. Granted, there are some capable reporters who attempt to warn the administration and the citizens of the dangers inherent in closing up City Hall. When McGruder computed figures to warn the public of the city's impending financial danger he was on the right track, albeit late. But where was that information when the public was forced to take sides in the council and City Hall battle of the income tax? If Clevelanders were ignorant about the financial situation in Cleveland, how were they expected to deal with it?

That the entire media was completely out of touch with what was happening in Cleveland is evident by their coverage of the 1971 campaign. To the reporters, Ralph Perk was just a boring speaker. He wasn't exciting enough to cover. The media couldn't see beyond the man to the people.

After the campaign the media admitted that they were out of touch. "We were just talking to each other," said Fred Griffith of WEWS. Thomas Vail of the *Plain Dealer* admitted that the mediators remained in their ivory towers. The editors of one newspaper, when told that *Perk* was winning, were absolutely stunned.

Now that it's all over, the reporters are "discovering" the ethnics who, they claim, put Ralph Perk in office. But few have taken the time to understand these groups of people who have lived in Cleveland for two generations.

Who are these ethnics who suddenly displayed their power in Cleveland? Who are these people labeled racists by the poll-takers, the intellectuals, and the liberals? The ethnics will tell you that *their* ancestors did not own slaves but, in fact, were serfs until about two hundred years ago. And yes, they will admit they have lived in the same neighborhood for years, and they like it. A home is very important to them. They believe in communities, autonomous communities, just like the blacks do today. They don't need to be told about stereotyping. They know about name-calling: hunkie, dago, spic, Polack, and now, racist, fascist, and pig. They listen to the rationale of the melting pot, but they like the food of their ancestors and the native dances and the rituals. And they try to make "good" Americans out of their children.

It took the blacks, who had been deprived of their own heritage, to rile the ethnics. African art, music, and food found its way into the universities. While the children of ethnic parents were being told to melt, the children of the black community were just beginning to discover a history of their own. The intellectuals and the liberals, who never could understand the European ethnic pride, were supporting the search for black pride. This just didn't make sense. Not to the ethnics in Cleveland. They felt alienated.

No one, it seemed, felt compassion for them. In their eyes the media ignored them and concentrated upon the black community.

In the black community the hard working, industrious homeowners were equally disenchanted. Particularly the citizens in Glenville. What did the name Glenville mean to them? Not what it meant to the press.

Shady glens and little streams were responsible for the name Glenville, and through the years it was identified as the Gold Coast, Oatmeal Row, and the garden spot of the county.[10] Early German immigrants there served rabbit stew every Sunday. Later salted herring from Iceland was the featured food as the Jewish immigrants settled in the section. The Negro residents moved into the area in the early forties. The history of pride in the area is evidenced in *every* group that became a part of it. The Negro citizens organized committees on health and welfare, safety, education. The Glenville Area Community Council was organized in 1945 to look into population shift, the inadequacies of existing social services, the housing, the recreation facilities, the noticeable tensions in race relations. For over twenty years Glenville worked hard to stop the deterioration in the neighborhoods. Street clubs gave certificates to those owners who improved their property. George Edwards, music teacher and civic leader, has a collection of slides featuring some of the most beautiful gardens in Cleveland. The pictures were taken in 1969 and 1970—not years ago. The message of the devotion to community involvement was overshadowed by the Glenville shoot-out, and for every step forward the concerned citizenry made to improve their community, the constant identification with killing and disaster by the media set them back even farther.

When the press fails to be aware of impending change, when newsmen by their own admissions say they don't know what's going on in their city, when news is irrelevant because information is fragmentary, then society faces a real danger. The media needs to restore the confidence of the people of Cleveland, to improve the quality of the reporting. To do so they must take a good look at themselves, redefine their role in society, accept the reality that they *do* affect the behavior of the people they cover. Journalists must become more knowledgeable. In short, journalists must become a part of the city of Cleveland.

For Cleveland is not the same as it was ten years ago, or even four years ago. More citizens are now aware of the real problems confronting the city. The era of studying the problem should be over; the time to try out the new methods is here. We do not need a Doxiadis, who prefers the Mediterranean, to ponder over the city of Cleveland. A new council has the opportunity to introduce new politics. The negotiation must come before the decision is made, not after the fact.

Faith in Cleveland means faith in its people, the ones who doggedly hang on and say "stay and build." Visible signs already are appearing. A new university, a justice center, perhaps a jet port in the lake, and many, many other projects that will revitalize the city.

A young black student is putting together a film about the Martin Luther King, Jr., Shopping Center. He wanted to tell a story about the need for the center in the Hough area. He came to class with shots of vandalized homes, children burning trash in vacant lots, boarded-up, burned-out stores, old women lugging heavy bags of groceries. After he viewed his film, he went out and turned the camera upon the men working on the shopping center, a new housing project, a new high-rise for the elderly. "I have to finish with a future," he said. The future holds no promise if factions in the city continue their rhetorical game where one side must win and the other lose or stalemate is reached. Until more emphasis is placed on deliberative problem-solving and less on accusation and justification, Cleveland will not achieve the dream inscribed many years ago on the walls of City Council:

> Cleveland—a city that has achieved pre-eminence in industry, commerce and culture through enterprise of men and women who exercise scientific knowledge, inventive genius, productive labor and wise management, taking advantage of their favorable location on the greatest of all inland waterways and the proximity of rich mineral resources—has brought into being, in the finest tradition of local self-government, a community self disciplined where those of every race, of all creeds and of whatsoever national origin, live and work in harmony so that they may transmit to posterity a city with an enlightened vision and a civic soul.

This is the same Cleveland of the grassroots confrontation. This is the Cleveland dream, and this is reason enough for it all.

NOTES

CHAPTER 1—THE COMING TO BE

1. Mary Land, "The Malcontents and the Melting Pot: The Cleveland Story" (M.A. thesis, Western Reserve University, 1946), as cited in pp. 176–77.
2. William Ganson Rose, *Cleveland: The Making of a City* (Cleveland: World Publishing Co., 1950), p. 979.
3. Walter Abbott, "Cleveland: A City Collapses," *Forum Magazine*, September 1938, pp. 99–103.
4. Walter William, "Cleveland's Crisis Ghetto," *Transaction*, September 1967, p. 41.
5. Cleveland Urban League, Research Department, *The Negro in Cleveland, 1950–1963: An Analysis of the Social and Economic Characteristics of the Negro Population, the Changes between 1950 and 1963* (Cleveland: 1964), p. 40.
6. Mr. Rawlings did not mention the sources of his evidence, but an examination of school enrollment figures, ratios of white and non-white births, real property inventories, and other periodic "census" studies would, no doubt, have reflected the increase in Negro population.
7. Lewis G. Robinson, *The Making of a Man* (Cleveland: Green & Sons, 1970), p. 142.
8. Cuyahoga County, Ohio, Grand Jury, "Special Grand Jury Report Relating to Hough Riots, Cleveland, 1966" (Louis B. Seltzer, Foreman).
9. Robinson, *Making of a Man*, p. 158.
10. Ibid., p. 159.
11. Ibid., p. 162.
12. Ibid., pp. 162–3, 165.
13. John Skow, "The Question in the Ghetto: Can Cleveland Escape Burning?," *Saturday Evening Post*, July 29, 1967, p. 40.

CHAPTER 2—THE MOVEMENT FOR CHANGE

1. The distinction is one of moral purpose. Although rhetoric is an amoral art which can be used to support both good and bad causes,

the implication here is that an Aristotelian would argue to persuade his audience to worthwhile action, whereas the Sophist's goal would be victory regardless of the moral quality of the action or the honesty of the arguments used to effect it.

2. Leland M. Griffin, "The Rhetoric of Historical Movements," *Quarterly Journal of Speech* 38, no. 2 (April 1952): 184–88.
3. *Cleveland Plain Dealer*, November 9, 1967.
4. Each of these "issues" was developed in a separate news release sent to all media in the early stages of the primary campaign.
5. See fn. 4.
6. The remark was repeated several times at many small gatherings arranged by the Celeste organization on the west side. On September 28, 1967, I attended and recorded the proceedings at one such meeting in the basement of a private home near Kamms Corners, West 165th and Lorain Avenue. Included among the audience of thirty persons was a five-man unit from WKYC-TV.
7. See fn. 6.
8. *Cleveland Press*, July 10, 1967.
9. *Cleveland Plain Dealer*, August 17, 1968.
10. James H. McBath and Walter R. Fisher, "Persuasion in Presidential Campaign Communication," *Quarterly Journal of Speech* 55, no. 1 (February 1969): 18.
11. Stokes did not specify the particular incident when Locher failed or refused to see Martin Luther King.
12. Carl B. Stokes, television speech, WKYC-TV, October 3, 1967.
13. Of the ten speeches by Seth Taft I recorded, all carried documented statements of this nature.
14. Cuyahoga County Democratic Committee letter, no. 67–8, September 30, 1967.
15. Carl Stokes, speech delivered at Gunning Field, Puritas Avenue, Cleveland, September 17, 1967.
16. Adair transferred to the news staff of WKYC-TV in 1970, but WJW retained its first place in the local ratings.
17. "TV Under Fire," *U.S. News and World Report*, July 15, 1968, p. 37.
18. Robert MacNeil, "The News on TV and How It Is Unmade," *Harper's*, October 1968, pp. 75–76.
19. Abraham Lincoln, *The Collected Works of Abraham Lincoln*, ed. Roy P. Basler (New Brunswick: Rutgers University Press, 1953), 1:383.
20. C. David Morlensen, "The Influence of Television Policy," *Quarterly Journal of Speech* 54, no. 3 (October 1968): 77.

21. Kurt and Gladys Engel Lang, "Television and the Intimate View of Politics," *Journal of Broadcasting* 1 (Winter 1956–57): 54.
22. Whitney M. Young, Jr., speech delivered at Antioch Baptist Church, Cleveland, October 4, 1968.

CHAPTER 3—CRISIS AND CONSUMMATION

1. References are to Stokes's reconciliation with Democratic Party County Chairman Albert Porter after the primary election and his softening of the proposals to sell the Municipal Light Plant and the city-owned acreage which contains several small man-made lakes.
2. One of Taft's proposals for making government more responsive to people was the establishment of storefront branches of city government to handle complaints and facilitate communication.
3. *Washington Post*, October 24, 1967.
4. The city of Cleveland owns a parcel of land in nearby suburban Warrensville Township. Taft's plan was to create a "new town" on the property. How the issue was quashed by Stokes and then later adopted by him and parlayed into an issue will be seen in later chapters.
5. The consequences of Stokes's promise to reassign policemen to patrol duty is detailed in later chapters.
6. *Cleveland Plain Dealer*, Sunday Supplement, December 10, 1967.
7. Ibid.
8. Ibid., October 30, 1967.
9. Ibid., December 10, 1967.
10. In 1971 the City Club moved its facilities to the headquarters of the Women's City Club located in the Women's Federal Savings and Loan Building, but, despite the move, the men's City Club has maintained its exclusion policies.
11. Fred Vierow, City Club secretary, recalled these highlights of City Club forums in our conversation on May 5, 1969.
12. Stokes had claimed many times during the campaign that there was "hidden money" in various departmental accounts at City Hall which Locher could have used for needed projects. No such monies were located, and within six months of his election, Stokes was calling for an increase in the city income tax.
13. *Cleveland Plain Dealer*, January 14, 1968.
14. The theory of four evolutionary stages in public controversy was conceived by Dr. Carroll C. Arnold, Professor of Speech, Pennsyl-

vania State University. Permission to use this framework for analysis of the rhetorical conflicts which have occurred in Cleveland was granted by Dr. Arnold; however, the authors take full responsibility for interpretations and applications of Dr. Arnold's theory as they appear in this book.

CHAPTER 4—THE PERIOD OF ADJUSTMENT

1. *Cleveland Plain Dealer*, November 11, 1967.
2. Ibid., November 9, 1967.
3. James Naughton, *New York Times Magazine*, February 25, 1968, p. 26.
4. *Cleveland Plain Dealer*, January 18, 1968.
5. Ibid., January 28, 1968.
6. *Cleveland Press*, January 26, 1968.
7. This is the same Frank Celeste who opposed Stokes in the primary. Several key people of Celeste's campaign staff were to ally themselves with the Stokes administration.
8. *Cleveland Plain Dealer*, November 17, 1968.
9. Ibid., July 21, 1968.

CHAPTER 5—FALLEN IDOLS

1. According to the "Chronological Report of Events from 2:30 P.M. Tuesday, July 23 to 8:30 A.M. Sunday, July 28 on Glenville Area Disturbance Issued from the Office of Mayor Carl B. Stokes, City of Cleveland," a shot was fired at 8:25 P.M., but the police did not know where or at what. Also at 8:25 P.M. William C. McMillan, tow-truck operator, was wounded by sniper fire. At 8:30 three more patrolmen were injured and one patrolman killed. At 8:40 two of the snipers were killed and one wounded. By 9:30 the dead count was up to seven and the wounded, fifteen. At 10:11 the first prisoners connected with the shootings were taken by Mobile Patrol 591. The shooting ended at 12:30 A.M. when Fred (Ahmed) Evans, 37, 12312 Auburndale Avenue, was arrested at 1384 Lakeview.
2. Pride, Inc., 11106 St. Clair Avenue NE, ran a day-camp program for about six hundred hard-core unemployed and operated three rumor-control centers to try to control racial disturbances, according to Baxter Hill, director. He also claimed that Pride, Inc. sponsored surveillance teams which photographed prostitutes and

their dates and forwarded photographs to the police. An $80,000 grant to Pride, Inc. administered by the Mayor's Council on Youth Opportunity which came from Cleveland: NOW! funds and the Greater Cleveland Associated Foundation incurred the wrath of the United Pastors (formerly Negro Pastors) Association's Committee of Concern.

3. According to the Masotti Report, Forbes was uncertain whether he should speak to the police in the surveillance teams and ask them to leave but decided that since the officers were from a special unit they would not recognize him or listen to him. He then decided to call the safety director.
4. Chapter 3, page 7 of the original Masotti Report also states that "the precise manner in which the shooting began is still uncertain." Whereas *Shoot-Out in Cleveland*, the published version of the report, stated that "a small, well-equipped army of black extremists were responsible for the bloodshed," the original version does not make this claim.
5. Chief Blackwell started for the area under fire but was ordered back to City Hall. The safety director also remained at City Hall.
6. In August the Grand Jury of Cuyahoga County met and returned seven first degree murder indictments against Fred (Ahmed) Evans. On May 12 a jury found Evans guilty of first degree murder on all seven counts.
7. Both daily newspapers documented this fact two days after Evans's capture. I interviewed a sergeant at police headquarters who claimed he also heard Evans make this statement.
8. "Chronological Report of Glenville Disturbance," p. 6.
9. Ibid.
10. Ibid. p. 13.
11. Radio, television, and newspapers reported that the mayor announced the crisis to be over after the 11:00 A.M. news conference.
12. *Cleveland Plain Dealer*, August 10, 1968.
13. Ibid.
14. The Lemberg Center received a copy of the original Masotti Report. Dr. Ralph Lewis sent me a xeroxed copy of the report. Dr. James Norton of the Greater Cleveland Associated Foundation told me he never saw the report.
15. *Cleveland Press*, May 21, 1969.
16. Louis H. Masotti and Jerome R. Corsi, *Shoot-Out in Cleveland*, ed. Anthony E. Neville (New York: Bantam Books, 1969), p. 103.

CHAPTER 6—FROM POLICY TO CRISIS

1. *Cleveland Plain Dealer*, November 17, 1968.
2. William Ganson Rose, *Cleveland: The Making of a City* (Cleveland: World Publishing Co., 1950), pp. 82, 382.
3. Cleveland City Charter, Chapter 25, Section 115.
4. Cuyahoga County, Ohio, Grand Jury Report, April 1969 Term, p. 3. The report is addressed to the Honorable Judge George J. McMonagle, Presiding Judge, April Term 1969, Criminal Court, and is signed by Joseph H. Nook, Foreman, September 12, 1969.
5. Ibid., p. 4.
6. Ibid., p. 5.
7. Dr. Thomas further reported that only the most meager instructions on interpreting the personality indices were distributed to the interviewers and that the only guidelines were a set of sample questions, some of which vaguely pertained to police work. The twenty-minute interviews were conducted in bedrooms of the Statler Hilton Hotel following procedures identical to ones outlined on page 156. (Her assessment of the interviewer's role coincided with mine.)
8. A tragic incident which took place on April 3, 1971, seemed to bear out Chief Gerity's claim. Apparently depressed and frustrated by the prospect of having to take a new exam because he had been passed over for promotion a third time, Patrolman Thomas F. McLaughlin went berserk while on duty, shooting two fellow officers, killing one.
9. *Cleveland Press*, May 15, 1969. The following excerpt from the Cleveland City Charter, Chapter 27, Section 129, clarifies Judge Mitchell's decision:

   > Tests required by the Civil Service Commission shall be practical and shall relate to matters which fairly measure the relative fitness of the candidates to discharge the duties of the positions to which they seek appointment. No question in any such test shall relate to political or religious opinion, affiliation or service; and no appointment, transfer, lay-off, promotion, reduction, suspension, or removal shall be affected or influenced by such opinion, affiliation or service.

10. Cuyahoga County, Ohio, Grand Jury Report, April 1969 Term:

    > In the latter part of March 1969, after a lawsuit was decided on March 18, 1969, the parties being the *State of Ohio ex rel. Peter Kilbane v. City of Cleveland and the Civil Service Commission, et al*, Judge Thomas Mitchell, who presided in that lawsuit, ordered that the prosecuting attorney and grand jury look into whether

or not there had been any violations of laws by anyone in connection with the January 23 Police Promotional Examination given by the Civil Service Commission. This referral to the prosecutor and grand jury was of course prompted in part by the fact that during that lawsuit, a witness, Lt. John Apanites of the Cleveland Police Department, declined to give to the Court the source from whom he had allegedly obtained a copy of the January 23rd Police Promotional Examination.

11. Ibid., pp. 3–4, 11, 25.
12. *Cleveland Press*, October 3, 1969.
13. Ibid., July 17, 1969.
14. Ibid., August 27, 1969.
15. Ibid., August 28, 1969.
16. Ibid., August 26, 1969.
17. Ibid., September 13, 1969.
18. Ibid., September 26, 1969.
19. "Rabbi" David Hill and his chief assistant, James Raplin, were eventually convicted of blackmail as a result of methods they used during the McDonald's boycott. Out on bail while appealing his conviction, Hill told *Cleveland Press* writer Bob Williams on January 16, 1971, that the settlement of the disagreement had done nothing to help the black community. "Black capitalism is no different than white capitalism. The sales agreements aren't worth the paper they are written on as far as increasing the economic power of the black community." Hill charged that while the restaurants are black-owned, "the poverty around them is still there, the hamburgers cost as much, and the black community is not profiting."
20. For background on housing and urban renewal, see Rose, *Cleveland*, pp. 341, 605, 629, 851, 915, 920.
21. Robert Bernard Navin, "Analysis of a Slum Area in Cleveland," prepared for the Cleveland Metropolitan Housing Authority with the counsel of Howard Whipple Green, 1934, p. 1.
22. See fn. 20.
23. James Q. Wilson, "Planning and Politics: Citizen Participation in Urban Renewal," *Journal of the American Institute of Planners* 29, no. 4 (November 1963): 242.
24. *Cleveland Press*, June 13, 1969.
25. Ibid.
26. Ibid.
27. *Near-Town News*, January 1970.
28. "Downtown Is for Everyone," editorial, *Cleveland Press*, February 16, 1970.

CHAPTER 7—TIME OUT FOR ARBITRATION

1. *Cleveland Press*, August 25, 1969.
2. Cleveland City Charter, Chapter 27, Section 139: "No person in the administrative service of the city shall directly or indirectly give, solicit or receive, or be in any manner concerned in giving, soliciting or receiving any assessment, subscription or contribution for any political party or purpose whatever. . . . No person in the service of the city shall use his official authority to influence or coerce the political action of any person or body, or to interfere with any nomination or election to public office. No person in the classified service of the city shall act as an officer of a political organization or take part in a political campaign, or serve as a member of a committee of any such organization, or circulate or seek signatures to any petition provided for by primary or election laws, or act as a worker in favor of or in opposition to any candidate for public office."
3. Letter dated August 26, 1967, prepared on letterhead of the Cuyahoga County Democratic party, addressed to Robert J. Kelly and signed by Samuel R. Gerber.
4. I called Dr. Mary Jean Thomas and asked her to view the WJW-TV eleven o'clock news. Even though she was alerted to hearing the word and knew in what sentence it was contained, she did not detect the word "nigger" or even "near" or "nearby." It sounded to her more like a glottal closure on the first attempt to pronounce "neighbor" and like Kelly had repeated the word "neighbor" after choking or gagging slightly on the first attempt. Such an occurrence would not be uncommon if a speaker were suffering such manifestations of a head cold as postnasal drip.
5. On December 12, 1969, the *Cleveland Press* published articles by reporter Paul Lilley which alleged that a similar "2 percent club" was being operated in the Cuyahoga County Engineer's office. Although Lilley had statements of several employees and former employees of the office that such kickback operations existed, no formal investigation by the county prosecutor followed. During budget hearings in the spring of 1971, County Commissioner Seth Taft questioned County Engineer Albert Porter about the reported presence of a "flower fund" in his office. Porter replied that he would answer for the conduct of his office only to a "cognizant body." Because of the structure of the Ohio state and county governments, only the electorate, a grand jury, or a trial jury would constitute such a "cognizant body."

6. *Cleveland Plain Dealer*, October 15, 1969.
7. By noon of November 4, 1969, the *Cleveland Press* was headlining the presence of policemen in polling places. In television interviews carried that evening on WKYC-TV, reporter Virgil Dominic queried Arnold Pinkney, Stokes's campaign manager, and attorney Paul Walter about the matter. Pinkney said that off-duty police officers had been intimidating black voters. Attorney Walter had advised off-duty police volunteers not to budge despite a decision by Law Director Clarence James that the policemen's actions violated the provisions of the Cleveland City Charter.

   On election day, November 3, 1970, I noticed that WKYC-TV reporters were duly authorized challengers in Bay Village. I called County Democratic Chairman Joseph Bartunek to inquire about the issuance of such credentials to newsmen. Bartunek informed me that the Ohio secretary of state authorized the issuance of witness and challenger credentials to newsmen. In 1971 newsmen received these credentials again, this time authorized by council and mayoral candidates. WKYC had people in every key precinct to *report*, not to challenge. Using polling places for commercial purposes is not exercising one's right as a private citizen. The media publicized the police and the polls but failed to put their own house in order.
8. *Cleveland Plain Dealer*, November 5, 1969.

CHAPTER 8—ENDGAME

1. *Cleveland Plain Dealer*, January 26, 1970.
2. *Cleveland Press*, July 11, 1970.
3. Ibid., July 30, 1970.
4. *Cleveland Plain Dealer*, July 29, 1970.
5. Ibid.
6. Ibid., September 19, 1970.
7. Ibid.
8. Ibid., October 19, 1971.
9. *Cleveland Press*, October 18, 1971.
10. Ibid., August 8, 1963.

INDEX